# Change in
# Use of Land

To our former and present students of
the Hong Kong Polytechnic, Hong Kong Polytechnic University and
the University of Hong Kong

# Change in Use of Land

## A Practical Guide to Development in Hong Kong

**Lawrence Wai-chung Lai**

BSocSc (Hons), MSocSc (Econ), PhD (HKU); LLB (Hons)(London); MTCP (Sydney); MRAPI, MHKIP, MCILT, MIAAEM, FPFM, MWES, Registered Professional Planner

**Daniel Chi-wing Ho**

BSc (CNAA); MBA (CUHK); PhD (HKU); FPFM, FRICS, FHKIS, Registered Professional Surveyor (BS), Authorized Person

**Hing-fung Leung**

BSc (Building Studies), BBuilding, PCLL(HKU); LLB (London); LLM (Wolv); MA(CityU); FRICS; FHKIS, FCIArb, FHKIArb, Registered Professional Surveyor (QS), Barrister of the High Court of Hong Kong

香港大學出版社
HONG KONG UNIVERSITY PRESS

**Hong Kong University Press**
14/F Hing Wai Centre
7 Tin Wan Praya Road
Aberdeen
Hong Kong

© Hong Kong University Press 2004

ISBN 962 209 707 3


All rights reserved. No portion of this publication may be reproduced or transmitted in any form or by any means, electronic or mechanical, including photocopy, recording, or any information storage or retrieval system, without permission in writing from the publisher.


Secure On-line Ordering
http://www.hkupress.org


British Library Cataloguing-in-Publication Data
A catalogue record for this book is available
from the British Library.

Printed and bound by Kings Time Printing Press Ltd., Hong Kong, China

# CONTENTS

| | | |
|---|---|---|
| Preface | | vii |
| 1 | The Importance of Use and Change in Use | 1 |
| 2 | Dual Development Control under the Land Lease and Statutory Town Plan | 7 |
| 3 | What Is a Use? | 13 |
| 4 | Change in Use and Development Control under the Land Lease, Town Plans and the Buildings Ordinance | 23 |
| 5 | The Need for Making a Planning Application to Enable a Change in Use under the Town Planning Ordinance | 29 |
| 6 | 'Temporary Uses' and 'Existing Uses' on Private Land under a Statutory Town Plan | 33 |
| 7 | The Possibility of Making a Planning Application and Steps in Checking Whether a Use Requires Planning Permission | 37 |
| 8 | The Relationship among Lease Modifications, Planning Permissions and Building Permissions in the Development Cycle | 41 |
| 9 | Planning Applications, Reviews and Appeals | 61 |
| 10 | Lease Modifications and Waivers | 67 |
| 11 | Building Applications and Appeals | 75 |
| 12 | Enforcement of Leases, Town Planning Ordinance and Buildings Ordinance | 85 |
| 13 | Development Blight | 93 |

| | | |
|---|---|---|
| 14 | Information Regarding Leases, Statutory Town Plans and Building Plans | 95 |
| 15 | Problem sets | 97 |

Appendices
    Appendix 1: Town Planning Board Guidelines (as at 8 April 2004) — 113
    Appendix 2: Aggregate Statistics Regarding Planning Applications 1975–2002 — 115
    Appendix 3: Probit and Logit Estimates of Non-Aggregate Statistics Regarding Planning Applications — 193

References — 225

Index — 233

# PREFACE

There are two major conceptual difficulties confronting a person who is unfamiliar with property or building development and property management in Hong Kong. The first difficulty is the complexity involved in the ascertainment of the permitted and permissible use and development intensity of the land, and the possibility and extent of the change in such use and intensity. The other difficulty is due to two factors. First, there is the sophisticated inter-relationship among various types of procedures, notably applications for modifying a government (Crown) lease (lease modifications and waivers), planning applications and building applications. Second, there is the complicated relationship between these procedures and various kinds of contractual and statutory enforcement measures taken by the government. These difficulties have been compounded by the frequent minor revisions to the Town Planning Ordinance since 1990, the sheer mass of building laws and the 'internal' nature of land administration.

To overcome these difficulties, resourceful individuals (notably developers without requisite in-house professional staff) would normally retain experienced Registered Professional Surveyors (RPS) with qualifications from the Royal Institution of Chartered Surveyors (RICS) and Hong Kong Institute of Surveyors (HKIS) and Registered Professional Planners (RPP) in private practice. RICS qualifications and experience are important quality assurance signals as the common law, especially the United Kingdom law, is of persuasive influence in Hong Kong courts and tribunals, not to mention that the local surveying practice has a strong British affiliation. Furthermore, as Hong Kong is an open and international city, professionals with an international profile are useful human capital. Where legal issues are involved, the service of lawyers may be required.

To better understand the need for and type of professional services, a person should have some working knowledge of the said couple of difficulties. Nissim's *Land Administration and Practice in Hong Kong* and Roberts and Siu's *Valuation of Development Land in Hong Kong* are useful publications that focus on the land administration aspects of development.

As a more focussed complement to the works of Nissim and Roberts and Siu, this book is a succinct guide to tackling the inter-related and interdisciplinary difficulties mentioned above. It provides an account of the concepts of use and change in use of land, followed by an outline of the concepts of, and procedures for, lease modifications and waivers; planning applications, reviews and appeals; building applications and appeals. It also gives an overview of government enforcement against contravention of lease conditions (lease enforcement); provisions of statutory town plans prepared under the Town Planning Ordinance (planning enforcement) and provisions of the Buildings Ordinance (enforcement against unauthorized building works). Finally, it gives an idea of the meaning of development blight and a guide to the source of information regarding lease conditions, statutory town plans and approved building plans as well as the decisions of various statutory bodies involved in the development process.

To stimulate thoughts and offer advice for further inquiry, a number of 'problems' based on real-life scenarios encountered by the authors in their experience as teachers, consultants and practitioners, are provided in the last chapter in addition to three appendices and a selected list of references at the end of this book. These problems should be useful to those preparing for their 'APC' HKIS qualifying examinations. We also hope that our efforts would help reduce the costs of property owners by helping them avoid unnecessary litigation with the government as they gain more knowledge of the relevant institutional, procedural and policy arrangements.

For practitioners and policy analysts, the detailed appendices in this book provide vital statistical information on both aggregate and non-aggregate development applications. They enable better appreciation of the chance of success of applications for specific uses, locations or sizes of development on a zone-by-zone basis in the light of refutable hypotheses.

Lawrence Wai-chung Lai, Daniel Chi-wing Ho, and Hing-fung Leung
Department of Real Estate and Construction
The University of Hong Kong

King-tong Liu
BSc (Econ) (London)(Hons); LLB (Zhongshan); FRICS, FHKIS, Registered Professional Surveyor (GP)

Zhi Han
BSc (Surveying)(Hons), PhD (HKU); MRICS, MHKIS, Registered Professional Surveyor (GP)

Ping Yung
BSocSc (Surveying)(Hons), PhD candidate (HKU)

April 2004

# 1 THE IMPORTANCE OF USE AND CHANGE IN USE

The concepts of 'use' and 'change in use' of land (which legally include buildings) are probably the most important and, at the same time, most difficult concepts in planning, building and development, and property management practice in Hong Kong.

## Why Must a Landowner Understand the Nature of Use and Change in Use?

These two concepts are important to the property owner (the lessee or grantee of government land or assignee of shares in property developed on such land) because the use of land, and therefore the change in the use of land, is not a matter of unconstrained or unconditional free choice of the property owner.

Indeed, both the use of land and the change in use of land are *heavily regulated* and prior permissions from various authorities of the Hong Kong Special Administrative Region (the government) are often required. In case the property owner is a company, these concepts are important to the investor who buys shares of the company.

The concept of 'use' is important to the property owners, as investors and consumers, for a number of reasons:

(a) First, a necessary factor in the *valuation* or *value appraisal* of a piece of property is the accurate determination of all possible and permissible existing and future uses of the property. This factor is important to the investor for assessing investment return to land or shares in companies that hold land property.

(b) Second, an important constraint that delimits *the extent of private property rights in land* is the correct identification of all permitted uses for, and/or uses prohibited/excluded from, the land. This constraint must be accurately identified by the owner or user of land because action or inaction based on mistaken or negligent identification by the owner, user or the property manager may lead to various 'enforcement' measures by the government (which may result in fines, title defects or even loss of title). Such measures may be a matter of breach of the land contract/grant and/or violation of the written law as embodied in various ordinances. Correct identification of the relevant constraint is also significant to the neighbour of land if that neighbour owns a legal estate or an equitable interest (such as an easement in the form of a right of way) that may be affected by any proposed change in use of the servient land.

## Why Must An Estate Surveyor Know about the Nature of Use and Change in Use?

An *estate surveyor* must understand the nature of use and change in use because of at least six reasons:

(a) In a *valuation* exercise, there is a need to interpret not only the uses (often expressed as 'user') and building covenants specified in the lease but also the effects of the provisions of statutory town plans on the covenants and various types of notices issued under the Town Planning Ordinance (Chapter 131, Laws of Hong Kong) to regulate unauthorized change in use.

(b) In ascertaining the possibility for *lease modification* or *short-term waiver*, there is a need to interpret not only the user and building covenants in the lease, but also the effects of the provisions of statutory plans on the covenants as well as the implications of administrative zoning delineated in administrative town plans.

(c) A surveyor can help make a planning application, attend a review or appeal (under the Town Planning Ordinance). In processing a planning application, planning review or planning appeal for a *change in use*, there is a need to understand the provisions of the Town Planning Ordinance.

(d) In negotiating *compensation* payment in land resumption under the Lands Resumption Ordinance (Chapter 124, Laws of Hong Kong), there is a need to consider relevant administrative town plans or development plans.

(e) In processing conveyancing matters for property in the rural New Territories, there is a need to appreciate the nature and implications of *enforcement notices* under the Town Planning Ordinance as encumbrances.

(f) In processing *lease enforcement* matters of a site, there is a need to appreciate the legal and valuation implications of statutory plans applicable to the site.

## Why Must a Lawyer Need to Know about Use and Change in Use?

A lawyer, whether a solicitor or barrister, needs to know about town planning because of at least ten reasons:

(a) In the *conveyancing of units* in a property, there is a need for the solicitor to check the *user* and this involves the interpretation of 'lease conditions', i.e. covenants in government leases and conditions for land sale, grant, surrender, exchange etc. (which will be further explained), and the 'Deed of Mutual Covenants' (DMC) in the light of relevant statutory town plans and 'planning conditions' (such as the requirements and stipulations of a 'Master Layout Plan' (MLP) (Lai et al. 2004), which may or may not be incorporated as part of the lease or the DMC) affecting the building and its environment (e.g. reclamation/highway/drainage projects).

(b) In the *conveyancing of a site*, there is a need for the solicitor to check (i) the *user* and this involves the interpretation of lease conditions and the DMC in the light of any statutory town plans and planning conditions (such as the requirements for a Master Layout Plan (MLP), which may or may not be incorporated as part of the lease; an environmental impact assessment (EIA); and other impact assessment) affecting the building and its environment (e.g. reclamation/highway/drainage channel projects); (ii) the site classification and plot ratios for the site under the Buildings Ordinance (Chapter 123, Laws of Hong Kong) as may be affected by a statutory town plan.

(c) In processing *conveyancing matters* for property in the rural New Territories subject to a past or present Interim Development Permission Area (IDPA) Plans, there is a need for the solicitor to appreciate the nature and implications of *enforcement notices* under the Town Planning Ordinance as encumbrances.

(d) In handling litigation involving *defeasibility of titles* in conveyancing, a solicitor/barrister should appreciate the implications of the non-fulfilment or breach of the provisions of the Town Planning Ordinance or planning conditions.

(e) In negotiating *compensation* payment in resumption, there is a need for a lawyer to consider relevant development plans.

(g) In processing *lease enforcement* matters of a site, there is a need for a lawyer to appreciate the legal implications of statutory plans applicable to the site.

(f) A solicitor can make or be involved in matters arising from *planning applications*. In processing a planning application, review or appeal to a *change in use*, there is a need to understand the provisions of the Town Planning Ordinance.

(g) In exercising due diligence in raising *title requisitions* regarding latent defects of the property, a solicitor acting for a purchaser in conveyancing needs to visit the property before completion with relevant experts and documents. The documents should include the applicable statutory town plans, occupation permits and approved building plans.

(h) In exercising due diligence for a client in the acquisition of shares of a company holding land assets, a solicitor needs to understand the effects of amendment to the zoning of the applicable statutory town plans and/or results of planning applications upon the value of the land assets.

(i) A barrister may be instructed to represent parties to a *planning appeal* before the Appeal Board (and further appeals); an enforcement action under the Town Planning Ordinance before a magistracy court (and further appeals); or a building appeal before the Building Tribunal under the Buildings Ordinance, which may or may not involve issues of the contravention of statutory town plans or a notice of an order under the respective ordinance.

(j) Direct professional access by planners to barristers is possible nowadays.

To minimize the chance for making negligent statements, it is advisable for lawyers to consult a Registered Professional Planner (RPP) and an Authorized Person (AP) before offering advice in respect of planning and building matters.

## Why Must an Authorized Person Know about Use and Change in Use?

An Authorized Person (AP), who may be an architect, a structural engineer or a building surveyor, must understand planning for at least three reasons:

(a) An AP can make or be involved in matters arising from *planning applications*. In processing a planning application, review or appeal to a *change in use*, there is a need to understand not only fundamental planning principles but also the provisions of the Town Planning Ordinance.

(b) In the preparation of a building plan application to the Building Authority, there is a need for the AP to ascertain the *user*. This involves the interpretation of lease conditions in the light of statutory town plans and planning conditions, assuming that planning permission has been granted (such as the requirements for a Master Layout Plan [MLP], which may or may not be incorporated as part of the lease; an Environmental Impact Assessment; and other impact assessment) affecting the building and its environment (e.g. reclamation/highway/drainage channel projects).

(c) In the preparation of a building plan application to the Building Authority, there is a need for the AP to ascertain the site classification and plot ratios for the site under the Buildings Ordinance as may be affected by a statutory town plan.

## Why Must a Person Concerned with Environmental Protection Need to Know about the Nature of Use and Change in Use?

A person who is keen on protecting the environment and ecology must understand town planning because various types of town plans have different implications for environmental protection in either forward planning or development control (notably planning applications and impositions of planning conditions), which may or may not reinforce the environmental protection clauses in the lease and/or specific environmental legislation.

## Why Must a Homebuyer or Investor Need to Know About the Nature of Use and Change in Use?

A homebuyer or a property investor needs to know more about town planning before making a purchase decision because of the reasons below:

(a) A homebuyer must be able to *interpret various types of town plans* and relevant building plans and their inter-relationships in order to ascertain the *present and future state of affairs and environment* of the property. Some of the common questions are: Would present seaviews or 'garden views' be protected in future? What kinds of use will be permitted or built by government on the 'Government/Institution and Community' (G/IC) zones? Would a funeral parlour or a church be built there? When exactly will such facilities be built? What would happen to 'Unspecified' zones?

(b) A homebuyer or investor must understand the town planning system and procedures in order to make a *proposal* or an *objection* to various types of town plans to protect or further his/her interest.

(c) A homebuyer and seller should know whether a property has any unauthorized use or unauthorized building work that may contravene the lease or Buildings Ordinance, rendering the title of a property defective.

(d) An indigenous villager who wishes to build a *small house* or use land for other *highest value use* must understand the provisions of relevant statutory town plans, especially those originated from the Interim Development Permission Area Plans.

(e) A property investor who has interest to buy, or has already acquired land in the New Territories, must understand the provisions of relevant statutory town plans, especially those originated from the Interim Development Permission Area Plans.

The purpose of government regulation of land uses and their changes is often explained in terms of the idea of forward planning and development control.

Forward planning is a government activity; it refers to the specification of parameters, rules, standards, guidelines, and procedures for land uses and built-forms by the government for private individuals in relation to land, or planning and development thereon.

Development control refers to the government processes or orders which ensure that matters specified or restricted in the forward planning process are followed or observed by private individuals, as backed by enforcement action based on contract or legislation in case of violation, contravention or non-compliance.

# 2 DUAL DEVELOPMENT CONTROL UNDER THE LAND LEASE AND STATUTORY TOWN PLAN

The key means used by the Hong Kong government to regulate land uses and the changes in such uses for a piece of land under private ownership are contractual and statutory, respectively through:

(a) the Government (previously Crown) Lease or lease conditions[1] (the land lease, which was either an indenture executed by deed, executed by signing, sealing and delivery; or a simple contract under hand which has become deemed to be a lease, which we may call a 'statutory lease', under the Conveyancing and Property Ordinance (Chapter 219, Laws of Hong Kong) for the piece of land at all time from its allocation; and

(b) any statutory town plan (draft or approved) produced under the Town Planning Ordinance (Chapter 131, Laws of Hong Kong) that may be imposed on the same piece of land from time to time before or after the execution of the lease; and any country park map (draft or approved) or designation under the Country Parks Ordinance (Chapter 208, Laws of Hong Kong).[2]

## Government Leases

'Government Leases' in Hong Kong were represented as 'Crown Leases' before the Joint Declaration of the Government of the United Kingdom of Great Britain and Northern Ireland and the Government of the People's Republic of China on the Question of Hong Kong (the Sino British Agreement or Joint Declaration of 1984), made on 19 December 1984 and ratified on 27 May 1985.

---

1. Government departments use the term 'lease conditions' to refer to both the covenants in a Crown (Government) Lease executed by deed and conditions of sale/grant/re-grant/extension etc. entered into by simple contract, which eventually become statutory leases when all positive covenants are fulfilled.
2. Section 16 of the Country Parks Ordinance refers to the Director of Lands as the 'Land Authority'.

*8  Change in Use of Land*

The leases refer to the title documents that grant land from the government to lessees (some of whom are grantees), who are usually developers. Such title documents must be registered and are the most important 'roots of titles' in conveyancing in Hong Kong.

The title documents executed in early years (before the 1960s) in Hong Kong Island, Kowloon and the New Territories are indentures (i.e., deeds).

The title documents executed since the late 1960s have been simple contracts under hand and generally described as Conditions (of Sale, of Exchange, or of Grant, depending on circumstances). Upon the compliance of all positive covenants, a Certificate of Compliance (CC) can be obtained and the title documents are deemed to be leases under the Conveyancing and Property Ordinance. The term of the lease or conditions starts to run from a specified date which may or may not be the date of the execution of the deed or the making of the agreement.

## Common Types of Land Leases

There are five main categories of land leases in Hong Kong. They are as follows:

(a) Block Crown (Government) Leases for clusters of 'private agricultural lots' and 'private building lots' in rural New Territories originally held under Imperial Chinese customary laws by 'indigenous villagers' when the British took over the Territories in 1898;

(b) conditions for 'New Grant Lots' in the New Territories, which were originally under government ownership, having had no prior history of indigenous ownership, and later sold or granted to private individuals;

(c) Crown (Government) Leases and Conditions of Sale executed for land parcels in Hong Kong Island, Kowloon and New Kowloon originally held under government ownership and later sold by the government to private individuals;

(d) Conditions of Regrant and Conditions of Renewal, respectively, for land re-granted and lease renewed for land parcels in Hong Kong, Kowloon and New Kowloon; and

(e) Conditions of Exchange executed for a major revision in the boundary or of the terms of a lease, for instance where land parcels under fragmented ownership are assembled and surrendered to government in exchange for a single site *in-situ*. The surrender of a group of land parcels under several ownership under a Block Government Lease in exchange for a development site is a typical example of an *in-situ* exchange.

A Block Crown (Government) Lease for each Demarcation District (DD) contains a survey map on which the location and boundaries of individual lots are indicated with numbers assigned to denote the lots, and a schedule that lists the name of the owner(s), the land use(s) (such as 'house', 'dry cultivation', 'wet cultivation', 'latrine' and 'grave') and rent collected for each lot indicated on the survey map. The information in the Block Crown Lease was collected by Indian surveyors in the beginning of the last century soon after the New Territories had been leased to the British by the Imperial China in 1898. The *Melhado Case* of 1983 affirms that the written materials in the schedule of a Block Crown Lease are only descriptive and do not amount to be restrictive covenants. All Block Crown Leases have an expiry date in the year 1997 but this has been automatically been extended to the year 2047 under the New Territories Leases (Extension) Ordinance (Chapter 150, Laws of Hong Kong) in accordance with the Sino-British Agreement.

Mostly located along roads developed when the New Territories were opened up, 'new grant lots' have conditions that make reference to various 'gazette notices' (or 'GN') that specify the general land use and development restrictions common to a specific vintage of these lots. A well-known example of such notices include 'GN 364 of 1934'. (Other better known examples are 'GN 365 of 1906'; 'GN 570 of 1924' and 'GN 720 of 1984'.) The tenure for the conditions for New Grant Lots in the New Territories that have an expiry date in the year 1997 has been automatically extended to 30 June 2047, subject to payment of government rent equivalent to 3 per cent of the rateable value of the property for the time being, under the New Territories Leases (Extension) Ordinance pursuant to the Sino-British Agreement.

The Crown (Government) Leases for land parcels in Hong Kong Island, Kowloon and New Kowloon have various terms of years. Some, common for land parcels in oldest urban areas on Hong Kong Island, have terms as long as 999 years. Some have a term of only 99 years, with no right of renewal. Most conditions granted before 1997 have a typical term of 75 years, which is either automatically renewable for another 75 years or non-renewable. All leases and pre-1997 conditions for land parcels in New Kowloon, i.e., those located to the north of Boundary Street, have an expiry date in the year 1997 but this date has also been automatically extended to the year 2047 under the New Territories Leases (Extension) Ordinance in accordance with the Sino-British Agreement.

Since the execution of the Joint Declaration, the Hong Kong government has begun selling or granting land parcels for a term up to 30 June 2047, whether they are in Hong Kong, Kowloon or the New Territories. These conditions are subject always to a rent equivalent to 3 per cent of the rateable value of the property, as revised by the Rating and Valuation Department from time to time, to be placed from the date of the return of sovereignty over Hong Kong to China on 1 July 1997.

## Statutory Town Plans under the Town Planning Ordinance

The Town Planning Ordinance in Hong Kong was enacted in 1939 to establish and empower an appointed Town Planning Board to produce statutory plans. The first statutory plan was not prepared until the 1960s. Due to the effect the *Singway Case*, namely that all statutory plans at the time were null and void for uncertainty, the 'section 16 application' procedure, which survives to date, was added to the Town Planning Ordinance in 1974. However, the basic structure of this ordinance remained the same until 1990, when a Town Planning Amendment Bill was passed so that in 1991 the planning legislation was substantially amended by the Town Planning (Amendment) Ordinance. The major amendments include those which (a) empower the Director of Planning to design Interim Development Permission Areas (IDPA) and to provide him enforcement power and the court sanction against unauthorized development in these areas whether under IDPA plans (first produced in 1990) or subsequent plans; (b) establish an appointed Appeal Board to hear and decide appeals against decisions of the Town Planning Board; and (c) require the submission of draft plans for approval by the Governor/Chief Executive-in-Council by the Town Planning Board.

When a draft plan has been prepared by the Town Planning Board, the notice of its preparation and exhibition must be published in the Government Gazette. The Board has a statutory duty to supply a person the plan at a cost it decides. The Town Planning Board's homepage is at http://www.info.gov.hk/tpb. The current statutory plans in force can be viewed from the government website for town planning, http://www.ozp.tpb.gov.hk, and all current and past statutory plans can be inspected at Planning Department and purchased from the Survey and Mapping Office of the Lands Department.

For the purpose for making a planning application, there is a need to examine the latest relevant statutory plan.

The life of a statutory plan made under the Town Planning Ordinance begins with the publication of the notice of its draft in the Government Gazette.

For making an application for review to the Town Planning Board or appeal to the Appeal Board under (respectively, section 17(1) and section 17B of) the Town Planning Ordinance, it is the statutory plan in force on the date of the application that is relevant and this plan may or may not be the current plan.

## Country Parks Designated under the Country Parks Ordinance

Under the Country Parks Ordinance applications to 'new development' inside country parks or marine parks should be made to the Country and Marine Parks Authority (previously Country Parks Authority): the Director of Agriculture, Fisheries and Conservation (previously the Director of Agriculture and Fisheries), who is advised by a Country and Marine Parks Board (previously the Country Parks Board). Decisions of this authority have not been published or made available to the public.

# 3 WHAT IS A USE?

## Uses in the 'User Clauses' in Land Leases

The old '999-year lease' is often misleadingly referred to as an 'unrestricted lease',[1] as it permits any type of use of land, save a specified list of uses, known as 'obnoxious' or 'offensive' trades, stipulated in the so-called 'offensive trade clause'.

Other than the 999-year leases, most lease documents contain specific 'user clauses' that define:

(a) uses and/or type of buildings that are permitted; and/or
(b) uses and/or type of buildings that are not permitted.

The intensity and other dimensions of the permitted uses are often further defined in other clauses or conditions in terms of such development control parameters or variables as building height; number of storeys; number of parking spaces; set-back; site coverage; plot ratios; physical manifestation of foundations and retaining walls.

The wordings of the covenants, terms or conditions contained in the lease conditions might not always explicitly or clearly spell out the exact kind of uses and development that is allowed. Court clarification of the exact meaning of a use or a form development is not uncommon in case there is a conflict in opinion between the government and the land user occurs.

Since the early 1980s, the Conditions of Sales or Grant in respect of government land parcels sold or grant executed have their user clauses and development conditions specified in great detail. They have lengthy and elaborated specifications for the design of the building, user(s) for each floor and even the maximum and minimum GFA for the site.

---

1. An example is the lease for Quarry Bay Marine Lot No. 1, Tong Chong Street and Hoi Wan Street.

## 14  Change in Use of Land

In Crown (Government) Leases and Block Crown (Government) Leases, old Conditions and New Grants, the user clauses and development conditions could be highly simplistic. For instance, the Block Crown Lease often simply states 'house' and 'building' in the schedule.

Some common examples of user clauses and development conditions in old 'lease conditions' are as follows:

(a) User clauses, limiting uses to:
- non-industrial purposes only
- residential use only
- commercial purposes only
- commercial/residential purposes only
- private residential purposes only
- industrial purposes only
- industrial/godown use/factory building only

(b) Building covenants or development conditions, which permit for the building only of:
- a European-type house
- one detached or semi-detached residence (house or dwelling) (of European-type) for the residence of a simple family
- detached or semi-detached residences
- a house not exceeding '35 feet' (10.67 metres) high
- a factory or warehouse

Crown Leases and New Grants were executed more than 50 or even 100 years ago when the town planning, environmental, building style and design were completely different from what we take for granted for the modern world today. (It is a complicated academic and professional issue as we consider how a building developed in this century should be controlled by a description in a lease executed several generations before. As mentioned above, for instance, should the 35-feet height ceiling allow for a car park floor? Could a 'house' be in the form of flatted development? Could a 'hotel' be regarded as 'a private residential purpose'? The various coverage of the term 'house' in the old leases is of great benefit as it allows a high degree of flexibility in interpretation. However, there are always cases where the interpretation between the government and the land user is not in agreement. For example, a developer may say a car park floor in addition to the 35-feet limit should be allowed whereas the government may not think so.)

Practice Notes issued by the Lands Administrative Office of the Lands Department sometimes help clarify the stance of the government regarding lease interpretation, but only the court has the final word when a dispute cannot be resolved by mutual agreement. As regards the 'house' example mentioned above, a Practice Note states that 'a building with one main entrance and one secondary entrance together with such means of escape as may be required under the Buildings Ordinance to serve the buildings (provided that the means of escape are designed and constructed to be for exit purpose only and can be opened only from the inside)' is one house. Residential flats within a building meeting the 'house' criteria are acceptable as house. However, the Notes also state that the following examples are not accepted as 'house':

(a) a multi-storey commercial/residential development with shops on the ground floor, each shop having its own separate access to and from the street;
(b) a joint development having the characteristic of one house but constructed over two lots, the leases of which each contains a clause that the owner 'shall not erect other than one house'; and
(c) a building meeting all the 'one house' criteria but with a free-standing guard house or electrical and mechanical (E & M) room.

## Uses in Statutory Town Plans

There is no statutory definition of any land use or any class of land use zone in the Town Planning Ordinance. The *Review of Master Schedule of Notes to Statutory Plans* agreed by the Town Planning Board on 21 June 2002 for public consultation does not alter this situation, though it streamlines the existing lists of definitions of terms.

The statutory town plan in Hong Kong is a kind of land use zoning plan. The zoning system in Hong Kong has a racial segregation origin (Lai and Yu 2001; Lai 2002), imposed by a series of ordinances, namely the European District Reservation Ordinance of April 1888; which was replaced, in turn, by the Hill District Reservation Ordinance of April 1904 and the Peak District (Residence) Ordinance of May 1918 for the Peak on Hong Kong Island and the Cheung Chau Reservation Ordinance of August 1919 for the island Cheung Chau. Both the Peak District (Residence) Ordinance and the Cheung Chau Reservation Ordinance were repealed in 1946.

Racially-based zoning is now illegal under the Hong Kong Bill of Rights Ordinance (Bill of Rights) (Chapter 383, Laws of Hong Kong) and the Basic Law of the Hong Kong Special Administrative Region of the People's Republic of China (the Basic Law).

## 16  Change in Use of Land

Modern statutory planning of town and country in Hong Kong has been carried out under two major pieces of legislation, the Town Planning Ordinance 1939 and the Country Parks Ordinance 1976, and their amendments. No statutory plan had been prepared under the former until many years after the publication of the so-called Abercrombie Report of 1948 (Lai 1999) and the latter was enacted about 10 years after the Talbots Report (Talbot and Talbot 1965) had been published. Each ordinance establishes its own planning body, namely the Town Planning Board and the Country and Marine Parks Authority.[2] The Country and Marine Parks Authority is the planning authority for land which covers more than 70 per cent of the land of the territory whereas the Town Planning Board deals with all land outside the country parks. Once the notice of a draft country map is published in the Government Gazette under section 9(1) of the Country Parks Ordinance, any 'new development', under section 10(1) of the Country Parks Ordinance requires prior permission of the Country and Marine Parks Authority though such development may be permitted by any 'lease condition'. Section 10(3) of Country Parks Ordinance gives a partial and open-ended definition of 'development' (which includes 'any material change in the use of any buildings or other land') that is similar but not identical to that in section 1A of the Town Planning Ordinance. Section 16 empowers the Country and Marine Parks Authority to take enforcement action against those who contravene the country parks maps. The statutory power of the Town Planning Board to make plan and exercise development control in lands already designated as country parks by the Country and Marine Parks Authority means that new development in such lands may require concurrent development permission by two authorities.[3] (Yet, most people, such as developers and proprietors, tend to focus on the activities of the Town Planning Board as the Board is dealing with land or greater economic value that is either urbanized or in the process of urbanization. In addition, there are many others who are concerned with the urban environment as well as the impact of proliferation of urban activities upon the urban fringes which are regarded as having significant visual, ecological or sentimental values, real or imaginary, as a matter of degree or as matter of kind.)

---

2. Unlike the Town Planning Board, the Country and Marine Park Board is advisory, though the Country and Marine Parks Authority has a statutory duty to consult the Board.
3. This is so notwithstanding that the Notes to statutory town plans often relegate matters inside Country Park Zones on them to the Country Parks Ordinance.

Since the establishment of the Planning Department in 1990 as an independent government department, there has been much legislative activism to expand the Town Planning Ordinance. Following the Town Planning Amendment Bill of 1990, the Town Planning (Amendment) Ordinance was introduced in 1991 as a means to extend statutory plan coverage to *all lands* (including country parks) in Hong Kong especially private lands in the New Territories outside the country parks and new towns. Another major Town Planning Bill was announced for public consultation in July 1996, followed by another bill in January 2000, and one more in May 2003.

Yet, it is noteworthy that there has never been any attempt to develop an elaborated set of Town Planning Regulations, which could serve technical purposes such as those in the Building Regulations within the ambit of the Buildings Ordinance. As a result, the interpretation of almost all technical matters regarding statutory town plans has to rely on inferences from the statutory Notes to the plans and 'definitions of terms' prepared by the Town Planning Board, wordings in administrative documents such as the Town Planning Board Guidelines (Appendix 1), Hong Kong Planning Standards and Guidelines (HKPSG) and Town Planning Board Guidance Notes (Guidance Notes) prepared by the Town Planning Board, Explanatory Statements attached to the plans prepared by the Planning Department, and the Hong Kong Planning Standards and Guidelines (HKPSG) issued by the government.

In fact, there has been no major attempt by the government to issue as many practice notes, such as those issued to Authorized Persons (AP) and professional planners. Neither the Town Planning Bill 1996, the Town Planning Bill 2000, nor the Town Planning (amendment) Bill 2003 bothered itself with the task of determining technical planning matters on an unambiguous statutory base and promote scientific application of planning as a professional endeavour. (This state of affairs shapes the way in which decisions are made by the Town Planning Board when exercising its discretionary powers.)

The planning appeal mechanism commenced operation in November 1991 under the Town Planning (Amendment) Ordinance 1991 (hereinafter also referred to as 'the Town Planning Ordinance' unless otherwise specified). It is the final resort within the framework of the ordinance for a person who feels aggrieved by the outcomes of the planning application and review procedures. These outcomes include the situations where the decisions of the Town Planning Board are to reject the applications categorically, or where the decisions to approve are attaching planning conditions that are unacceptable to the applicant. The applicant is entitled to (become an appellant in) an appeal to an appointed statutory body, the Appeal Board (often referred to as the Town Planning Appeal Board), which has a membership that is completely different from that of the Town Planning Board. This Appeal Board may reverse the decision of rejection and/or striking out or amending the imposed planning conditions to the appellant's favour.

Article 6 of the Basic Law expressly protects private property, in accordance with the Sino British Agreement of 1984. (The implications of the Agreement and the Basic Law in respect of private property rights over land apparently have not attracted much attention of the academic or legal drafter of the Town Planning (Amendment) Ordinance, though it often compromises, if not nullifies, common law rights conferred by the land lease without compensation.)

The statutory land use zoning plan defines for each class of zone specific land uses in terms of two lists of uses (Column 1 uses and Column 2 uses) in the 'Schedule of Uses' in the Notes and in terms of 'planning intention'[4] or other information in the Explanatory Statement and the Notes to the plan. However, it does not provide any definition of each land use in either Column or the Explanatory statement. The legal meaning of a use, such as a house in a Green Belt Zone, is to be decided by the government town planner and, in time of dispute, the court. The leading case is the *Wah Yick Case*.

However, the Town Planning Board does maintain and make available to the public, at no cost, a list of definitions for land use items found in each of the two types of statutory town plans. One of the lists, applicable to plans with a history of an Interim Development Permission Area (IDPA), is called 'Definitions of Terms for Rural Outline Zoning Plans and Development Permission Areas Plans' approved by the Town Planning Board in April 1994 and last updated on 27 April 2001. The other list, with a longer history, for plans without a history of IDPA, is known as 'Definitions of Terms Used in

---

4. Originally only stated in the Explanatory Statement, this expression has recently been inserted below each zone in the Schedule of Uses in the Notes in some Outline Zoning Plans. This is a good reform as the public can now raise objections to the planning intention thus stated when notice of a relevant statutory plan is published in the gazette. No one can raise any objection to the Explanatory Statement as it is expressly stated as being 'not part of the plan' prepared under the Town Planning Ordinance.

Statutory Plans', and was updated on 18 August 1990 and 27 April 2001. The *Review of Master Schedule of Notes to Statutory Plans,* agreed by the Town Planning Board on 21 June 2002 for public consultation, would streamline the terms under both lists and standardize existing item under both Columns 1 and 2. This list of definitions is updated from times to times but does not form part of (or referred to) the statutory town plan (including the Notes) or its Explanatory Statement.

In addition to the list of definitions of land uses, the Planning Department also produces sets of Town Planning Board Guidelines and Guidance Notes for specific uses or zones.

The concept of 'use' is often involved in evaluating the implication of a statutory zone for an intended 'change in use'.

## The Concept of 'Change in Use' in Government Leases, Building Control and Planning Enforcement

One scenario in which the concept of 'change in use' is significant is the situation where the government is exercising enforcement actions, in her contractual or statutory capacity, against current land uses which are considered to be in breach of lease/conditions of the Buildings Ordinance or the Town Planning Ordinance.

While the meaning of uses under lease/conditions is largely a matter of lease interpretation informed by case law, there are statutory definitions of 'change in use' under both the Buildings Ordinance and the Town Planning Ordinance.

Section 25 of the Buildings Ordinance deals with the 'change in *use of a building*'. Section 25 (3) of the Buildings Ordinance states:

> The use of a building shall be deemed to be materially changed – (a) where the carrying out of building works for the erection or a building intended for such use would have contravened the provisions of this Ordinance; or (b) where the Building Authority could have refused to give approvals of plans of such building works under section 16(1)(g).

Section 16(1)(d) of the Buildings Ordinance is significant as it refers to the discretionary power of the Building Authority in refusing to approve building plans on the grounds of contravention of plans prepared under the Town Planning Ordinance.

The key referent for ascertaining the change in the use of a building is the 'permit to occupy a new building,' commonly referred to as an Occupation Permit (OP).

Section 1A of the Town Planning Ordinance gives partial and open-ended definitions of:

(a) 'material change in the *use of land or buildings*', which is stated to 'include depositing matter on land, notwithstanding that all or part of the land is already used for depositing matter, if the area, height or amount of the deposit is increased.' (Under this wide definition, farming may require planning permission even if it is carried out in an Agriculture Zone[5] where the farming activities involve depositing new top soils after a long period of cultivation.)

(b) 'existing use'[6] 'in relation to a development permission area',[7] which means 'a use of a building or land that was in existence immediately before the publication in the Gazette of notice of the draft plan of the development permission area'.

This wide definition is adopted by the government to give a broad meaning of 'development' to tackle 'unauthorized development' under section 20(7) in respect of an interim development permission area and a development permission area; sections 22 and 23 of the Town Planning Ordinance. Section 1A of the Town Planning Ordinance defines 'development' in a way similar to that under section 10 (3) of the Country and Marine Parks Ordinance. 'Development' is defined by the former as 'carrying out building, engineering, mining or other operations in, on, over or under land, or making a material change in the use of land or buildings'. 'Development' is defined by the latter as 'carrying out building, engineering, mining or other similar operations in, on, over or under land, or the making a material change in the use of any buildings or other land other than ...'.

---

5. The drafting of the statutory town plans may further restrict agriculture. Although agriculture is a 'Column 1 use', the drafting of the Notes entails that it is not always permitted where excavation or filling is involved.
6. The Chinese translation 'present use' is a poor one as 'existing use' in effect refers to an old use with reference to an IDPA or DPA Plan.
7. Section 20 (7) also refers to this meaning. But it would be a serious mistake to disregard the provision of the IDPA Plan, if there is one, or OZP itself, as the real cut-off line for 'existing use' is really the IDPA Plans.

## The Concept of Change in Use in Applications under Statutory Town Plans

The concept of 'change in use' is also significant is the situation when a proprietor wishes to develop a *proposed* land use or building lawfully in compliance with the Town Planning Ordinance. This situation covers several sub-scenarios about which many students are frequently confused, namely:

(a) objecting a draft plan: making an objection to a draft plan as a matter of a statutory right under section 6 of the Town Planning Ordinance, which may or may not involve (b) below; and
(b) rezoning proposals: requesting the Town Planning Board to amend a statutory town plan (being a 'draft plan': or an 'approved plan') in force, exercising its powers to make plans under section 3(1) of the Town Planning Ordinance, so that the proposed use can be carried out as a matter of course or may be carried out after a successful planning application. This may arise when the proprietor finds that there is no possibility of developing the use without contravening the town plan as a matter of course under Column 1, or making a planning application under Column 2 to the Notes (or cover pages) of a statutory town plan.
(c) planning applications under section 16 and subsequent reviews and appeals under sections 17(1) and 17B(1), respectively, of the Town Planning Ordinance for uses within Column 2 or outside Column 2, i.e., on the cover pages of the Notes to a statutory town plan — this is 'planning application' commonly understood.

The Town Planning Ordinance has specific provisions for handling objections to draft plans and planning applications (and further reviews/appeals, including a review by the Secretary under section 24 in respect an reinstatement notice issued under section 20[4]) but not for rezoning proposals.

# 4 CHANGE IN USE AND DEVELOPMENT CONTROL UNDER THE LAND LEASE, TOWN PLANS AND THE BUILDINGS ORDINANCE

Enforcement against or an application for change in use in Hong Kong varies due to differences in the types of applicable leases/conditions and town plans in the regimes of statutory enforcement.

It is impossible to specify all possible interactions between the land lease and various types of town plans that may be imposed on 'privately owned land', especially the 'private agricultural land' held under Block Government (formerly Crown) Leases in the New Territories. The scenarios presented in this chapter are only some of the commonly found situations in practice. These scenarios refer to private land parcels outside country parks.[1] The New Territories scenarios are presented first, as the situation there is most complicated.

## The New Territories

Not all areas in the New Territories have been covered by statutory town plans.

### Where There Is No Statutory Town Plans

*Where there is no district town plan of any kind (Scenario A)*

All land in Hong Kong is within the ambit of Territorial Development Strategy (Review) (TDSR),[2] Hong Kong Planning Standards and Guidelines (HKPSG) and a Sub-Regional Plan. However, by December 2002, there are still areas outside country parks that are not yet covered by any district town plan. A

---

1. As mentioned, both the Town Planning Ordinance and Country Parks Ordinance control development in the country parks.
2. The latest round of TDSR is called *Hong Kong 2030: Planning Vision and Strategy* ('HK 2030'), which commenced in the year 2000.

## 24  Change in Use of Land

good example is Ping Chau, Mirs Bay. (Another classic example was Discovery Bay on Lantau Island, which became subject to an OZP on 14 September 2001. This was more than twenty years after the development began to take shape according to a Master Layout Plan. This example attracted statutory control partly as a result of the Disney World project at Penny's Bay.)

In this scenario, government control of land use or built form is exercised on a contractual basis according to lease conditions, subject to whatever relevant ordinances, notably the Buildings Ordinance.

Change in use in this scenario not permitted by the lease requires lease modifications or waivers, which invariably involve payment of premia, followed by building applications, unless the works are exempted by the Buildings Ordinance.

In the New Territories, some categories of buildings, 'New Territories Exempted Houses' (NTEH), are outside the reach of the Buildings Ordinance. However, they are permitted if and only if they satisfy all policy and design requirements of the New Territories Exempted House (NTEH or 'small house') policy.[3] A 'small house' is the most common form of the NTEH.

For this scenario, the rule in the *Melhado Case* applies to the 'private agricultural lots' in the New Territories. For such lots, the lessees have a contractual right to use land for open storage, in so far as it does not involve building works. This common law rule has become subject to the Town Planning Ordinance since its amendment in 1991.

When an 'Interim Development Area Plan' (IDPA Plan) is imposed, the use 'immediately before' the date of the IDPA plan is 'existing use'[4] that is allowed to persist under the Town Planning Ordinance or the relevant statutory plan.

Therefore, a landowner has the economic incentive to maximize removal of natural vegetation covers, wet lands and open storage on land parcels not yet caught by IDPA Plans. This often leads to the complete destruction of ecologically significant habitats.

---

3. See Lands Department (1999), *Construction of New Territories Exempted Houses*. Hong Kong: Lands Department (Chinese publication).
4. The definition of 'existing use' under section 1A, which is relative to a DPA plan only, must be considered with extreme care. To fully appreciate the meaning of 'an existing use' in an area, one must read the entire Town Planning Ordinance and the drafting of applicable statutory plan and its history (whether there is an IDPA Plan or not).

*Where there are only non-statutory district plans (Scenario B)*

By 2002, there are still areas in the New Territories which are only covered by administrative town plans, as in the case of some populated 'outlying islands', notably Cheung Chau (Lamma Island and Peng Chau became subject to Outline Zoning Plan, respectively, on 25 August 2000 and 20 February 2001).

As in the first scenario, government control of land use or built form is exercised on a contractual basis according to 'lease conditions', subject to relevant ordinances, notably the Buildings Ordinance. The main difference is that in considering lease modifications and small house applications, the Land Authority would take into account the provisions of the relevant administrative town plans.

Change in use in this scenario requires lease modifications or waivers (if that use is not permitted by the lease), which invariably involve payment of premia, followed by building applications, unless the works involved are exempted by the Buildings Ordinance. If the proposal is consistent with the administrative zoning, then the applicant has a greater chance of success.

Applications for NTEH are permitted if and only if they satisfy all policy and design requirements of the New Territories Exempted House (NTEH) policy (the 'small house policy') as well as the provisions of the administrative town plans.

The rule in the *Melhado Case* also applies to land parcels in this scenario so far as 'Agricultural lots' are concerned, since this common law rule has not been displaced by any statutory town plan yet. For such lots, the lessees have a contractual right to use land for open storage, in so far as it does not involve building works caught under the Buildings Ordinance.

When an IDPA Plan is imposed, the use 'immediately before' the date of the IDPA plan is 'existing use' that is allowed to persist under the Town Planning Ordinance. Where an IDPA Plan cannot be imposed[5] but a DPA is, the use 'immediately before' the date of the DPA plan is 'existing use' that is allowed to persist under the Town Planning Ordinance.[6]

---

5. After the operation of the Town Planning (Amendment) Ordinance of 1991, the Director of Planning can no longer designate any 'interim development permission area'. See section 26(4).
6. Section 1A, Town Planning Ordinance.

As in the first scenario, a landowner has economic incentive to maximize destruction of wildlife habitats and open storage on land not yet caught by IDPA (DPA) Plans. Similarly adverse ecological consequences often occur.

### Where There Are Statutory Town Plans

*Where there are only statutory district plans and they have no history of IDPA or DPA Plans (Scenario C)*

This scenario is mainly found outside new towns. Development in this scenario is identical to that in the urban areas of Hong Kong Island and Kowloon. There is no enforcement provision in this scenario under the Town Planning Ordinance.

Enforcement of town plans in this scenario will rely on (a) the lease modification and enforcement mechanism, where there is a linkage clause in the lease stipulating compliance with town planning law provisions; and (b) the building plan permission and occupation permit system under the Buildings Ordinance. Note that the Building Authority has discretion not to follow the provisions in statutory town plans.

*Where there are only statutory district plans with a prior history of IDPA Plans[7] (Scenario D1) or where there are statutory plans that are either draft DPA plans with no prior history of IDPA Plans[8] or any subsequent statutory plans[9] arising from such draft DPA Plans (Scenario D2)*

This scenario is similar to Scenario C above except that there are provisions for enforcement under the Town Planning Ordinance for areas previously designated interim development permission areas (Scenario D1) or development permission areas (Scenario D2).

---

7. An Outline Zoning Plan with a history of an IDPA Plan is often called a 'Rural Outline Zoning Plan'.
8. These DPA Plans have no history of IDPA Plans as the applicable land was not designated IDPA before the Town Planning (Amendment) Ordinance of 1991 came into effect.
9. An Outline Zoning Plan with a history of a DPA Plan in this sub-scenario is also called a 'Rural Outline Zoning Plan'.

*Where there are both non-statutory and statutory district plans with no prior history of IDPA or draft DPA Plans (Scenario E)*

This scenario is mainly found within new towns. Development in this scenario is identical to that in the urban areas of Hong Kong Island and Kowloon. Other examples are Peng Chau and Lamma Island. In this scenario, there is no enforcement provision under the Town Planning Ordinance.

Enforcement of town plans will rely on (a) the lease modification and enforcement mechanism, where there is a linkage clause in the lease stipulating compliance with town planning law provisions; and (b) the building plan permission and occupation permit system under the Buildings Ordinance. Note that the Building Authority has discretion not to follow the provisions in statutory town plans.

## Hong Kong Island and Kowloon

### Where There Are Both Non-statutory and Statutory District Plans (Scenario E)

By 2002, virtually all land parcels in Hong Kong Island and Kowloon have been covered by both administrative and statutory town plans. (Land parcels not so covered by town plans are inside country parks.)

In this scenario, government control of land use or built form is exercised on a contractual basis according to lease conditions, subject to statutory town plans that may or may not displace or confer extra development rights and relevant ordinances, notably the Buildings Ordinance.

The rule in the *Melhado Case* does not apply, as almost all lands are subject to government leases with specific user restrictions. But open storage could be carried out as temporary uses.

There is no enforcement provision in this scenario under the Town Planning Ordinance.

Enforcement of town plans will rely on (a) the lease modification and enforcement mechanism, where there is a linkage clause in the lease stipulating compliance with town planning provisions; and (b) the building plan approval and occupation permit system under the Buildings Ordinance. Note that the Buildings Department has no discretion not to follow the provisions in such administrative town plans as Outline Development Plans.

28  Change in Use of Land

### *Where There Is No Statutory or Administrative Town Plan (Scenario F)*

To complete the picture, there is a mass of land not covered by any statutory or administrative town plan. This area is government land within the Tai Tam Country Park. The relevant development permission authority for this area is the Country and Marine Parks Authority.

Figure 4.1 below summarizes the types of statutory plans in the scenarios discussed.

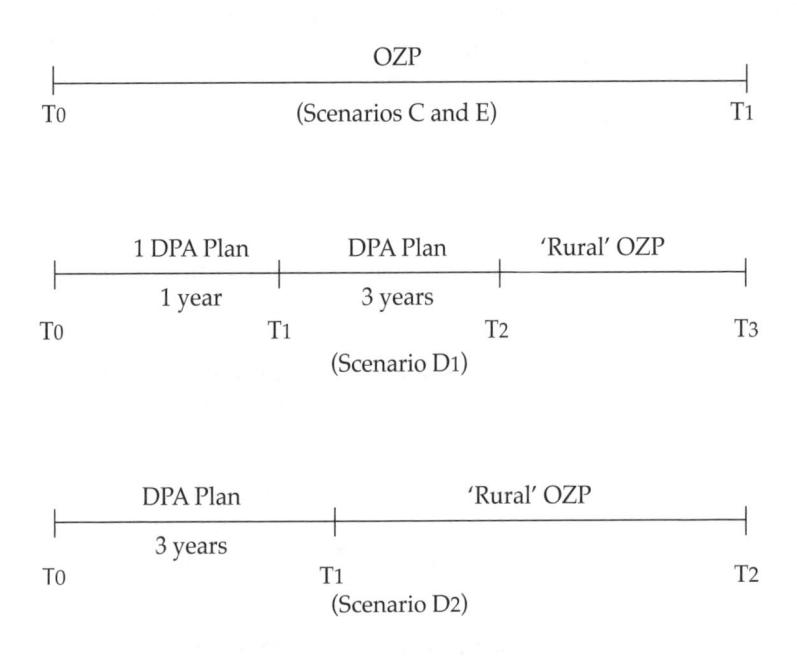

```
            OZP
|---------------------------------|
T0    (Scenarios C and E)         T1


    1 DPA Plan       DPA Plan      'Rural' OZP
|---------------|---------------|---------------|
     1 year           3 years
T0              T1              T2              T3
                (Scenario D1)


     DPA Plan              'Rural' OZP
|---------------|-------------------------------|
     3 years
T0              T1                              T2
                (Scenario D2)
```

Figure 4.1  Vintages of Statutory Town Plans under different scenarios

# 5 THE NEED FOR MAKING A PLANNING APPLICATION TO ENABLE A CHANGE IN USE UNDER THE TOWN PLANNING ORDINANCE

*12. When is a s. 16 application required?*

Each Outline Zoning Plan is accompanied by a *Schedule of Notes* showing the uses always permitted (Column One Uses) and uses that would require permission from the Town Planning Board (Column Two Uses) within a particular zone. There may be additional controls on developments within a particular zone and these are specified under the *'Remarks' column* in the Notes *for that land use zone*. You *only* need to apply for permission under s. 16 of the Town Planning Ordinance when your proposed use *or* development is under 'Column 2' or as required is under the 'Remarks' of the Notes.[1] (FAQ, June 2003: ttp://info.gov.hk/planning/info_serv/faq/index_e.htm http://info.gov.hk/planning/info_serv/faq/index_e.htm) [Emphasis added]

## Situations Where There Is No Need for Obtaining Planning Permissions

There is *no need* for planning permission obtained by a planning application under section 16 of the Town Planning Ordinance:

(1) Where the plan has no prior history of an IDPA or a draft DPA Plan
   a. for any 'existing use';
   b. for any temporary use that involves no building or work defined under the Buildings Ordinance;
   c. for any use always permitted in all zones as specified on the cover pages of the Notes; and

---

1. The FAQ answer is misleading. The 'Schedule of Notes' should read 'Schedule of Uses in the Notes'. There is no 'Remarks column' in any Notes. There are in fact 'Remarks' for some zones and written matters (paragraphed in small Roman numbers) stated before the Schedule of Uses. The 'Column 2' and 'Remark' distinction is far from being adequate.

d. for any Column 1 use (unless there is a remark regarding further restrictions such as those regarding plot ratios, number of storeys and building heights).

(2) Where the plan has a prior history of an IDPA or DPA Plan
   a. for any 'existing use' as defined under the Town Planning Ordinance: in essence, a use that existed immediately before the publication of the IDPA Plan (where the first plan is an IDPA Plan) or the draft DPA Plan (where the first plan is a draft DPA Plan) and has continued to be in existence without any material change;
   b. for such temporary use as specified on the cover pages of the Notes of the statutory plan, which involves no building work or other specified work (such as excavation, pond filling or 'filling of ponds') and does not last for more than two weeks;
   c. for any use always permitted in all zones as specified on the cover pages of the Notes of the statutory plan; and
   d. for any Column 1 use (unless there is a remark regarding further restrictions notably excavation and pond filling).

## Situations Where There Is a Need for Obtaining Planning Permissions

There is a need for planning permission obtained by a planning application under section 16 of the Town Planning Ordinance:

(1) Where the plan has no prior history of an IDPA Plan or a draft DPA Plan
   a. for any 'existing use' has ceased to exist or has been discontinued at the time the notice about the relevant plan is published in the gazette;
   b. for any Column 1 use where there is a remark regarding further restrictions (such as plot ratios); and
   c. for any Column 2 use, which is not or unless it is an existing use — the principal source of planning applications.

(2) Where the plan has a history of an IDPA Plan
   a. for any 'existing use' as defined under the Town Planning Ordinance (in essence a use that existed immediately before the publication of the IDPA Plan) which has ceased to be in existence or has been discontinued, or has witnessed a *material change* since the publication of the IDPA Plan;
   b. for such temporary use as specified on the cover pages of the Notes of the statutory plan and any use that involves building work; pond filling, excavation or lasting for more than two weeks — whether or

not it is triggered by an enforcement notice issued under the Town Planning Ordinance;
c.  for any Column 1 use where there is a remark regarding further restrictions, notably pond filling; and
d.  for any Column 2 use, whether temporary or permanent and whether involving building work or otherwise.

(3) Where the plan has no history of an IDPA Plan but of a draft DPA Plan
a.  for any 'existing use' as defined under the Town Planning Ordinance (a use, according section 1A, that existed immediately before the publication of the draft DPA Plan) which has ceased to be in existence or has been discontinued, or has witnessed a *material change* since the publication of the draft DPA Plan;
b.  for such temporary use as specified on the cover pages of the Notes of the statutory plan and any use that involves building work; pond filling, excavation or lasting for more than two weeks — whether or not it is triggered by an *enforcement notice* issued under the Town Planning Ordinance;
c.  for any Column 1 use where there is a remark regarding further restrictions, notably pond filling; and
d.  for any Column 2 use, whether temporary or permanent and whether involving building work or otherwise, which is not or unless it is an existing use.

# 6 'TEMPORARY USES' AND 'EXISTING USES' ON PRIVATE LAND UNDER A STATUTORY TOWN PLAN

## Temporary Uses

If a use is carried out on private land in the open air without involving any building or work defined in the Buildings Ordinance, then this use is often regarded as being 'temporary'. Where a temporary use is conducted on private land, whether or not there is a need to obtain planning permission for that use or its development would depend on the location of the land and the applicable type of statutory town plan.

### Where There Is No Statutory Town Plan

Where there is no statutory town plan, then there is no need (and in fact possibility) of obtaining any planning permission; the regulation of the use is primarily a contractual matter based on the land lease. Where the lease is a Block Government (Crown) Lease, the rule in the *Melhado Case* applies.

### Where There Is a Statutory Town Plan without a History of an IDPA or a Draft DPA Plan

Where there is an applicable statutory plan but its origin was not an IDPA Plan or a draft DPA Plan, then there is generally no need for planning permission for the temporary use. This 'toleration' of temporary use is defined on the cover pages of the Notes to the statutory plan.

Even if the temporary use does contravene the statutory town plan in this scenario, there is no possibility of enforcement against contravention under the existing Town Planning Ordinance.

## Where There Is a Statutory Town Plan with a History of an IDPA or a Draft DPA Plan

Where there is an applicable statutory plan and its origin was an IDPA or a draft DPA Plan, it is necessary to obtain planning permission for the temporary use if the use is not an existing use.

There is no need for planning permission where the use is 'existing' and there has been no material change to it. This 'toleration' of existing use is defined on the cover pages of the Notes to the statutory plan as well as in the Town Planning Ordinance. A crucial problem confronting the landowner is that he/she may not know for sure whether his/her perception of 'existing use' is shared by the Planning Department or accepted by the court as a matter of fact. This difficulty becomes a real crisis when the Director of Planning takes enforcement action on the grounds that such use is not considered by him/her as existing. This issue will be further discussed under the section on enforcement.

If the temporary use is not 'existing' but has been carried out or continued without planning permission, then the owner and/or occupier of the land are/is liable to enforcement action against contravention under the Town Planning Ordinance.

## Existing Uses

If a use is an 'existing use' in the sense that it is physically in existence at the time of the imposition of a statutory town plan affecting the land, then subject to some qualifications discussed below, there is generally no need for the lessee or occupier to discontinue the use or to obtain planning permission for the *continuation* of the use, though such use is not permitted under by the relevant zoning of the land. 'Town Planning Board Guidelines for Interpretation of Existing Use in the Urban and New Town Areas' (TPB PG-No. 24B dated June 2003) should be consulted to appreciate the Town Planning Board's interpretation of existing uses outside areas affected by Interim Development Permission Area Plans and/or Development Permission Area Plans.

### Where the Statutory Plan Has No Prior History of an IDPA or a Draft DPA Plan

Other than TPB PG-No. 24B, there is no statutory or administrative definition of an 'existing use' in this scenario. There is no need for obtaining planning permission for the use or development and this is expressed on the cover pages of the Notes to the statutory town plan.

According to TPB PG-No. 24B, the followings under a statutory town plan inside 'urban and new town areas'[1] need no planning permission: (a) any use of land or building which is 'in existence before the publication of any statutory plan covering the concerned area'; and (b) any use of a building 'as designated on the approved building plans/OP[occupation permit], or as approved under section 25 of the BO'. [Brackets added]

### Where the Statutory Plan Has a Prior History of an IDPA or a Draft DPA Plan

There is a partial statutory definition of an 'existing use' in this scenario, as provided expressly in section 1A of the Town Planning Ordinance, as well as indirectly on the cover pages of the Notes to the statutory town plan. There is no need for obtaining planning permission for such use if there is no actual intensification of the use, provided that the use has never been abandoned, discontinued or witnessing any '*material change*' since the relevant date on which the use is defined under the law.

---

1. The situation of statutory plans without a prior history of an IDPA or a draft DPA Plan for rural areas is not covered by this set of guidelines.

# 7 THE POSSIBILITY OF MAKING A PLANNING APPLICATION AND STEPS IN CHECKING WHETHER A USE REQUIRES PLANNING PERMISSION

## Possibility of Making a Planning Application to Enable a Change in Use Under the Town Planning Ordinance

It is only possible for making a planning application for a piece of land by any person to be lodged in under section 16 of the Town Planning Ordinance where:

(1) the land in question is covered by a valid draft or approved statutory town plan; and
(2) there is a need as mentioned in Chapter 5 to make an application under the town plan referred to in (1) above.

There is no possibility for a planning application for a piece of land to be lodged in under section 16 of the Town Planning Ordinance:

(1) where there is no statutory plan or zone covering the land in question;
(2) where the land is covered by a statutory zone in the plan with no prior history of an IDPA or a draft DPA Plan and the use or intended use for the land.
   a. needs not be applied for (as in the case where the use is an 'existing use'); it is always permitted in any zone as specified on the cover pages of the Notes, or is permitted as a Column 1 use for the specific class of zone as discussed in Chapter 5; or
   b. cannot be applied for, as it is not be found under Column 2 or Column 1, or anywhere in the Notes stating that the use or change may be permitted on a permanent or temporary basis.

## Steps in Checking Whether a Use Requires Planning Permission

To ascertain whether a use for a piece of land requires planning permission through an application under section 16 of the Town Planning Ordinance:

(1) Where the plan has no prior history of an IDPA or draft DPA Plan:
    a. identify the exact location of the land in question;
    b. obtain the latest Outline Zoning Plan (which consists of a zoning map and a set of Notes, both being statutory) together with a set of Explanatory Statement;
    c. identify the zoning of the land;
    d. obtain the latest set of 'definitions of terms' from the Town Planning Board;
    e. define the use, its intensity and scale;
    f. check whether the use is an 'existing use' which involves no new building work. If the answer to this question is yes, there is no need for planning permission. If the answer is no, take the next step;
    g. check whether the use is a temporary use (involving no building work). If yes, there is no need for planning permission. If no, take the next step;
    h. check the cover pages of the Notes to see whether the use is a use that is 'always permitted' in all zones. If yes, there is no need for planning permission. If no, take the next step;
    i. check Column 1 of the Notes to see whether the use is a use that is always permitted in the specific zone within which the land is located. If yes and there is no further restrictions specified against the use in the Column, there is no need for planning permission. If no, take the next step;
    j. if the use is a Column 1 use but there is a restriction, the use can be developed 'as of right' (provided that it is also permitted by the land lease and does not contravene any other ordinances) and there is no need for planning permission so far as the development complies with the restrictions. If the use exceeds the specified restrictions or if the use is not a Column 1 use, take the next step;
    k. check Column 2 of the Notes to see whether the use (with its intensity or scale) is a use that may be permitted in the specific zone within which the land is located. If yes, there is a need for planning permission. Apply under section 16 of the Town Planning Ordinance for permission. (If no, the only way to enable the use to comply with the town plan is to wait for or obtain government rezoning of the land so that the use becomes either a Column 1 or Column 2 use.)

(2) Where the plan has a prior history of an IDPA Plan, or a draft DPA Plan, and there is no enforcement notice requiring planning permissions:
    a. identify the exact location of the land in question;
    b. obtain the latest statutory plan, which is either an Outline Zoning

*The Possibility of Making a Planning Application and Steps in Checking a Use* 39

Plan, or its preceding Development Permission Area Plan, or the original Interim Development Permission Area Plan (the latter two consist of a zoning map and a set of Notes, both being statutory) together with a set of Explanatory Statement;
c. identify the zoning of the land;
d. obtain the latest set of 'definitions of terms';
e. define the use, its intensity and scale;
f. check whether the use is an 'existing use' that existed immediately before the publication of the IDPA Plan or the first draft DPA Plan, where there is no IDPA Plan, in the gazette and has existed since then without any 'material change'. If the answer to this question is yes, there is no need for planning permission. If the answer is no, take the next step;
g. Check the cover pages of the Notes to see whether the use is an exempted specified temporary use (involving no building work and is for a period less than two weeks). If yes, there is no need for planning permission. If no, take the next step;
h. check the cover pages of the Notes to see whether the use is a use that is always permitted in all zones. If yes, there is no need for planning permission. If no, take the next step;
i. check Column 1 of the Notes to see whether the use is a use that is always permitted in the specific zone within which the land is located. If yes and there is no further restrictions specified against the use in the Column, there is no need for planning permission. If no, take the next step;
j. if the use is a Column 1 use but there is a restriction, the use can be developed 'as of right' (provided that it is also permitted by the land lease and does not contravene any other ordinances) and there is no need for planning permission so far as the development complies with the restrictions. If the use exceeds the specified restrictions or if the use is not a Column 1 use, take the next step;
k. check Column 2 of the Notes to see whether the use (with its intensity or scale) is a use that may be permitted in the specific zone within which the land is located. If yes, there is a need for planning permission. Apply under section 16 of the Town Planning Ordinance for permission. (If no, the only way to enable the use to comply with the town plan is to wait for or obtain government rezoning of the land so that the use becomes either a Column 1 or Column 2 use.)

# 8 THE RELATIONSHIP AMONG LEASE MODIFICATIONS, PLANNING PERMISSIONS AND BUILDING PERMISSIONS IN THE DEVELOPMENT CYCLE

In order to appreciate the relationship among lease modifications, planning permissions and building permissions for change in use that may be required, an understanding of the steps involved in the development cycle for permanent use and development is helpful. Figure 8.1 shows the steps of an idealized development cycle for a green field site under complete government ownership.

## Idealized Development Process in Hong Kong

The first key event is the making of a decision by the government for the development of a new town or a new area (e.g., the Cyberport and Disney World). It is usually preceded or followed by a consultant study conducted by *planning consultants*.

The second step is land surveying by *land surveyors* if the survey plans of the town or area need to be produced or updated.

The third step is the preparation of the Layout Plans and Outline Development Plans (ODP). Layout plans are guides for major engineering works and the ODPs are guides for drafting the land documents, notably conditions of sale/grant and engineering conditions. For new towns, these plans are often drafted by consultants for adoption by the government.

Then, tenders for engineering works (such as those for reclamation; drainage; sewerage; and highways) are awarded to *building contractors*. This is followed by actual engineering work of site formation. The programming and control of such works are supervised by *civil engineers*. The programme for engineering works is contained in the Public Works Programme or a new town development programme.

In accordance with the land use zoning in ODPs, *estate surveyors* in the Lands Department prepare land documents for the disposal of land to the private sector (developers) and government departments. For the former, conditions of sale or grant, and for the latter, 'engineering conditions', are drafted for interdepartment consultation by circulation before adoption. For land parcels without specific long-term use or without committed development programme at the moment, Short Term Tenancy (STT) agreements are prepared by the Lands Department.

Developers then obtain land by auction, tender or grant (private treaty grant) in accordance with a land sale programme and government departments obtain land according to the Hong Kong Planning Standards and Guidelines (HKPSG). (Developers' bids in auction and tender are theoretically returned after detailed development feasibility studies. How much this is in practice is an interesting question. However, the base price set by the government in an auction or tender is judged by proper valuation methods.)

Lands without specific long-term use at the moment are allocated by the Lands Department under Short Term Tenancy (STTs) by tender. These STTs usually have a term of three years, with an option of renewal on a quarterly basis thereafter.

Upon acquiring land, a developer will usually proceed to develop the site rather than disposing it for temporary uses, as there is a general condition in the conditions of sale/grant for land to be developed within a certain time limit (e.g., three years) from the date land sale. Breach of this contractual condition, a building covenant (BC), may trigger a 're-entry' or repossession process by the government that extinguishes the title of the developer. This process is in practice subject to a discretionary policy of indulgence on payment of an additional charge ('premium for BC extension') or by free extension of the BC).[1] As there is often no statutory town plan at this stage, there is no need for the developer to check the need for or possibility of making a planning application. Thus, the developer will instruct its *Authorized Person*, who in this case is an *architect* with proper qualifications for architectural design and building plan submission to the Building Authority. Once the building plan is approved, the developer will proceed to award building contracts to building contractors for the necessary construction work.

In Hong Kong, 'pre-sale' and leasing of property (in case it is retained as investment property) before completion is common. As a Hong Kong building is normally multi-storeyed, property is sold as units which are collectively governed by a Deed of Mutual Covenants (DMC) executed by the developer and the first buyer, who is often an 'insider' of the developer. The DMC is

---

1. See Nissim (1998: 52–3).

drafted by a *solicitor*. It specifies (a) the total number of shares of a development, (b) the number of shares of individual units and (c) the number of shares of parking spaces. Upon the issue of an occupation permit, a property buyer can occupy his or her unit lawfully. When the positive covenants of the conditions of sale/grant are fulfilled, then all owners are deemed to have obtained legal titles to their property and the conditions become part of a government lease by operation of law. The Certificate of Compliance (CC) is evidence of these conveyancing technicalities.

The use of the property upon completion is mainly governed privately by the DMC and publicly by the provisions of the government lease and the Buildings Ordinance. The *town planner in private practice* may be of assistance in lease enforcement cases involving the interpretation of land uses and town plans. The expression 'town planner' is not protected by law but 'Registered Professional Planner' (RPP) is. However, there is no legal requirement for the instruction of an RPP in making an objection to a town plan or an application within its ambit.

Land allocated to government departments will be developed only when funding for specific works items is made available. The design of such works for departments other than the Housing Department, which designs its own property, is the work of the *architects* in the Architectural Services Department. The building plans of all government departments are exempted from the Buildings Ordinance. Like those for the private sector, construction works for government departments are carried out by building contractors.

When a new development area becomes mature in time (e.g., ten years), the notice of a draft Outline Zoning Plan (OZP) will be published in the gazette to control change in the use of the developed land. A property owner whose interest is adversely affected by the plan has a right to make an objection to the Town Planning Board. A *town planner* in private practice may be instructed to help raise an objection and make a counter-proposal to the Town Planning Board.

For land retained by developers as investment property, redevelopment is easy in the sense that there is no need for acquiring titles of units. For property sold as units, a developer may only develop the site of that property if he/she can acquire 100 per cent shares of the buildings. If not, he/she must at least acquire 90 per cent of the shares of the buildings and then request the government, under the Land (Compulsory Sale for Redevelopment) Ordinance (Ordinance No. 30 of 1998), to give permission for forced acquisition of the remaining shares so that it can collect 100 per cent shares to start the redevelopment.

44 *Change in Use of Land*

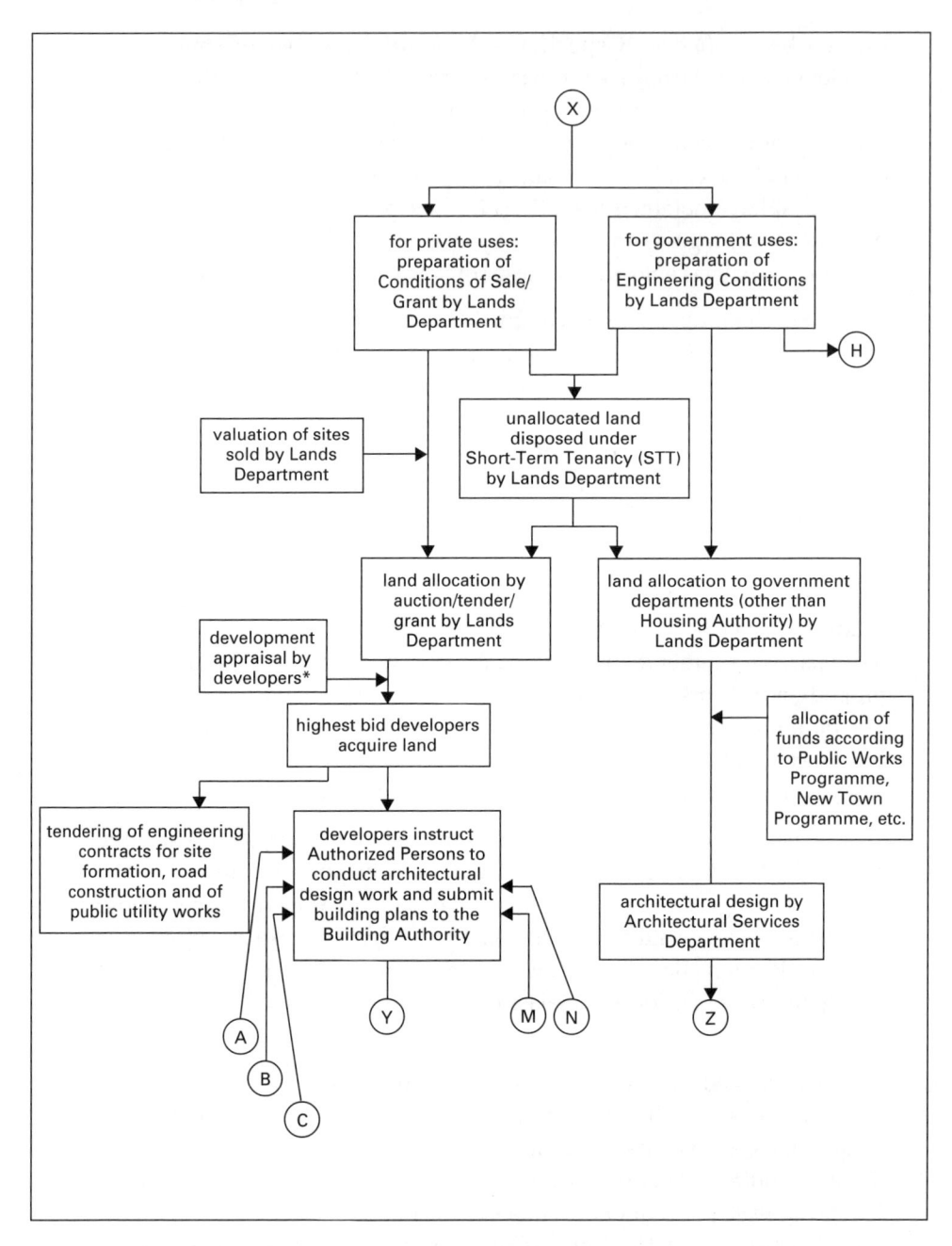

Figure 8.1 A flowchart showing the development cycle commencing with government planning studies on a greenfield site
\* This is a taught subject in surveying schools and generates a mountain of research publications on methods. In practice, 'bosses' of development companies make decisions on the basis of their intuition.

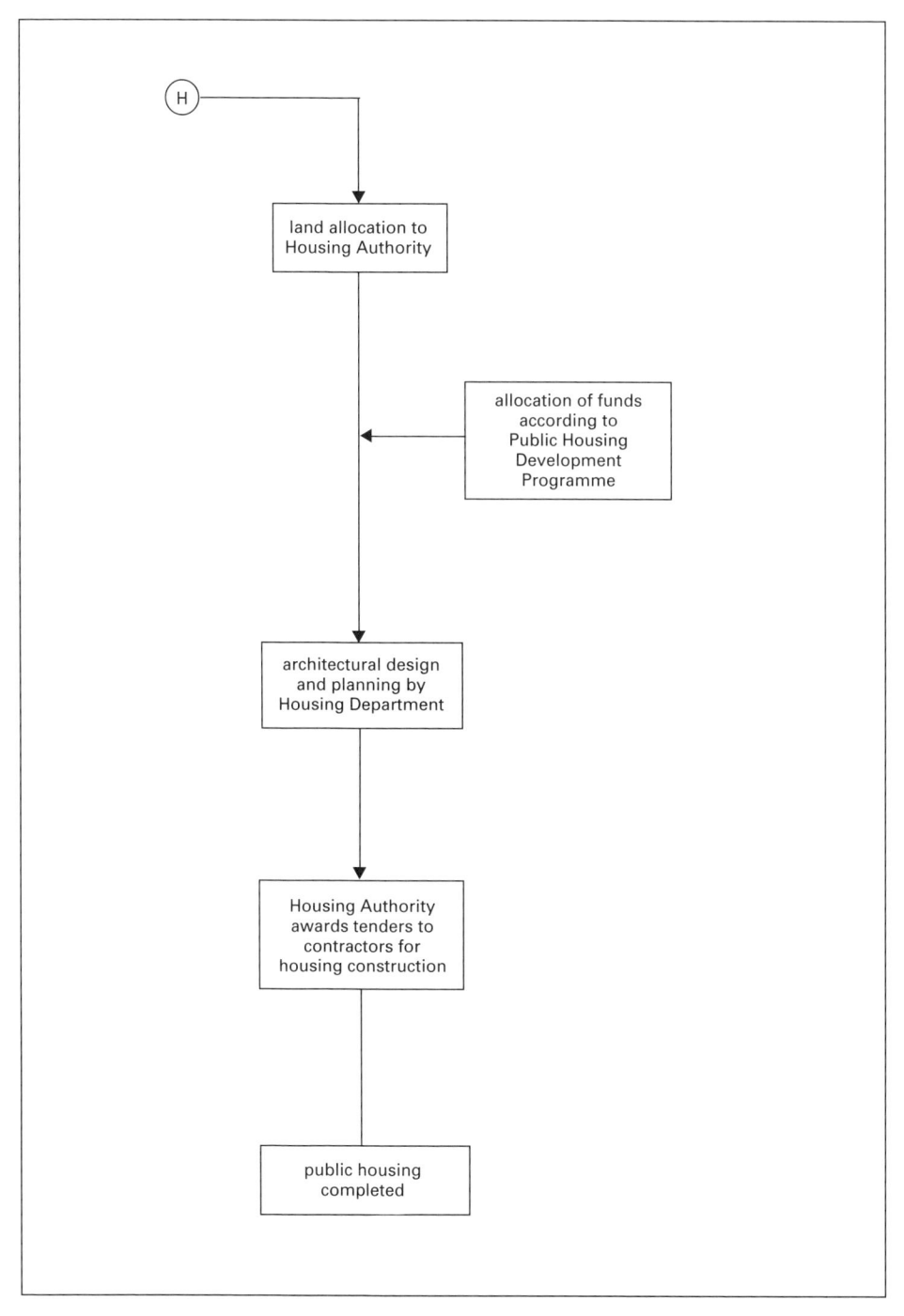

# Lease Modifications, Planning Permission and Building Permissions 45

Figure 8.1 (continued)   A flowchart showing the development cycle commencing with government planning studies on a greenfield site

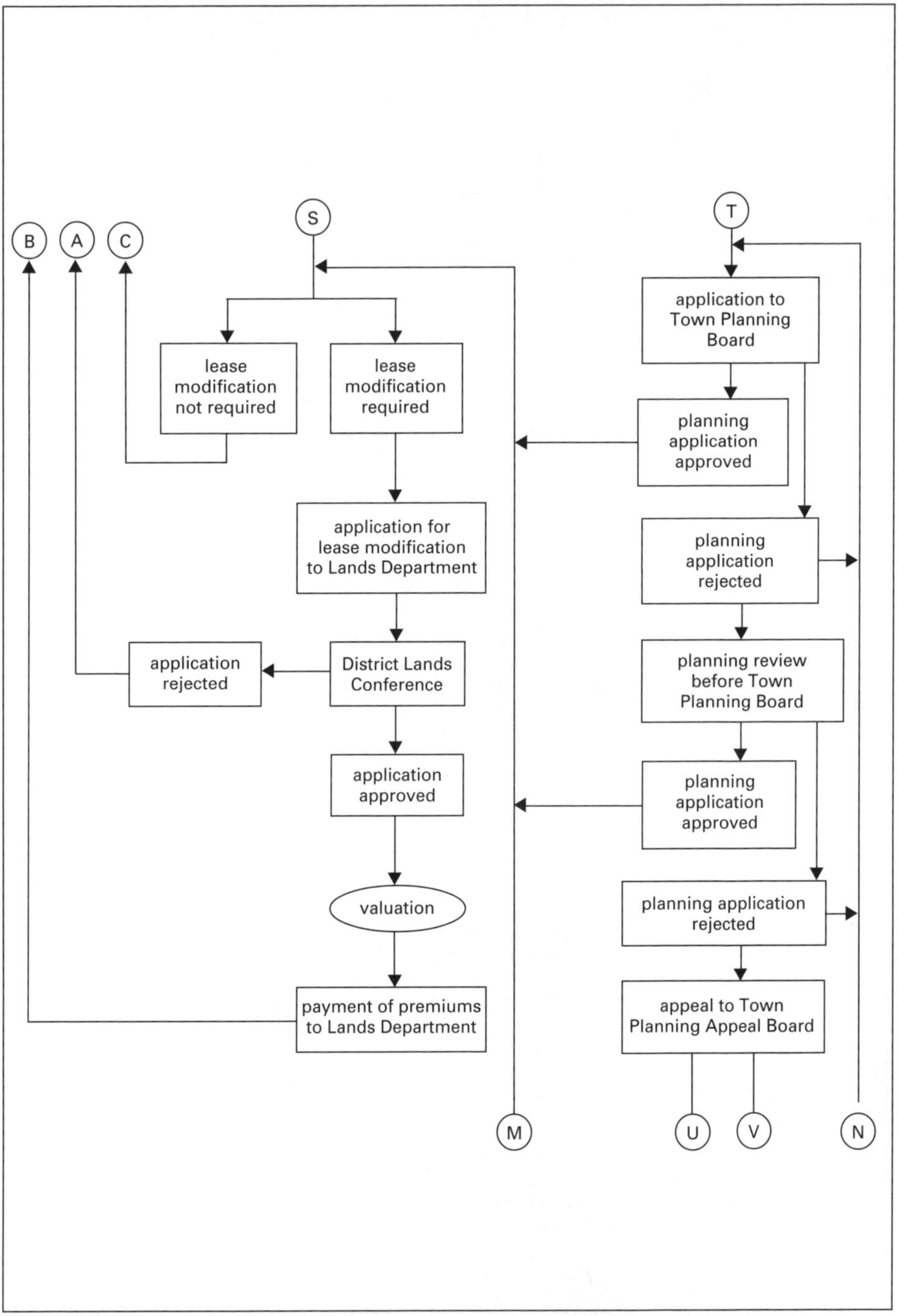

Figure 8.1 (continued)   A flowchart showing the development cycle commencing with government planning studies on a greenfield site

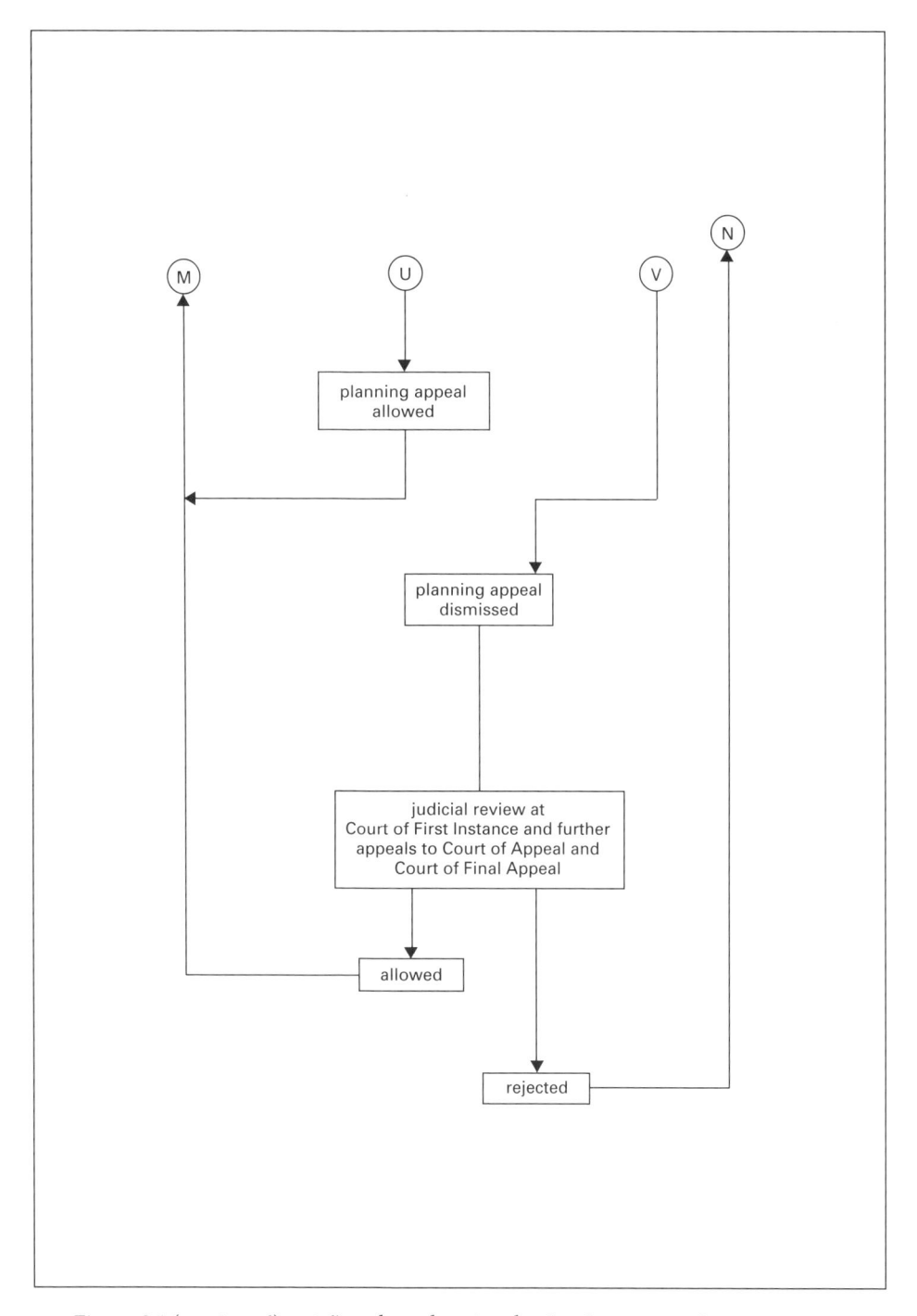

Figure 8.1 (continued)  A flowchart showing the development cycle commencing with government planning studies on a greenfield site

48　*Change in Use of Land*

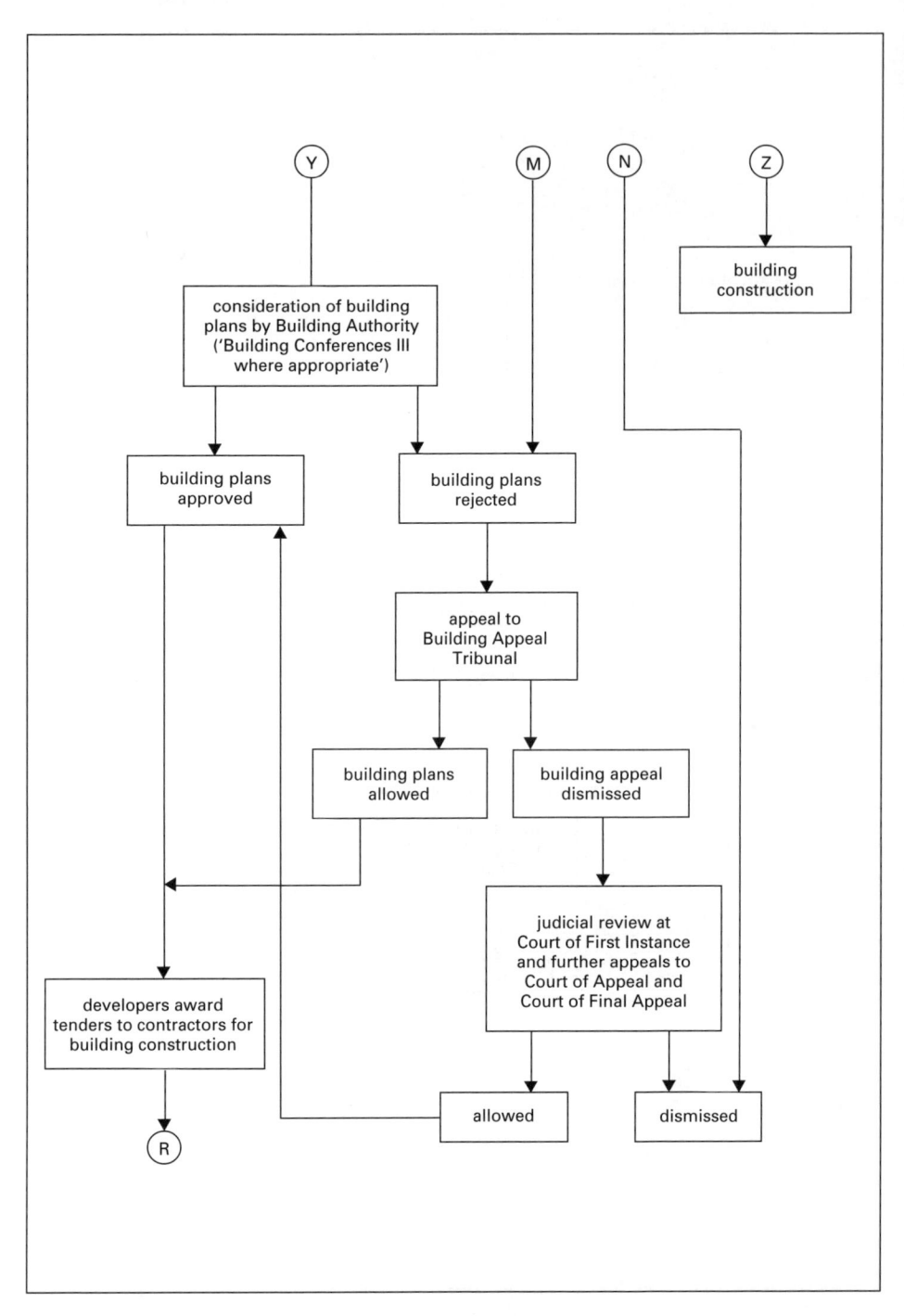

Figure 8.1 (continued)　A flowchart showing the development cycle commencing with government planning studies on a greenfield site

Lease Modifications, Planning Permission and Building Permissions  49

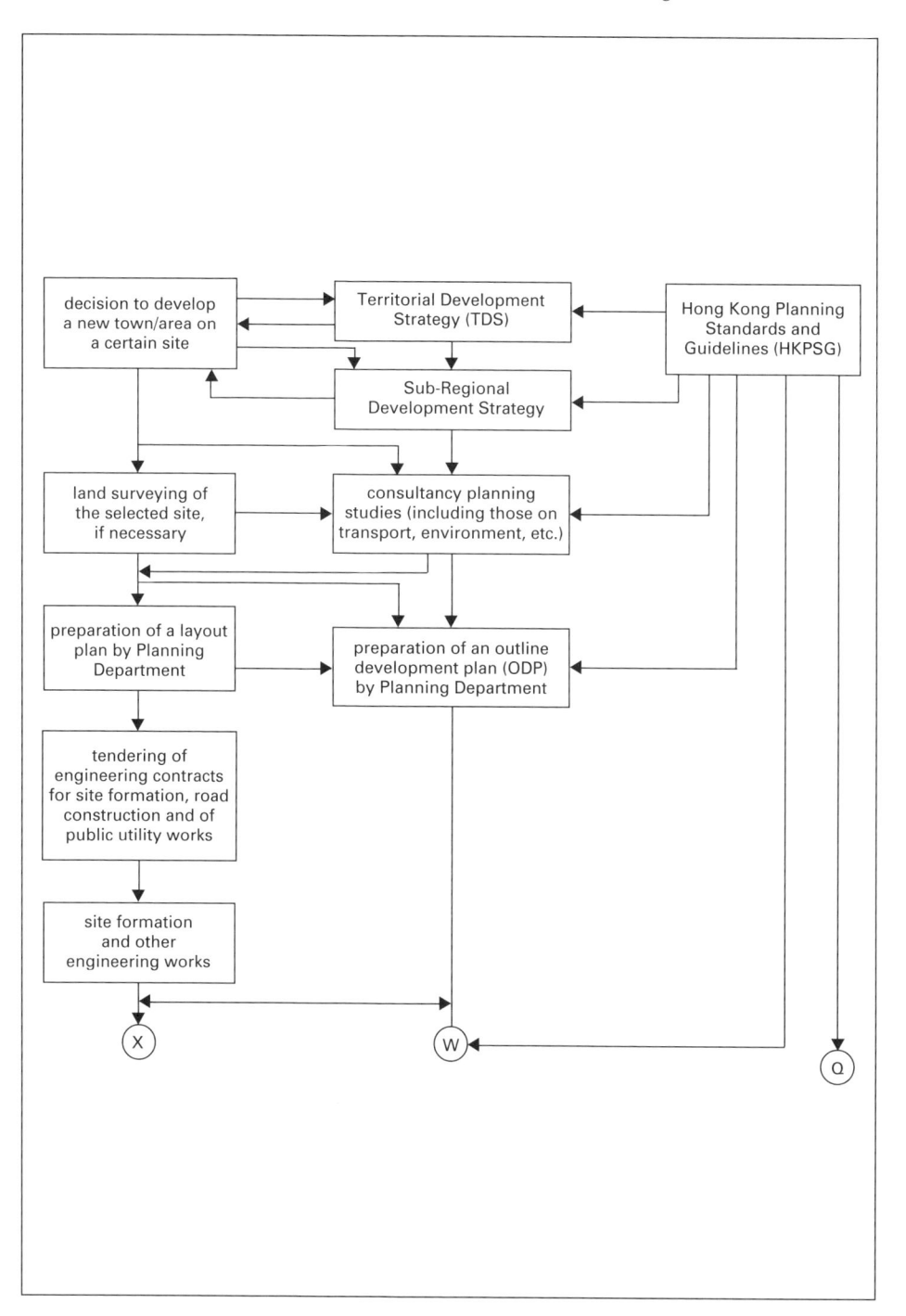

Figure 8.1 (continued)  A flowchart showing the development cycle commencing with government planning studies on a greenfield site

## 50  Change in Use of Land

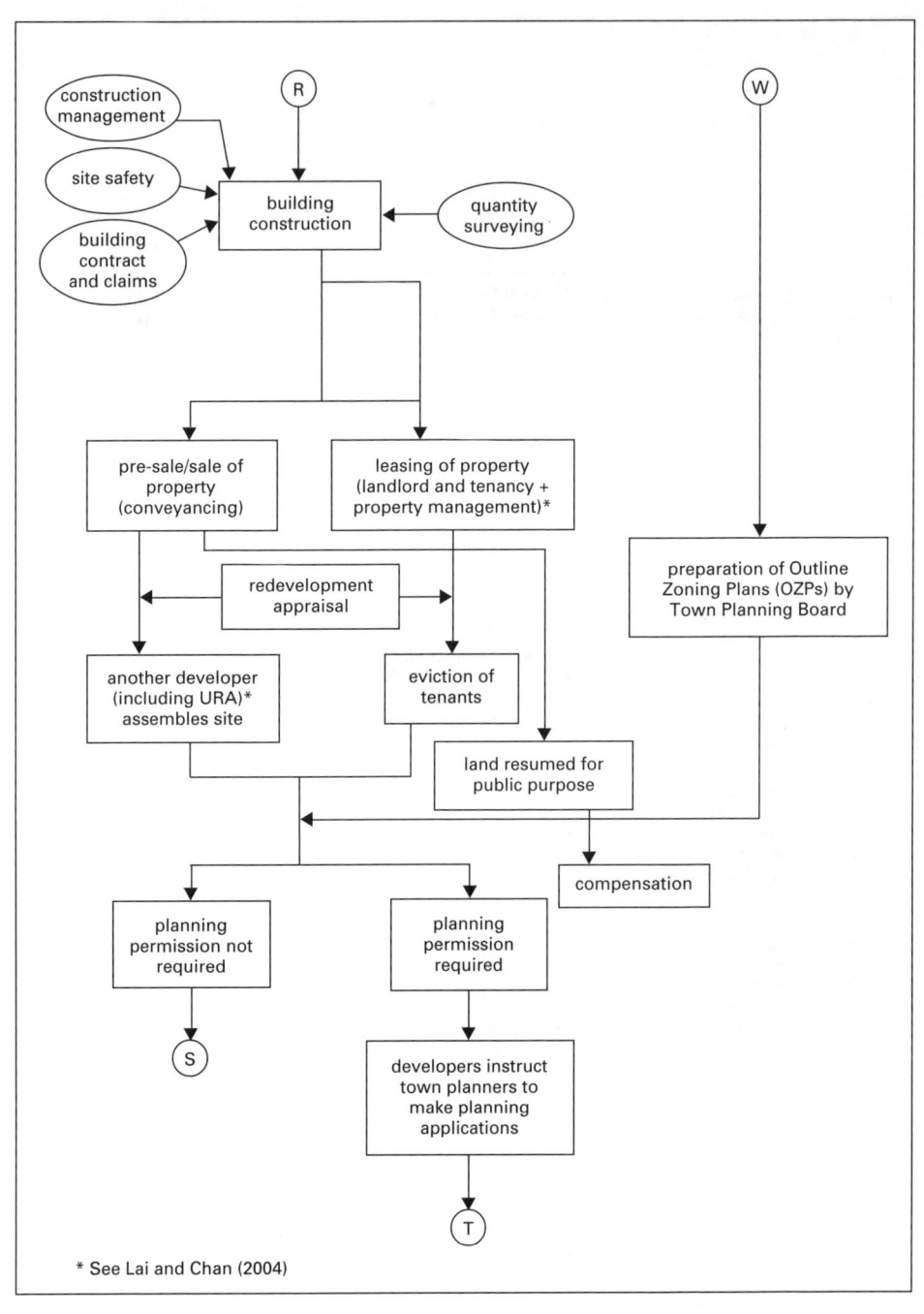

Figure 8.1 (continued)  A flowchart showing the development cycle commencing with government planning studies on a greenfield site

The developer will not contemplate redevelopment of its wholly owned building or acquiring shares of property of property under multiple ownership if in his or her investment analysis the redevelopment identifies no financial gains. Often such gains can be obtained if there is market for a better use, i.e., one that is more valuable than the existing one; and/or a more intensive form of development. To realize such change and/or intensification of land use, the developer may need to obtain either lease modification or planning permission, or both before any building application made is meaningful.

Without planning permission, a building plan submitted may be rejected on statutory ground for 'contravention of town plan'.

Without lease modification, if required, then the land with a building and an approved building plan, and even an occupation permit (OP), may attract re-entry by the government.

Where there is a need to make a planning application, review or an appeal (to the Town Planning Board, or Appeal Board, under the Town Planning Ordinance where appropriate) to obtain the requisite permission, a *town planner* in private practice may be instructed. In a planning appeal, *barristers* (and hence solicitors who must be retained in order to instruct the former) are often instructed to give legal opinion, make written submissions and appear in the appeal hearing.

## The Planning Authorities in Hong Kong

In substance, there are several planning authorities in Hong Kong, though in practice the planning authority refers to either the Town Planning Board or the Director of Planning, head of the Planning Department.

The Planning Department prepares administrative town plans (such as Outline Development Plans [ODPs] and Layout Plans) for land other than areas within country parks and planning documents, such as the Territorial Development Strategy (Review) (TDS or TDSR), Sub-Regional Strategy Review, development statements, and the Hong Kong Planning Standards and Guidelines (HKPSG), for the whole of Hong Kong.

The Director of Planning can designate under the Town Planning Ordinance any area in Hong Kong as an 'Interim Development Permission Areas' (IDPA), but this power does not statutorily extend to areas in which the first statutory plans are Outline Zoning Plans and, as a matter of practice, to areas already included in a country park map.

The Director of Planning can take enforcement actions under the Town Planning Ordinance against violation of provisions in statutory plans for areas for which the first statutory plans were Interim Development Permission Area Plans (IDPA Plans).

The Town Planning Board can prepare statutory town plans (namely Development Permission Area Plans and Outline Zoning Plans) for the whole of Hong Kong under the Town Planning Ordinance but in practice the development control and enforcement of these statutory plans do not extend to country park areas.

As mentioned above, these statutory plans are often superimposed onto land with pre-existing property rights, for which the planning and building control authority is the Land Authority (the Director of Lands), as far as government leases are concerned, and the Building Authority (the Director of Building) in respect of approved building plans.

The effective forward planning and development control work of the Town Planning Board, the Director Planning, and the Director of Buildings (once concentrated in the Director of Buildings and Lands) are confined to areas outside (a) country parks; and (b) the Housing Authority: once it obtains lands from the Land Authority.

The Director of Agriculture, Fisheries and Conservation designates Marine Fish Culture Zones under the Marine and other types of zones under the Marine Fish Culture Ordinance.

The Country and Marine Park Authority (the Director of Agriculture, Fisheries and Conservation) prepares and enforces statutory country park and marine park plans under the Country Parks Ordinance. Country parks occupy more than 70 per cent of land in Hong Kong.

The Housing Authority is the land, planning and building authority of its land holdings obtained through the Lands Department. It prepares planning briefs for its estates and architecture designs for its building stocks, awards tenders for the construction of its property, and conducts building inspections of its own property. The Housing Ordinance exempts the buildings constructed by the Housing Authority from the control by the Land Authority or the Buildings Ordinance; there is no need for a certificate of compliance or occupation permit for using a Housing Authority unit. As a result of unsatisfactory structural and quality problems of some old and recent Housing Authority buildings, the government has been considering the transfer of the inspection function to the Buildings Department.

## The Overlapping Forward Planning and Development Control Functions of the Planning, Land and Building Authorities

The functions of the planning, lands and building authorities are not only related but also overlapping in terms of forward planning and development control.

### Land Authority and Building Authority as forward planning and development control bodies

In the history of planning and development control of Hong Kong, the Land Authority was once the sole planning and development control authority. The functions of planning and development control have gradually been replaced, displaced or duplicated by the Building Authority and later the town planners in the government.

As early as 1840s, the Land Authority involved itself in forward planning by:

(1) 'laying out' districts;
(2) delineating within districts roads and land parcels;
(3) subdividing land parcels or lots;
(4) stipulating in lease documents development restrictions; such as those upon sub-division; right of ways in favour of adjoining property;
(5) stipulating in lease documents for each land lot 'user' (land use) or 'user restrictions', such as prohibition against offensive trades;
(6) stipulating in lease documents for each land lot building restrictions, such as the types of buildings permitted, for instance, 'European-type houses'; 'houses'; 'flats'; their height; and site coverage; non-building areas; set-backs; access location; plot ratios; maintenance of slopes and support to other properties, etc.

The activities as regards (1) and (2), laying out districts and roads, have been taken over by the town planners in the government. Further superimposed on such administrative town planning is statutory planning of the Town Planning Board.

All other forward planning methods have been retained and 'modernized' by the Land Authority when introducing 'Master Layout Plans' (MLP); 'Rate and Range'; and 'Design, Disposition, and Height (DDH) clauses.

However, most of the remaining and modernized forward planning methods have been 'borrowed' by both the Building Authority and the Town Planning Board:

(1) The Buildings Ordinance and its subsidiary legislation provide for a statutory requirements of building permissions and a system of building applications that add to the building planning stipulations in the lease; and a system of site classification for the purpose of calculating plot ratios for buildings as well as the statutory consideration of the 'immediate neighbourhood'.
(2) The Town Planning Board has introduced plot ratio and building height restrictions. These have been held as valid, *intra vires* planning concerns in the *CC Tze Case*.
(3) The Town Planning Board has imported from the Land Authority the concept of 'master layout plans' for the 'Comprehensive Development Area' (CDA) zones.

Since 1840s, the Land Authority has conducted development control by:

(1) considering applications for permanent lease modifications in respect of subdivision or combination of lots; change in user restrictions; change in building restrictions; and other types of development restrictions and temporary waivers of leases conditions; and
(2) enforcing breach of lease terms, including those related to user and building matters.

The introduction of the Buildings Ordinance means that the development control function of the Land Authority Department in respect of enforcing against unauthorized building has been substantially taken over by the Building Authority.

The introduction of the Town Planning Ordinance means that:

(1) The decision of the Land Authority in respect of a lease modification application becomes contingent upon the decision of the Town Planning Board in case planning permission is necessary.
(2) The decision of the Building Authority in respect of a building application also becomes contingent upon the decision of the Town Planning Board in case planning permission is necessary.

However, statutory town planning and the decisions of the Town Planning Board are also dependent on both the Land Authority and Building Authority in the following respects:

(1) Enforcement of statutory town plans (other than those with a history of interim development permission areas) relies on the Buildings Ordinance. Where planning permission for a site is required but is not obtained, the Building Authority may, under section 16(1)(d) of the Buildings Ordinance, reject the building plans submitted in respect of intended development of the site.
(2) 'Planning conditions' imposed by the Town Planning Board for an approved planning application are enforceable only when they have actually been incorporated in the lease as lease conditions. Indeed, the set of Notes to statutory town plans often imposes a general requirement for compliance with lease conditions. A planning condition may also impose a requirement for such compliance, or for obtaining the necessary modifications to lease conditions where they are required.
(3) Successful planning applications do not automatically entail successful lease modifications.
(4) Successful planning applications and lease modifications do not guarantee building permission.
(5) Where lease modification for a site is required but has not yet been obtained, the Building Authority may still process and approve building plans in respect of an intended development on the site. A written warning, however, will be made by the Building Authority that under section 14(2) of the Buildings Ordinance such building approval does not entail that lease modification will be granted by the Lands Department as a matter of course.

The splitting or the so-called 'defederalization' of the lands, building and planning authorities (the last is supported by the planners in the government) into three separate departments from the Public Works Department (and later the Buildings and Lands Department), has led to a higher degree of specialization (at the cost of some delays in the processing of development applications). This defederalization is definitely in the interest of 'empire building' of bureaucrats and perhaps also a means to prevent corruption.

### Overlapping development concerns in Hong Kong

Given the above definitions of 'planning' and 'development control', and the functional relationship among the three authorities, we shall now turn to the specific areas over which the Building Authority, Town Planning Board and Land Authority have overlapping control that cover a number of key tools, considerations or concerns in both planning and development. Figure 8.2 illustrates this observation.

56  *Change in Use of Land*

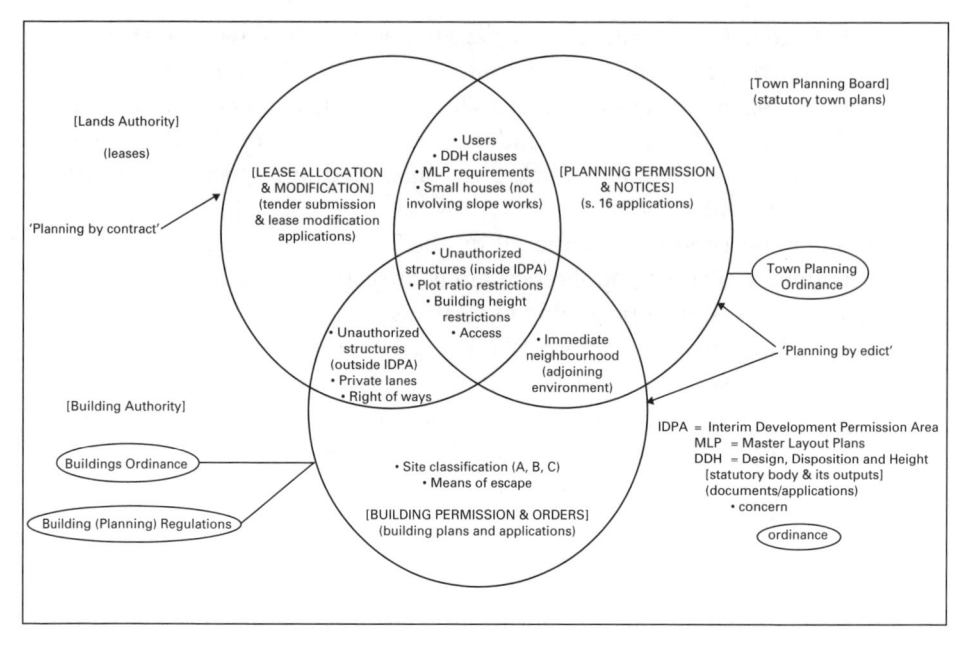

Figure 8.2  Some overlapping control of development by the planning, lands and building authorities

Both the Town Planning Board and Building Authority have specific statutory powers to deal with, respectively, 'section 16 planning applications' under the Town Planning Ordinance and 'building applications' under the Buildings Ordinance (and its subsidiary legislation). Such statutory powers are exercised without the consent of private individuals. The Land Authority handles allocation of leasehold interests to private individuals and their lease modification (waiver) applications on a contractual basis. The deed is a contract made by signing, sealing and delivery whereas the conditions made by a simple contract under hand that is deemed to be a lease under the Conveyancing and Property Ordinance. One may therefore describe government 'planning' by lease as 'planning by contract' (Lai 1994, 1998) or 'planning by consent' (Lai 1994, 1998) as the lease is an agreement with terms regarding land use and building forms enforceable by the court.

Though the three authorities have specific powers or independent contractual capacities, the tools, considerations or concerns for planning and/or development control in the exercise of such powers or capacities do overlap. The most common examples are presented in Figure 8.2 above. A total of six such tools, considerations and concerns can be found:

**Common Concerns of the Building Authority and the Town Planning Board**

*Development control*

The statutory interpretation 'immediate neighbourhood' under section 16(1)(g) of the Buildings Ordinance, its equivalent being the general concept of 'adjoining environment' or 'adjoining development' in the 'section 16 application' development control process under the Town Planning Ordinance. The focus of section 16(1)(g) of the Buildings Ordinance is building height and its derivative factors: fire prevention and escape (means of escape [MOE]), and access. However, in determining building appeals, the Building Appeal Tribunal does consider wider issues relating to the compatibility with adjoining land uses. These issues are also the emphasis of Town Planning Board decisions.

**Common Concerns of the Building Authority and the Land Authority**

*Forward planning*

The extinguishing or preservation of private lanes or right of ways is forward planning and development control concerns of both the Building Authority and the Land Authority. From their point of view, the consequence for public convenience and the legitimate interests of the public are of paramount importance. The particular concern of the Building Authority is the consequence for increase/decrease in plot ratio, and hence gross floor area (GFA). The Land Authority's specific concern is the premium payable as a result of the gain in value of the land as a result.

*Development control*

'Unauthorized' structures outside areas being covered or once covered by a statutory 'Interim Development Permission Area' (IDPA) plan prepared under the Town Planning Ordinance by the Director of Planning (not the Town Planning Board) or a draft 'Development Permission Area' (DPA) plan (where there is no previous IDPA Plan) are the common development control concerns of the Building Authority and the Land Authority, where such unauthorized structures constitute both a violation of express or implied conditions of sale/lease and the provisions of the Buildings Ordinance. The methods of 'enforcement' differ between the authorities. The Building

Authority may issue 'orders' for demolition whereas the Land Authority levy 'forbearance fees' and apply to the court for re-entry of the land. When making decisions about enforcement, the primary concern of the Building Authority appears to be immediate danger to the public. Their subsidiary considerations are fairness and ease of implementation, where there is no imminent safety threat. The primary consideration of the Land Authority appears to be purely financial. Note that structures erected contrary to the Buildings Ordinance or Town Planning Ordinance may or may not result in a breach of the lease, and vice versa.

## Common Concerns of the Building Authority, Land Authority and the Town Planning Board

*Planning and development control regarding building heights*

Building heights restrictions can be imposed as:

(1) a forward planning parameter as a mandatory ceiling in conditions of sale/lease conditions and/or statutory town plans; and/or
(2) a development control consideration or 'condition' as a matter of discretion of the Building Authority when considering building plans under section 16(1)(g) of the Buildings Ordinance, or of the Town Planning Board when considering section 16 planning applications.

The common concern is the visual impact and fire safety implications of building height on the adjoining environment, built and natural.

*Planning and development control regarding plot ratios*

Plot Ratio restrictions can be imposed as:

(1) a forward planning parameter as a mandatory ceiling in conditions of sale/lease conditions and/or statutory town plans; and/or
(2) a development control consideration or 'condition' as a matter of discretion of the Building Authority when considering building plans under section 16(1)(g) of the Buildings Ordinance or of the Town Planning Board when considering section 16 planning applications.

The common concerns connected with plot ratios are:

(1) building height; and
(2) the total amount of resulting gross floor area, a proxy for estimating

population, traffic implications and environmental impacts on the adjoining environment, built and natural.

*Planning and development control regarding access*

Access and parking specifications/requirements in forward planning and traffic impacts are development control factors, considerations and conditions frequently invoked by the three authorities in the exercise of their respective powers or capacities.

The common concern is convenience and safety.

# 9 PLANNING APPLICATIONS, REVIEWS AND APPEALS

## Planning Applications

Any person may make an application, often referred to as a 'section 16 application' (or 'planning application'), to the Town Planning Board for uses specified under Column 2 or on the covering pages (where appropriate for temporary uses within areas covered or once covered by Interim Development Permission Area plans) of the Notes of a plan prepared and a notice about it published in the gazette under the Town Planning Ordinance (the Ordinance). The Town Planning Board has produced a set of Guidance Notes[1] that advise applicants of the basic elements for making planning applications and changes to the statutory town plans or their notes.

The Notes are expressly stated as being 'part of the plan' so produced. Such a plan, whether it is a 'draft' or 'approved' plan, may be an Interim Permission Area (IDPA) Plan, a Development Permission Area (DPA) Plan or, more commonly, an Outline Zoning Plan (OZP).

A rezoning proposal that seeks to change the prevailing statutory zoning plan cannot be made under a section 16 application but may be made within the provisions of the Ordinance regarding plan-making.

The Town Planning Board is a statutory body comprising appointed official and unofficial members.[2] The Board is a 'public body' within the meaning of the Prevention of Bribery Ordinance. The Chairman of the Board is the Secretary for Planning and Lands, who may delegate his/her authority to

---

1. Guidance Notes: Application for Permission under section 16 of the Town Planning Ordinance (Cap. 131), Town Planning Board, undated.
2. Under section 2(4) of the Ordinance, the committee of the board must have three unofficial members to form meet the quorum of five persons. Under section 2A(5), the committee must have a majority of unofficial members whenever it is meeting.

the Director of Planning or Deputy Director of Planning. Other members of the Town Planning Board are notable figures appointed from the public. Most of these unofficial members are professionals, academics, politicians and learned individuals. Planning qualifications or experience, however, are apparently not conditions for appointment.

The applicant may or may not be the owner or occupier of the land involved. No fee was required to be paid to the government in making a planning (or rezoning) application until the Town Planning (Amendment) Bill 2003[3] becomes law. There is no limit on the number of planning applications on may make for a site or rule against concurrent applications (for different uses, designs or development intensities). Nor is there any time limitation on the making of another application after a previous attempt has failed.

There is no statutory requirement that the planning application needs to be made by persons with specific academic or professional qualifications, although the application must be made using a prescribed form, Form No. PLN-18, which can be obtained free of charge from the Secretary for the Town Planning Board. This form is a 4-page A4-size standard proforma, and may be completed in Chinese or English.

When preparing for a planning application, the applicant may wish to consult the relevant Town Planning Board Guidelines and Guidance Notes, which can be obtained free of charge from the Planning Department.

There is no statutory requirement for the submission of consultant reports or any other supporting documents for an application. However, the standard form contains references to the number of copies of such documents required when the applicant does provide such documents. It is common that a planning application is made by a planning consultant, usually a Registered Professional Planners (RPP) in private practice, who fills in the standard form and prepares supporting reports on behalf of an applicant for a 'section 16 application'. The planning consultant often also prepares documents for the subsequent planning review or appeal procedures where necessary.

There is no legally prescribed style for the supporting documents, but there must be a 'master layout plan' for applications for uses, or for development inside a Comprehensive Development Area.

---

3. Introduced to the Legislative Council on 21 May 2003, this bill proposes the introduction of a 'prescribed fee' for both rezoning and planning applications.

The Town Planning Board has two sub-committees, the Metro Planning Committee and the Rural and New Town Planning Committee (RNTPC). These committees deal with planning applications and reviews falling within their area jurisdictions. The Chairperson of the Committees may be unofficial members of the Town Planning Board. In deliberating decisions, the Board has the benefit of a Town Planning Board Paper prepared by the secretariat of the Town Planning Board that is staffed by professional planners of the Planning Department.

Under the Town Planning Ordinance, the Town Planning Board must make a decision in respect of an application within two months, but there is no equivalent statutory provision for 'deemed approval' as is the case for building plans submissions under the Buildings Ordinance shall no decision is made or a decision is made out of time by the Town Planning Board. Note that under s.16(3) of the Ordinance, the decision of the Board in respect of an application must be made in the absence of the applicant.

The decision of the Town Planning Board in respect of a 'section 16' application is communicated formally to the applicant in writing.

There is no legal requirement to register the Town Planning Board decision in respect of a 'section 16 application' with the Land Registry, except the master layout plan(s) for an approved application in respect of Comprehensive Development Areas Zones under s.4A(3) of the Town Planning Ordinance.

The decision for a valid application may either be:

(a) an approval without any condition (planning condition);
(b) an approval with certain conditions (planning conditions) to be fulfilled prior to, during or subsequent to actual carrying out of the use, work or building development; or
(c) rejection.

Where permission is granted, the life of the permission (which is usually two years for which extension may be considered on application) and planning conditions, if any, are stated in the letter to the applicant. Where permission is refused, the letter of the Town Planning Board would state the reasons for rejecting the planning application. **Appendices 2 and 3** provide, respectively, information on the statistical inquiry into aggregate and non-aggregate planning application data for various zones undertaken by Hong Kong planning researchers based in the Department of Real Estate and

Construction of the University of Hong Kong, and the Department of Building and Real Estate of the Hong Kong Polytechnic University.

## Planning Reviews

An applicant who makes a 'planning application' to the Town Planning Board under section 16 of the ordinance has a statutory right of a review ('planning review'). It is the same case under section 17(1) of the ordinance by the same Board if his/her application is rejected by The Town Planning Board. If the applicant is not satisfied with the conditions ('planning conditions') imposed by the Town Planning Board, he/she also has a statutory right of a review.

The review is restricted to the original application and no variation of the original application may be raised.

There is no prescribed form for making an application for a planning review.

The request for a review hearing must be made in writing to the Secretary of the Town Planning Board within 21 days of receiving the decision of the Town Planning Board. Within three months of the receipt of the written request of the applicant, the Town Planning Board must hear the review, having given 14 days' notice to the applicant.

The applicant, and his/her consultants, will be invited to appear before the Town Planning Board for the review. No third party is permitted to attend the Board's meeting for deciding section 16 applications or section 17(1) reviews.

The Town Planning Board's decisions regarding a section 16 application or a section 17(1) review, and relevant sections of the Town Planning Board Papers, are made known only to the applicant and are not published. However, the public may inspect, free of charge, past records of such applications or reviews at the Planning Department on request.

In its annual reports the Town Planning Board publishes the annual success and failure rates of all planning applications and reviews for the whole territory. These statistics are aggregate; therefore, they may not be useful for meaningful statistical analysis of the Town Planning Board decisions, or the success rates of various applications with reference to location, zone, and time.

## Planning Appeals

If an applicant is not satisfied with the decision of Town Planning Board in a review, he/she has a statutory right to make an appeal ('planning appeal') to an Appeal Board (or 'the Town Planning Appeal Board') under section 17B of the ordinance.

The applicant must file a written notice of appeal to the Appeal Board secretary within 60 days after receiving the review decision.

In an appeal hearing, the Town Planning Board is the respondent and the applicant is the appellant.

As a statutory body, the Appeal Board is also a public body with appointed members. The members, by law, must be different from those of the Town Planning Board. Under section 17A(2) of the Town Planning Ordinance, the members of the Appeal Board must not be members of the Town Planning Board. Neither should the member be a public officer, nor a Justice of Appeal.

The Chairperson and Deputy-Chairperson of the Appeal Board is in practice a member of the legal profession or of the judiciary, subject to sections 17A(2) and 17A(2A). Other members have similar qualifications as those appointed to the Town Planning Board. Again, there is no prescribed form or professional person for making a planning appeal. However, it is common that the appellant would employ legal practitioners and planning consultants to prepare materials for appearing before the Appeal Board. The appeal sessions of the Appeal Board are not open to the public.

The Appeal Board may confirm, reverse or vary the decision appealed against under section 17B(8)(b).

When considering an appeal, the Appeal Board has to take the plans as they are. It is its duty to see that permissions which should be given thereunder are given but 'only to the extent shown or provided for or specified in the plan' according to section 16(4). As stated by the Appeal Board in its decision allowing the *Henderson Case*, the Appeal Board must not trespass upon the Town Planning Board's plan-making function in considering an appeal. 'Whether the Appeal Board agrees with any plan or not is irrelevant. Its duty is to see that plans are faithfully implemented. If changes to any plan are desired, representations should be made to the [Town Planning] Board. It follows that if permission should be granted under a plan, the Appeal Board has no right to refuse permission even if it does not like or agree with the applicable plan' (para. 6, Appeal Case No. 13/93; brackets added).

The Appeal Board is not a court of law and the decision of one panel of the Board does not bind the other. However, the Building Appeal Tribunal has repeatedly stated that it would follow the rules in its earlier decisions (such as the *Cheer Kent, Jenxon Investment, China Engineers, Hedland Investments (2) Cases*; see Lai and Ho [2000, 2002]). The same practice can be found in many decisions of the Board of Review under the Inland Revenue Ordinance. Thus, we may say that the rules in earlier decisions of the Appeal Board should be of great persuasive weight if not regarded as precedents for subsequent decisions. Furthermore, the Appeal Board has the statutory power under section 17B(6)(d) to issue summons in writing to persons so that they appear before it to give evidence or produce documents. Those who ignore summons will be fined. It also has the statutory power to award costs.

Under sections 17A(13) and 17A(14), the Appeal Board shall make a decision in respect of a question by majority vote with the Chairperson having an additional casting vote. The decisions of the Appeal Board are recorded, made known to the appellants and available for public inspection at the Appeal Board secretariat. The Appeal Board has also reported and published eighteen of its decisions for the years 1991–1993 in *Town Planning Appeal Decisions Volume One 1992–1993*. This 81-page document can be purchased at the Government Publications Centre at a cost of HK$36. The first fifty decisions of the Appeal Board have been reported and published in Lai (1999, reprinted in 2001).

Copies of any decisions already made could be obtained from the Appeal Board secretariat at a cost of HK$ 8.5 per page in 1997. Recently, the cost has become HK$1.5 per page with a fixed search cost of HK$60 for each search. Chapter 3 in Lai (2003) gives a list of the 'rules' used by the Appeal Board to make decisions.

# 10 LEASE MODIFICATIONS AND WAIVERS

## Applications for Lease Modifications/Waivers and Statutorily Governed Applications

For 'permanent changes'[1] in the terms of a land lease, lease modifications are required. For temporary changes, 'waivers' are required. Unlike planning or building applications, lease modifications (waivers) are not statutorily governed. Though compliance with lease terms is often also a matter of planning conditions, the agreement to lease modifications and waivers is always a matter of contractual negotiation between the lessee and the government as landlord.[2]

As in the case of planning and building applications, the government plays a passive role and it is up to the lessee to make the application, which must be made to the relevant District Lands Office of the Lands Department that administers the land in question. There is no legal limit to the number of modifications, but the Lands Department has adopted a 'five-year rule' which disregards applications for major modifications within five years of the sale of a piece of land to the lessee.

An approved modification (waiver) can only take effect upon entering into an agreement for the proposed changes and the payment of 'premia' (waiver charges) mutually agreed, and upon the payment of an administration fee within a period of time specified by the District Lands Office.

The modification premium charged to the modification seeker represents the enhancement in value (or the difference in the 'after' and 'before' value of the best permissible use) due to the approved modification. If the

---

1. Permanent changes are changes that last until the lease naturally expires.
2. Whether government decisions related to leases can be subject to judicial review is an interesting academic question. See Law (1999) and *Director of Lands v Yin Shuen Enterprises Limited, Nam Chun Investment Company Limited*. FACV Nos. 2 and 3 of 2002 (the *Yin Shuen Case*).

enhancement is small, the government might only charge an administration fee. If the enhancement is due to the removal of an archaic term in the offensive trade clause in an old lease, a token premium may be charged.

The assessment of the 'before' and 'after' values is a matter of valuation. 'Hope values', or values in anticipation of betterment, resumption for development or redevelopment made possible by the government under the Lands Resumption Ordinance (Chapter 124, Laws of Hong Kong), or other activities may be taken into consideration for assessing the 'before' value.

The application for lease modification or waiver should be made, as a matter of practice, to the relevant District Lands Office of the Lands Department that administers the parcel(s) of land involved. For lease modification, the application must state the identity of the applicant and the proposed change to the original land lease. The application must be accompanied by a bundle of documents including:

(1) a location plan to a scale of 1:1000 in case the property is under Block Crown (Government) Lease;
(2) two copies of the original land lease with all previous modifications and attachments (and all other title documents) certified by the Land Registry; and
(3) two copies of the ownership records of the land also certified by the Land Registry.

For a piece of property under unitary ownership, an approved modification for any permanent change to the old lease or conditions is conveyed by either a simple 'modification letter' or a 'land exchange' document involving a 'surrender-and-re-grant' procedure. (In the past, a 'deed of variation' was always executed for modification of a Crown Lease, as at common law a deed can only be modified by deed, whereas the 'modification letter' was only used for modifying conditions, as there is no need to use a deed to modify a contract. This distinction has been abandoned in favour of the exclusive use of the modification letter due to the operation of section 14A of the Conveyancing and Property Ordinance. An example is the modification of 'subsection 1 of section F of Quarry Bay Marine Lot No. 1, the remaining portion of section F of Quarry Bay Marine Lot No. 1' to allow for the building of a pedestrian footbridge across King's Road to a mass transit railway station. Thus a modification letter is statutorily deemed to be a deed. This new practice of using a modification letter to modify a deed may also be said to be consistent with the rule in *Walsh v Longsdale* that an agreement to make a lease is in equity equivalent to a deed.)

The modification letter can be a simple letter, or one to which a set of elaborated conditions is attached.

The surrender-and-re-grant procedure is followed normally where the modification sought involves boundary adjustment, and/or extinction of road or service land. If the modification is too complicated to be handled by a modification letter, as in the case of development projects involving site assembly or subdivision, the surrender-and-re-grant procedure is also normally followed. Either way, the modification runs with the land and governs all subsequent redevelopment.

For a piece of property under unitary ownership, an approved waiver for temporary changes to the old lease or conditions is conveyed by a 'waiver letter'.

Where multiple ownership is involved, the approved modification is effected by a 'no objection letter' stating that the Lands Department would not object to a certain proposed change. The effect of this letter also runs with the land, though this is often expressly limited to the life of the building found on the land.

The modification letter or the set of re-grant conditions has to be registered with the Land Registry in order to become part of the title documents of the land. All title documents are public documents.

As lease modification (waiver) is a matter of mutual agreement to change a pre-existing contract (i.e. the lease), there is no appeal procedure for an unsuccessful application whether the amount of the premium (charge) is an issue or not.

Though there is no legal requirement for so doing, the landowner or developer who wishes to apply for a lease modification (waiver) often instructs an *estate surveyor in private practice*. This is so by virtue of the expertise of the estate surveyor in lease interpretation and valuation, a skill that is required for lease terms and premium negotiation.

## When Is Lease Modification Required?

Lease modification (or waiver) is required whenever *an intended use(s)* and/or its (their) development intensity (e.g., plot ratios, building height, and number of storeys) on a piece of land is/are not permitted under the terms of the land lease *for that same piece of land*. This is required whether the use is to occur permanently (or temporarily) in an existing building, or upon redevelopment during the term of the lease.

Lease modification is also required where the intended use or development is to occur *on a site that is different in terms of boundary and/or on a buildable area from an existing one* due to the need to close existing (or opening up) lanes or roads, and/or to amalgamate with an adjoining private lot with a view to maximizing the development potential of the site. An example is exploiting achievable GFA under the Buildings Ordinance. Lease modification in this situation typically involves a 'surrender-and-re-grant' process by which the old lot is surrendered in exchange for the re-grant of the new lot *in situ* (and hence 'in situ-exchange') under a completely revised set of conditions in consideration for a premium.

Lease modification is also necessary if a developer wishes *to alter any of the development restrictions for a smaller site carved out from a larger parent lot*, where that is not prohibited by the lease. After privately executing a deed poll that enables the sub-division, the developer then applies for the modification of the relevant lease terms for the smaller site.

The concept of 'lease modification' overlaps, but it is not identical to either 'surrender-and-re-grant' or 'extension'. Surrender-and-re-grant and extension can occur without any modification to the covenant of an existing lease (executed by deed or deemed to be so by the Conveyancing and Property Ordinance) when:

(1) an old private lot is surrendered in exchange for an entirely separate government lot that is in a different location and is in no way physically connected with the old lot (referred to as 'non in-situ exchange'); and
(2) adjoining piece(s) of government land is (are) granted to a lessee or grantee on the same terms of the original lease/grant by 'Conditions of Extension' or an 'Extension Letter'.

Lease modification or waiver *for a use that has been carried out* in existing premises is sometimes required by the relevant District Lands Office in connection with lease enforcement actions. An application is subject to interdepartmental consultation by circulation before it is decided by the District Lands Conference (DLC).

A typical lease modification scenario is one in which an *intended* development is to be built on several pieces of land, subject to leases with different terms or conditions, or to terms or conditions that prevent or restrict site amalgamation acquired by a developer for a *higher value* use (with a view to gain or realize more development potential under the Buildings Ordinance). In this scenario, the modification involves a proposed 'surrender-and-re-grant' of the land parcels. This means that the proposed surrender of the lands involved in exchange for the re-grant of all land as one single plot of land subject to an entirely fresh lease with new conditions.

## Steps in Checking Whether Lease Modification Is Required

It must be stressed that any discussion about the need for lease modification assumes that (1) the intended change in use is of a higher value than that permitted by the terms of the existing lease, and (2) there is a net gain in value when taking into account the transaction costs (including the premium, administrative fee and any ensuing government rent payable; the costs of obtaining planning permissions if required; the costs of obtaining building permissions; the lost in rents as result of redevelopment; the building costs of redevelopment; the costs of compensating existing tenants, etc.) involved in modifying the lease. The gain in value is largely a matter of two factors: (1) a new user that is more valuable per unit area, and/or (2) a greater achievable GFA. This is an financial or business consideration that must be borne in mind by a rational investor. Generally speaking, it would be unwise for a landowner to surrender a 999-year lease in exchange for a re-grant of land that achieves no or little gain in GFA for a specific use on a much shorter term (e.g., up to the year 2047). This is so unless the government compensates the tremendous loss in rights with premium[3] or significant benefits in another dealing with the landowner. Where the modification is by deed, no consideration needs to be paid by the government for a lessee who surrenders to the government some valuable land rights such as marine rights.

Subject to sound financial consideration, if an intended use or development is contradictory to, or restricted, or not permitted, by the covenants, terms or conditions stipulated in the Government Leases or Conditions, then no matter how insignificant such contradiction, restriction or lack of permission may be, there is a need for lease modification. This is even more so where compliance with the lease is a condition of the planning permission or a requirement under the statutory town plan, but the intended use is not permitted by the existing lease conditions. Thus, the steps to take are:

(1) Determine the intended use.
(2) Read the entire lease or set of conditions and previous modifications, waivers or extensions, if there are any. If the intended use is permitted by the lease conditions, there is no need for lease modification. If not, go to the next step.

---

3. See the Deed of Variation dated 21 October 1999 for Inland Lot 6622, the site of the Consulate General of the United States at 26, Garden Road, Hong Kong.

(3) Evaluate whether the intended change in use requires planning permission.
(4) Based on the results of the above, evaluate if there is any reasonable net gain in value if lease modification is granted. If there is no reasonable gain in value, give up the idea of lease modification and seek other means to maximize the use value of the site under the existing lease. If there is a reasonable gain in value and there is no need for obtaining planning permission, proceed to apply for lease modifications. If planning permissions are required, obtain planning permissions first *before* applying for lease modifications.

## For a Use or Development in an Existing Building

For a use or development intended to be or currently being carried out on a premises of a building, the first step is to check whether the use or development is consistent with the lease conditions or the terms of the DMC. If the intended use is to be carried out (or the existing use continued) and is not permitted, then lease modification is necessary.

However, lease modification in this context is meaningful only if such change is also permitted or permissible by the statutory town plan and the building plan.

## For Redevelopment

For an intended use to be carried out upon redevelopment, the first step is to check whether the use and its scale of development are permitted by the existing lease. If neither is permitted, then lease modification is necessary.

Lease modification in this context is meaningful only if the intended use or scale of development is permitted or permissible by the statutory town plan. Where the use requires planning permission, that permission must be obtained as otherwise no building approval can be obtained even where the lease is modified.

The standard lease modification procedure is summarized in Figure 10.1.

## Lease Modifications and Town Plans

In considering an application for lease modifications and the premium payable, the Lands Department would have regard to not only the relevant statutory town plans prepared under the Town Planning Ordinance, but also the provisions of such applicable administrative town plans as Outline Development Plans approved by the Committee on Planning and Lands.

*Lease Modifications and Waivers* 73

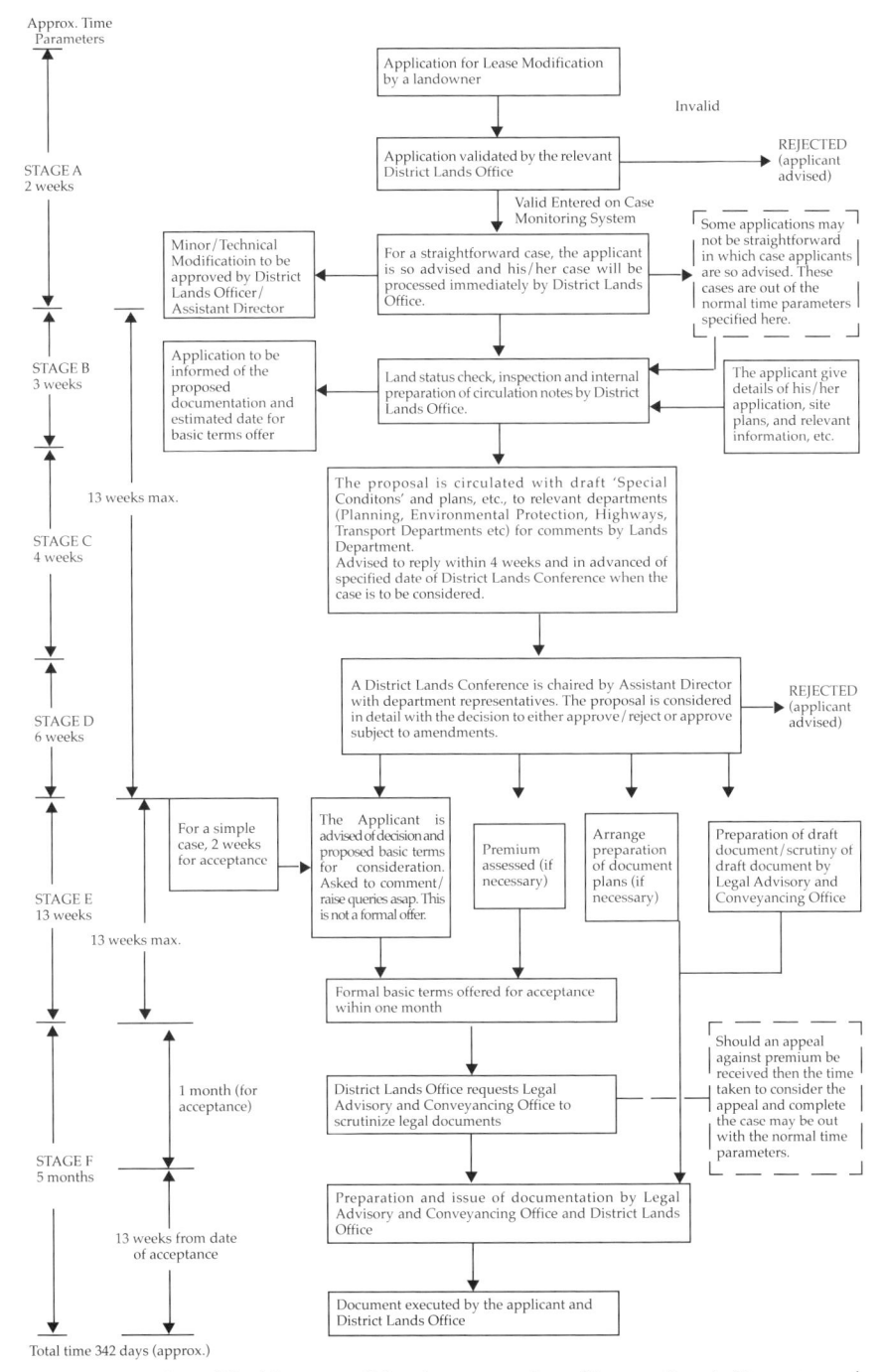

Figure 10.1 Simplified lease modifications procedure (Source: Lands Department)

# 11 BUILDING APPLICATIONS AND APPEALS

The conceptual and actual development process analysis discussed in Chapter 8 shows that building approvals are the key in the development cycle. It is the most important stage of actual property development. Successful planning and lease modifications will amount to nothing if permission for the proposed building plans is refused. In Hong Kong, buildings are expensive commodities. It pays to work faster. Besides, planning permissions have only a short life-span of two to three years. Thus, the building appeal procedures provide a developer hope of overcoming the final hurdle to building construction.

## Building Authority and Legislation

The Buildings Ordinance and its subsidiary legislation provide the legal basis for the work of the Building Authority, whose main duty is to plan and control building development in respect of health and safety of occupants in buildings. The preamble to the Buildings Ordinance reads:

> To provide for the planning, design and construction of buildings and associated works; to make provision for the rendering safe of dangerous buildings and land; and to make provision for matters connected therewith.

The administration of the Buildings Ordinance is vested with the Buildings Department. The Director of Buildings is the Building Authority.

The Buildings Ordinance provides the legal framework within which the following key aspects of building planning and development control are regulated:

(1) planning in terms of control on plot ratio, site coverage, open space, lanes, etc.;
(2) design in terms of provision of lighting and ventilation, projections;
(3) construction in terms of loading requirements, structural use of materials, retaining walls, etc.;

(4) associated works in terms of erection of hoarding, covered walkways, demolition, etc.;
(5) safety in terms of provision of means of escape, staircases, structural stability, etc.; and
(6) dangerous buildings in terms of inspection, application of closure orders, issue of orders for repair or actual carrying out of the repair works, etc.

Under section 41 of the Buildings Ordinance, all 'buildings' in Hong Kong are subject to control of the except:

(1) buildings belonging to the Crown or to the Government;
(2) buildings upon any land vested in or under the control of the Housing Authority; and
(3) buildings upon any land vested in any person on behalf of the People's Liberation Army.

Therefore, in general, any private development project for whatever uses (or users) will be subject to control under the Buildings Ordinance. However, under section 41(3) and section 41(3A) of the Buildings Ordinance, building works in existing buildings which 'do not involve the structure of any building may be carried out in any building without application to or approval from the Building Authority'. One example is interior renovation work involving demolition of non-structural walls that does not affect fire protection.

Thus, the scope of control under the Buildings Ordinance includes:

(1) control on all new building developments, e.g., office buildings, residential blocks and other associated works such as foundation, demolition, structural and drainage works;
(2) control on specialized use of existing buildings, e.g. kindergartens, home for the elderly, cinemas, restaurants, etc., by a system of licensing;
(3) control on dangerous buildings, dangerous signs and slopes by a system of inspection, order and enforcement;
(4) control on unauthorized building works by a system of inspection, order, prosecution and enforcement;
(5) regulation of emergency service to damaged buildings and scaffoldings, hoarding, signs, etc., in times of typhoon, flooding, fire damage, etc.
(6) administering of the Buildings Ordinance in respect of prosecution, disciplinary actions, appeals, litigation and legislative review.

The Buildings Ordinance (Application to the New Territories) Ordinance (Chapter 121) allows the Building Authority to exempt certain works in the New Territories from the provisions of the Buildings Ordinance. One example is the 'New Territories Exempted House' such as a 'small house'.

Subsidiary legislation to the Buildings Ordinance regulates specific dimensions of building planning and building works. The main pieces of subsidiary legislation include:

(1) Building (Administration) Regulations;
(2) Building (Construction) Regulations;
(3) Building (Demolition Works) Regulations;
(4) Building (Planning) Regulations;
(5) Building (Private Streets and Access Roads) Regulations;
(6) Building (Refuse Storage Chambers and Chutes) Regulations;
(7) Building (Standards of Sanitary Fitments, Plumbing, Drainage Works and Latrines) Regulations;
(8) Building (Ventilating Systems) Regulations;
(9) Building (Oil Storage Installations) Regulations; and
(10) Building (Energy Efficiency) Regulations.

In addition to the ordinance and regulations, there are a number of codes of practice prepared by the Building Authority, which cover such aspects as fire safety, energy conservation, and structural design, for practitioners. These codes serve as 'deemed to satisfy' designs. They supplement and elaborate on the statutory requirements stipulated in the ordinance and regulations.

There is also a set of Practice Notes for Authorized Persons (PNAP), prepared also by the Building Authority, which updates current practice in respect of procedures and discretion of the Building Authority.

## Building Development Approval

Under section 14 of the Buildings Ordinance, approval should be obtained from the Building Authority, to whom applications should be made, before the commencement of any construction work. As in the case of a planning application, there is no limit on the number of building applications one may make for a site, and there is not any rule against concurrent applications (for different uses, designs or development intensities). Neither is there any time limitation on the making of another application after an earlier attempt has failed. However, unlike a planning application, every building application must be accompanied by a fee payable to the government. The fee for new non-industrial buildings exceeding 10,000 square metres GFA as of 31 March 2004 is HK$ 2,750 per squared metres with a minimum charge ofHK$343,400 for every application.

Under section 4(1) of the Buildings Ordinance, any person for whom the building works is carried out shall appoint an Authorized Person (AP) acting as the co-ordinator of the works.

Under section 3 of the Buildings Ordinance, Authorized Persons are architects, structural engineers or building surveyors who have proven local experience and are registered. In general, an AP provides professional advice to the client, prepares development proposals, carries out supervision and co-ordinates with the Buildings Department regarding approvals, amendments, testing, inspection and upon final completion of work on a building site.

The process for approving the building plans for a new development project under the Buildings Ordinance takes two stages to complete. The first stage of the process is the approval of development drawings and associated designs by the Building Authority. Under the current 'centralized processing system' (as per PNAP 30), the Buildings Department will circulate the building plans submitted by the Authorized Person to all relevant government departments for 'comments', concurrence, or approval. The results of plan vetting and comments by various government departments, as required under various ordinances, will be incorporated in a letter of approval or disapproval to the applicant. Here we shall concentrate on the approval process that occurs within the Buildings Department, which serves the Building Authority under the Buildings Ordinance.

Once the building plans for a development proposal submitted by the Authorized Person is received, the Building Department will check the following fundamental aspects of the building proposal (PNAP 99):

(1) density: site parameters, plot ratio, site coverage;
(2) safety: means of access for fire-fighting and rescue, means of escape in case of fire, fire resistance and compartmentation, geotechnical assessment of potential landslip hazard;
(3) health and environment: lighting, ventilation, open space; and
(4) fundamental issues under allied legislation: fire safety, Outline Zoning Plans, access for persons with a disability, airport height restrictions and railway protection.

In accordance with section 30(3) of the Building (Administration) Regulations, the Building Authority should notify the Authorized Person within 60 days upon submission of plans as to whether the plans submitted are approved or not. The building plans are deemed to have been approved if notice is not given by the Building Authority within the statutory period. (Note that no similar deemed approval is provided for planning applications.) Thus staff of the Building Department have to meet the 60-day deadline, otherwise the developer's building plans will be deemed approved.

The second stage of the building plan approval process is the granting by the Building Authority, on application of the Authorized Person, of consent to commence work under section 14(1)(b) of the Buildings Ordinance. Under section 32 of the Building (Administration) Regulations, with a statutory period of 28 days, the Building Authority must notify the Authorized Person of his or her decision. Actual building construction work can lawfully start as soon as the consent is given.

## Grounds for Refusal of Building Plans

Unlike the Town Planning Board, which need not have regard to any statutory consideration in addition to the applicable statutory zoning plan, the Building Authority can only refuse a building plan submission where it contravenes one or more statutory grounds. Refusal of plans of building works, street works or consent to commence work shall be made in accordance with section 16 of the Buildings Ordinance. What follows are common statutory grounds for refusing to grant building permissions:

(1) plans submitted are not as prescribed by the regulations;
(2) plans submitted are not endorsed or accompanied by a certificate from the Director of Fire Services;
(3) plans are not submitted using the prescribed forms;
(4) carrying out of works would contravene the Buildings Ordinance or other enactment, or would contravene any draft or approved plan prepared under the Town Planning Ordinance;
(5) inadequate documents to support the proposal as prescribed by the regulations;
(6) prescribed fees are not paid;
(7) the carrying out of the building works would result in a building differing in height, design, type or intended use from buildings in the 'immediate neighbourhood' or 'previously existing' on the same site;
(8) new access is likely to be dangerous or prejudicial to the safety and convenience of traffic;

(9) further and better particulars are needed for consideration;
(10) not satisfied with the further particulars submitted in accordance with the above;
(11) the new building works required demolition of building which renders adjacent buildings dangerous;
(12) site formation works, piling works, excavation works or foundation works render adjacent land and building dangerous;
(13) the proposed domestic use is likely to be contravene section 49 of the Building (Planning) Regulations and used for dangerous trades such as storage of dangerous goods, motor repair shops, paint shops, etc.;
(14) plans for proposal where land is under resumption;
(15) unsatisfactory connection to public street;
(16) proposal inadequate in respect of resisting landslide debris in Area Number 1 of the Schedule Area;
(17) unjustified use of hand-dug caissons; and
(18) incompatibility with sewage tunnel works under section 17A.

The granting of an approval may be subject to specific conditions, such as the erection of shoring to adjacent buildings.

## Modifications of Building Plans

Due to various reasons, the Authorized Person may find it hard to fully satisfy certain provisions of the regulations. Under section 42 of the Buildings Ordinance, the Authorized Person can apply to the Building Authority for exemption from and/or modification of the Buildings Ordinance and regulations so that the building plans may be approved.

The application for modification must be made in a prescribed form. The Building Authority will consider every case on its own merits and shall not be required to take into account any statutory exemption or modification granted in the past.

In any case, items modified shall not prejudice the standard of structural stability and public health. The usual items that require modifications include inadequate lighting and ventilation to toilets, slight excess of gross floor area by way of additional cladding to external walls, erection of canopies over street for protection of public and the like.

## The Building Appeal Tribunal

Part VI of the Buildings Ordinance deals with appeal against decisions or orders made by the Building Authority.

Under section 44 of the Buildings Ordinance, 'a person' can appeal against decisions of the Building Authority, objecting the refusal of plans or discretion exercised by the Building Authority under the Buildings Ordinance.

Under section 45 of the Buildings Ordinance, the Governor (Chief Executive) shall appoint persons to form an Appeal Tribunal Panel to deal with the appeal cases. The period of appointment of panel members shall not be more than three years.

Upon receipt of a 'notice of appeal', the Governor (Chief Executive) shall appoint, from the Appeal Tribunal Panel, a tribunal consisting of a Chairperson and no fewer than two members to hear the appeal.

The Chairperson must be qualified for appointment as a District Court Judge under section 5 of the District Court Ordinance (Chapter 336, Laws of Hong Kong). Like the Town Planning Board, the composition of the tribunal is such that the majority of the members cannot be public officers. Those public officers acting as Chairpersons or members of the tribunal shall act in their personal capacity and not subject to any direction to consider the case as they are public officers.

Under section 53(A) of the Buildings Ordinance, the Chairperson and members of the Appeal Tribunal and any witness, counsel, solicitor or legal officer appearing before the Appeal Tribunal shall have the same privileges and immunities similar to a judge of the High Court in relation to civil proceedings.

Any person who refuses or fails without reasonable excuse to comply with any order or directions of the Appeal Tribunal or interferes with the proceedings commits an offence and is liable to a fine of $100,000 and to imprisonment for six months.

## Procedures of the Building Appeal Tribunal

Under section 38(1B) of the Buildings Ordinance, the Chief Executive in Council may by regulation provide for the procedures regarding appeal and the practice and procedures of the Appeal Tribunal. The Building (Appeal) Regulations gives details of the procedures under this section of the ordinance.

Notice to appeal must be made to the Secretary to the Appeal Tribunal in the prescribed manner within 21 days of the notification of the decision under appeal.

Within 28 days from the serving of the notice of appeal, the appellant shall provide the Secretary of the Appeal Tribunal and the Building Authority with the following documents:

(1) particulars of the decisions the appeal relates;
(2) the grounds of appeal, if not already specified;
(3) a detail description of matters relating to the appeal;
(4) documents to be produced for the hearing;
(5) description of related property or land and declaration of any interest of the appellant on such property or land; and
(6) particulars of the witnesses the appellant intends to call.

Upon receipt of the above documents, the Building Authority shall, within 28 days, furnish to the Secretary and the appellant any documents, representations in writing, etc., in his/her custody, which he/she considers would assist the Tribunal to determine or otherwise dispose of the appeal. Either party can request the other party to furnish further particulars relevant to the case. The Tribunal may dismiss the appeal if the appellant is unable to furnish the required documents or comply with the request. However, the Chairperson may extend the time limit as stated above upon application by either party to the appeal.

Under section 49 of the Buildings Ordinance, the Appeal Tribunal may hold a preliminary hearing to determine whether there is a good cause for a full hearing. The appeal may be dismissed if there is no such good cause. A 21-day notice shall be given to each party on the date, time and place of the hearing. The appellant may withdraw his/her appeal or abandon any part of it by giving notice in writing to the Secretary and to the Building Authority.

## Conduct of the Building Appeal Tribunal

As in the case of a planning appeal, all decisions have to be made by a majority vote of the members of the Appeal Tribunal (under section 50 of the Buildings Ordinance). The Chairperson shall have a casting vote if there is an equality of votes. **Where there is any question of law, the Chairperson can refer to the Court of Appeal for its decision by way of case stated.**

Under section 9(1) of the Building (Appeal) Regulation, the hearing of an appeal shall be in public. The Chairperson may order the hearing or part of it to be held in private by considering views or the private interest and claim to privilege of any party to the appeal.

The Building Authority or the appellant may be represented in person, by counsel, or by solicitor. With the approval of the Chairperson, the Building Authority or the appellant may be represented by any person authorized by the party concerned in writing.

In the course of proceeding, the Appeal Tribunal (or by order a public officer) may enter and inspect any land or premises it considers relevant for the appeal, including opening up, taking samples and removing anything that obstruct the access.

As far as evidence is concerned, the Appeal Tribunal adopts a more relaxed and liberal approach than the court. The Appeal Tribunal may receive all kinds of evidence, whether or not it is oral and documentary, on oath or affirmation.

The Appeal Tribunal can issue summons to the effect requiring any person to give evidence and produce any document. The decision of the Appeal Tribunal can confirm, vary, or reverse the decision that is appealed against or substitute with another order it thinks fit.

Details of the appeal are to be recorded including details of the appellant and witness, evidence given, the decisions, reasons and any order for cost. **The decision may be published in full or in part, whether or not the hearing is held in public or private**. Members of the public can inspect decisions of the appeals at the Buildings Department. Chapter 2 of Lai and D. Ho (2000, 2002) gives a list of the 'rules' used by the Appeal Tribunal to make decisions in some areas of interest.

The Appeal Tribunal can make order to cover the cost of the hearing and determination, but will not award any compensation in relation to the appeal. If the cost is awarded against the appellant, it shall be recovered in accordance with section 33 of the Buildings Ordinance. It is similar to recovery of cost incurred by the Building Authority in carrying out works, supervision, abortive visits and other services for a particular person or project. Any costs awarded against the Building Authority shall be paid out of the general revenue.

# 12 ENFORCEMENT OF LEASES, TOWN PLANNING ORDINANCE AND BUILDINGS ORDINANCE

## Lease Enforcement

A typical government lease contains clauses or provisions that expressly state that when any obligation, term or condition is not fulfilled and/or when any restriction is violated, the government can re-enter the land. These clauses or provisions are often referred to as 're-entry clauses'. Some examples of obligations, terms or conditions that trigger decisions to re-enter, as evidenced in a 'Memorandum of Re-entry' or a 'Vesting Notice', are:

(1) the obligation for the lessee to develop land purchased from the government within a certain period of time (with the social and economic concern that scarce land resource should not be wasted or allowed to be idle);
(2) user restrictions; and
(3) the need to comply with the Buildings Ordinance and Town Planning Ordinance.

Re-entry of land under re-entry clauses is a matter of contract enforcement based on mutually agreed terms. Though re-entry may be triggered by violation of an ordinance specified in the lease conditions, this must not be confused with land resumption of the land or enforcement against a certain use or development of the land under various ordinances.

Re-entry is a matter of lease enforcement. It is the contractual right of the government based on its contract with the lessee. The government will decide as to whether or not such right is exercised when a breach occurs. There is no duty on the part of the government to re-enter; thus a third party cannot compel the government to re-enter or complain against the government when it chooses not to re-enter.

The Lands Department conducts land inspection from time to time and where it discovers that there is a breach of lease terms, it would as a matter of practice issues a warning letter to the occupier and the lessee of the land.

## 86   Change in Use of Land

The warning letter regarding a breach of user or development restrictions typically contains the followings:

(1) a description of the use or development that is found on the land;
(2) a warning that the said use or development is in breach of the terms of the lease;
(3) a request that such use or development must be immediately discontinued (with a 28-day grace period);
(4) the consequences of ignoring the request;
(5) the need to pay the government a fine ('forbearance fees') should the use or development in question is not discontinued in 28 days and such a fine is payable for as long as the use or development to be discontinued remains on the land, whether or not the land is eventually re-entered; and
(6) an indication that the use or development may become permissible under the Town Planning Ordinance.

The forbearance fee is a charge that affects the title of the property, with serious implications for conveyancing.

The institution of 'forbearance fee' while the use or development to be discontinued remains on the land is a consideration for the government in refraining from immediately exercising its contractual right to re-enter land.

## Lease Enforcement and Planning Applications

The indication in the warning letter that the use or development may become permissible under the Town Planning Ordinance implies that lease modification or waiver for accommodating the use or development would be supported if an application is made upon obtaining the requisite planning permission. Here is a typical example: an occupier of a multi-storey building under lease conditions for a factory building is said to have been in breach of lease conditions by operating office activities on the premises. The lease enforcement notice served to the occupier and the owner of shares of the factory building often suggests that the owner obtain planning permission and apply for lease modification (the application for a 'no objection' letter) to 'regularize' the office uses.

However, whether a planning application for a use in breach of the lease conditions can be validly made to the Town Planning Board is not determined by the Lands Department, but the provisions of the applicable statutory town plan (see Chapter 7).

## When Served with an Enforcement Notice by the District Lands Office

The property owner should not ignore an enforcement notice served to him/her whether or not the breach alleged by the District Lands Office has been caused by him/her or the tenant.

The property owner should first find out as to whether there is a real breach of the lease as a matter of law (lease interpretation). This is particularly crucial for older leases, which are less specific in the definition and description of the user or other restrictions. Prompt legal advice should be sought. If there is no resource to do so, immediate compliance with the notice should be considered. Before costly litigation is contemplated, the owner should communicate with the District Lands Office about the legal advice he/she obtains. The District Lands Office would seek legal advice from the Legal Advisory and Conveyancing Office (LACO) of the Lands Department before deciding upon the case of alleged breach.

Whether or not there is a breach at law, the property owner should then find out as to whether the extent of breach, as a matter of fact, is accurate. The owner can approach the relevant District Lands Office for clarification, and this can be best achieved by a joint site visit to the premises so that the location and extent of the alleged breach can be delimited.

In any case, the aggrieved landowner should seek legal advice as regards the payment of the 'forbearance fees' if the alleged breach of use is not discontinued in 28 days.

## Planning Enforcement

A major amendment to the Town Planning Ordinance was made in 1991 to extend explicitly the jurisdiction of planning legislation to the entire territory of Hong Kong.[1] Previously, it was presumed that the reference to 'existing and potential urban areas' in the preamble of the Town Planning Ordinance had excluded the rural areas of the New Territories, i.e., areas outside designated new towns.

Under the provisions of the amended Town Planning Ordinance, Interim Development Permission Area (IDPA) could be designated and IDPA Plans were prepared by the Director of Planning before the Town Planning

---

1. Town Planning (Amendment) Ordinance 1991 (4 of 1991).

(Amendment) Ordinance 1991 came into operation.[2] Introduced in 1990 under a Town Planning Amendment Bill, the IDPA plans were first replaced by successively refined Development Permission Area (DPA) plans[3] and eventually by Rural Outline Zoning Plans.[4] In an area for which an IDPA plan was produced, a material change in the use of land or development constituted an offence, unless it was approved by the Town Planning Board or permitted as of right (under Column 1 or on the cover pages of the Notes) by the relevant statutory plan after the gazette date of the notice of the IDPA Plan.

After the operation of the Town Planning (Amendment) Ordinance 1991, the Town Planning Board could designate Development Permission Area (DPA) and draft DPA Plans. The draft DPA Plans were replaced by Rural Outline Zoning Plans eventually.[5] In an area for which such a DPA plan was produced, a material change in the use land or development constituted an offence, unless it was approved by the Town Planning Board or permitted as of right (under Column 1 or on the cover pages of the Notes) by the relevant statutory plan after the gazette date of the notice of the applicable IDPA Plan.

The relevant provisions, which include definition of the offence, its remedies and its statutory defences, are generally described as 'planning enforcement' provisions. According to these provisions, the Planning Department may either serve an Enforcement Notice under section 23 requiring rectification (failure to comply entails prosecution),[6] or proceed to prosecute directly under section 20(7). The accused may avoid prosecution or conviction if they obtain

---

2. Section 26, Town Planning Ordinance.
3. Section 20, Town Planning Ordinance. This section dictates that DPA plans can only be produced for areas previously covered by IDPA plans prepared under section 26. This means that enforcement provisions cannot be extended to cover new towns or the old urban areas for which Outline Zoning Plans were the first statutory plans prepared.
4. See Note 9, Chapter 4, ante.
5. See Note 9, Chapter 4, ante.
6. Section 23(1), Town Planning Ordinance. This can be served on the owner, occupier or a person who is responsible for the alleged unauthorized development. The follow-up option to an 'Enforcement Notice' may be a 'Stop Notice' issued under section 23(2), or a 'Reinstatement Notice' issued under sections 23(3) and 23(4).

planning permission,[7] or they can show that the uses in dispute are in fact 'existing uses',[8] i.e. uses that had existed 'immediately before' the date of the IDPA.

On conviction under either section 20(8) or section 23(6), an accused is liable to pay fines. The amount of fines has been increased successively. Conviction for an offence after a notice under section 23(6) may also attract a daily fine. The levels of sentencing in recent years in respect of conviction under the Town Planning Ordinance are shown in Table 14.1.

Failing to comply with a notice served under section 23 may entail loss of goods due to seizure, detention or disposal by the Planning Department. The *Consultative Paper on the Town Planning Bill* (June 1996) proposes a number of further amendments, notably the penalty of imprisonment, personal liability for company directors and Cho/Tong managers,[9] and the admissibility of photographic evidence.

The planning enforcement law creates a statutory strict liability criminal offence for unauthorized changes in use 'being found'[10] after the date of IDPA on the current owner, occupier or user's land.[11] No *mens rea* or actual conduct[12] of the accused is necessary to establish the offence and there is no provision for jury trial. The mischief[13] that the law is said to target is the uncontrolled proliferation of open storage uses on land governed by agricultural leases.

---

7. Sections 21(c); 23(1)(b)(ii); 23(9)(d), Town Planning Ordinance.
8. Section 1A of the Town Planning Ordinance defines 'existing use in relation to a development permission area'. However, rural outline zoning plans with a history of an IDPA refer back to the dates of their IDPA designation.
9. Cho or Tong is the body corporate for a 'clan'.
10. This is definitely the situation for offences committed under the old section 23(6) in which the offence was 'where there is or was unauthorised development'. The wordings 'no person shall undertake or continue development' are retained in section 20(7) and section 21(1) seems to suggest requirements of certain acts to form the *actus reus* of the offence. However, in the majority of the cases, it seems that only the situation of land as seen in aerial photos or ground photos matters.
11. This is expressed clearly for section 23 offences. The usual practice for sections 20(7)(1) and 21(1) is against the user.
12. See note 9, ante.
13. See *Consultation Paper on Town Planning Bill* (Hong Kong: Hong Kong Government, 1996), pp. 1–15.

## Table 14.1  Planning Enforcement Statistics: 1991–2001

| | 1991 | 1992 | 1993 | 1994 | 1995 | 1996 | 1997 | 1998 | 1999 | 2000 | 2001 |
|---|---|---|---|---|---|---|---|---|---|---|---|
| New Unauthorized Developments Detected | | | | | 379 | 769 | 847 | 765 | 560 | 507 | 981 |
| Enforcement Notices | 2 | 105 | 504 | 157 | 374 | 1061 | 1664 | 1345 | 865 | 450 | 649 |
| Stop Notices | 0 | 7 | 15 | 0 | 0 | 0 | 0 | 7 | 0 | 0 | 0 |
| Reinstatement Notices | 0 | 0 | 4 | 5 | 38 | 87 | 72 | 15 | 3 | 0 | 0 |
| Compliance Notices | 0 | 0 | 40 | 151 | 179 | 643 | 1405 | 1158 | 1389 | 627 | 449 |
| Convictions under s. 23(6), Number of Persons Convicted | | | | | 100 | 153 | 24 | 118 | 39 | 8 | 12 |
| Convictions under s. 21(2), s. 20(7 & 8), Number of Persons Convicted | | | | | 55 | 89 | 17 | 12 | 6 | 18 | 21 |
| Convictions under s. 23(6), Number of Cases | | | | | N/A | 56 | 11 | 44 | 14 | 2 | 3 |
| Convictions under s. 21(2), s. 20(7 & 8), Number of Cases | | | | | N/A | 77 | 14 | 9 | 6 | 15 | 20 |
| Average fine for convictions under s. 23(6) | | | | | $45,578 | $39,230 | $21,125 | $26,392 | $22,410 | $9,555 | $4,625 |
| Average fine for convictions under s. 21(2), s. 20(7 & 8) | | | | | $34,945 | $47,410 | $61,180 | $31,417 | $61,717 | $19,306 | $9,.571 |

Source: Planning Department (Compiled by Liu, 2003)

## Planning Enforcement and Planning Applications, Reviews and Appeals

The Town Planning Ordinance clearly provides, as reflected also in planning enforcement notices, that a person who has carried out unauthorized development may obtain planning permission from the Town Planning Board for that unauthorized development. This person has a statutory right to make a planning appeal to the Appeal Board against the decision of the Town Planning Board under the Town Planning Ordinance, in case his/her application fails after a review by the Town Planning Board. Such right for his/her application to be treated fairly by the Appeal Board should not be prejudiced by the fact that he/she is subject to an enforcement action or even under prosecution. This is so even though there are a few planning appeal cases that suggest, erroneously, that planning appeals arising from planning enforcement actions, must be dismissed. (Such suggestion is erroneous because it in effect attempts to deprive the person served with an enforcement notice of his/her statutory right under the ordinance to rectify his/her unauthorized use. See Lai [1999, 2003].)

## When Served with an Enforcement Notice under the Town Planning Ordinance

Upon receipt of a planning enforcement notice, one should take note of the following:

(1) Do not ignore the notice, or one runs the risk of being arrested and eventually convicted of a criminal offence; one's title to land may also be rendered defeasible.
(2) Seek legal advice immediately.
(3) Take 'reasonable steps' and comply with the notice where the allegation is correct.
(4) However, there is no need for self-incrimination by confessing or making a 'plea in mitigation' before staff of the Planning Department, as the department is not a court of law and is in fact the party that takes prosecution actions.
(5) Contest the notice at court only where there are strong legal grounds, good evidence and financial resources.

## Enforcement against Unauthorized Building Works

Section 24 of the Buildings Ordinance provides that where any building works have been or are being carried out in contravention of any provision of the ordinance, 'the Building Authority may by order require the demolition of the same'. This order is the 'section 24 Order'. A typical example of such contravention is the addition of structures without prior permission. A 'section 24 Order' would be registered against the title of land, rendering it defective.

The Building Authority has the discretion not to issue any such order. Yet, it does not mean that retrospective approval for the unauthorized work can be given. The Buildings Ordinance does not allow retrospective approval, even where such approval would have been granted if a building plan was actually submitted for the structure under a 'section 24 Order'.

# 13 DEVELOPMENT BLIGHT

Generally, a landowner would unwelcome the imposition of any administrative or statutory government measure that would add to the cost or reduce prospective revenue for his/her property, especially one that would halt or prevent a change in the use or development of land. Such unwelcome measure, particularly one that is uncompensated and could create development blight, may come along in the form of:

(1) a building moratorium such as that imposed on sites in the Mid-Levels after the June 18th Incident involving the collapse of a building at Kotewell Road in 1972;
(2) a development moratorium under the Antiquities and Monuments Ordinance (Chapter 53, Laws of Hong Kong); and
(3) down-zoning under the Town Planning Ordinance (e.g. the reduction of plot ratio or building height, Comprehensive Development Area designation with a view for urban renewal by the Urban Renewal Agency, Site of Special Scientific Area [SSSI] or Conservation Area zoning), the Country Parks Ordinance (country park or Special Area designation); and
(4) closure or narrowing of streets.

There may or may not be provisions for objection and/or compensation for the restrictions on development. Generally, a development moratorium is the worst constraint as it prohibits demolition or alteration of any part of a building.

# 14 INFORMATION REGARDING LEASES, STATUTORY TOWN PLANS, AND BUILDING PLANS

The HKSAR government has vastly expanded the scope and depth of its electronic services to the public. On the one hand, this has rendered the study of land use and change of use less costly. On the other hand, the quality and design of various systems vary and co-ordination is wanting. The reader should therefore constantly update his/her knowledge of various rapidly developing systems by making full use of the non-electronic systems of information.

## Leases

Leases and conditions, as well as their variations, modifications and extensions, are public documents because title documents must be registered with the Land Registry. Copies of these title documents can be purchased from the Land Registry by any person. They can also be ordered through an electronic system called the 'Direct Access System (DAS)'.

Electronic version of government land survey documents, which contain information about the location and boundaries of land lots (viz. 'Geographic Information System' or GIS), can be purchased from the Lands Department.

## Statutory Town Plans and Decisions Made by the Planning Boards

Statutory town plans are public documents and can be inspected free by any person at the Planning Department. The documents can also be purchased from the Lands Department. The latest statutory plans that are in effect can be seen on the Planning Department's website.

Apart from personal data, information regarding decisions of the Town Planning Board for section 16 applications or section 17(1) reviews can be inspected free at the Planning Department. Since 4 April 2003,[1] data on section

---

1. The press release can be accessed at:
   http://www.info.gov.hk/gia/general/200304/04/0404087.htm

16 applications and decisions about them from June 1990 have been made available to the public in the following website: http://www.ozp.tpb.gov.hk/epa/.

Master Layout Plans approved by the Town Planning Board can be inspected, as a matter of statutory right, at the Land Registry.

Copies of the planning conditions for approved section 16 applications can be inspected and purchased from the Planning Department, while copies of planning appeal decisions can be purchased from the Appeal Board secretariat.

## Building Plans and Decisions Made by the Building Appeal Tribunal

Copies of approved building plans can be inspected and purchased from the Building Department, although the copyright of these plans belong to the Authorized Persons who make them.

Copies of building appeal decisions can be inspected at the secretariat of the Building Appeal Tribunal and the Hong Kong Institute of Engineers (HKIE).

# 15 PROBLEM SETS

The scenarios described in this chapter are based on real-life practice. They serve to stimulate interesting discussion. In the following discussion, the reader is reminded that the 'notes' for various zones are those adopted for the latest Outline Zoning Plans.

1. Mr A has lost his case in a section 16 application and is considering a review or appeal. He would like to know if there are supporting legal grounds and the procedure for applying for a review and appeal. Advise him.

2. Planning control was substantially changed in the amendment of the Town Planning Ordinance in 1991. After the amendment, a big difference exists between rural and urban land. What is the difference? What gives rise to such discrepancy? Are various provisions in the Town Planning Ordinance the reason for the discrepancy?

3. There are different notices that can be issued in planning enforcement cases under the Town Planning Ordinance. What are these notices and their respective purposes?

4. A is a novice developer who intends to start a development in the New Territories. He has looked at the relevant Outline Zoning Plan of the area of development but does not understand it. He finds two columns in the notes to the plan. He would like to know what he has to do if:
    (a) his intended use falls within column 1 but not column 2;
    (b) his intended use falls within column 2 but not column 1; and
    (c) his intended use does not appear in any of the columns.

    In any case he wants to go ahead with the development. Advise him.

5. A has just found out that his intended use for a piece of land he owns does not fall within any of the columns in the notes to the Outline Zoning Plan. He intends to go ahead with his planning application. If the application fails, he will file for a planning appeal. He would like to

know how the Town Planning Board and the Town Planning Appeal Board operate respectively, and if there are any differences. Advise him.

6. In terms of purpose and constitution of members, what are the differences between:
   (a) the Town Planning Board and the Town Planning Appeal Board; and
   (b) the Town Planning Board and the Court of First Instance?

7. Mr A owns an industrial building, which he bought last year. The building was built some fifteen years ago. Mr A has recently discovered that the land on which the building is situated is zoned for residential use in the Outline Zoning Plan. He knows that all development must comply with the Outline Zoning Plan and is worried that the government may take action against him. Advise him as to whether the Planning Department could take action in this case, and under what circumstances the department could do so.

8. The Buildings Department is often described as the department that enforces planning control of urban land in Hong Kong. However, in the Town Planning Ordinance, the Planning Authority (i.e. the Director of Planning) is the only body that enforces planning control. Discuss why the Buildings Department is described as such.

9. What are the respective tribunals in each of the following cases:
   (a) section 16 application under the Town Planning Ordinance;
   (b) section 16A application under the Town Planning Ordinance;
   (c) section 17 application under the Town Planning Ordinance;
   (d) planning enforcement action by the Planning Department under the Town Planning Ordinance;
   (e) enforcement of lease covenants by the government

10. In a set of typical government lease conditions, there are general and special conditions. What are their differences? What are the typical conditions for each of these categories?

11. In a government lease, there often exists forfeiture clause. Discuss:
    (a) the nature of a forfeiture clause;
    (b) the purpose of such clause;
    (c) the procedure to take an action pursuant to a breach of the forfeiture clause.

    Give an example of a typical forfeiture clause.

12. Discuss the differences between lease conditions and the Town Planning Ordinance in their respective roles in planning control in terms of:
    (a) the sources of law;
    (b) the enforcing agents;
    (c) the actions that may be taken; and
    (d) the consequences on the defendant if the action is successful.

13. Planning through the use of government leases is often described as 'planning by contract'. In law, covenants relating to land may bind not only the purchaser of the land but also its subsequent purchasers. It may therefore be said that the mechanism in fact goes beyond the contract. Discuss the legal basis as to how covenants may bind subsequent purchasers of land in Hong Kong.

14. A is the government lessee of a piece of land in the New Territories and has been using it to store LPG gas. Under the law, a licence must be obtained from the relevant government department for the storage of such an amount of LPG gas. A has no such a licence. After perusing the lease conditions, A finds that there is a covenant prohibiting the government lessee from using the land for the storage of such an amount of gas. A would like to know what possible actions are available to the government pursuant to the covenant.

15. Planning control through the use of lease covenants is part of our history. Clauses such as 'user restriction clause', 'rate and range clause' and 'user clause', have been used in the past to fulfil the purpose of planning control. Discuss various kinds of clauses that the government has used in the past for planning control.

16. Discuss the differences in the roles of planning control and those of the Buildings Ordinance and government leases.

17. Discuss the effect of the Consent Scheme, which was designed for the purpose of pre-sale of property and the protection of purchasers, in planning control.

18. Mr Chan owns a first-floor unit of a piece of land under a 999-year 'unrestricted lease', which is zoned 'Residential 1' in the Outline Development Plan and 'Commercial' in the Outline Zoning Plan. The Occupation Permit for the unit is residential use and the unit is used as a flat. Mr Chan wants to change the use of the unit from flat to restaurant. Advise Mr Chan of the necessary procedure for ensuring that the proposed restaurant use can be properly carried out.

*100 Change in Use of Land*

19. Mr Cheng owns a piece of land under a 999-year 'unrestricted lease', which is zoned 'Commercial/Residential' in the Outline Zoning Plan. The site has been occupied by a building used as a cinema since 1965. Advise Mr Cheng of the necessary planning, lands and building plan application procedures for realizing the following redevelopment proposals: (a) a modern cinema; (b) a hotel; (c) an office building; (d) an office building with shops on the first three floors; and (e) an office building with a motor vehicle showroom on the ground floor.

20. Mrs Woo owns a piece of land under a Crown lease with the user restricted to 'Residential only' and a building covenant requiring any building plan on the land to comply with 'the Buildings Ordinance of 1964'. The statutory zoning of the site is Residential (Group B). The site has been occupied by a building used as a block of ten flats, each having the identical amount of shares since 1965. All flats have been leased to tenants since 1965 who, until recently, were paying sub-market rents as a result of the 'security of tenure' provision of the Landlord and Tenant Ordinance. Two tenants have refused to pay and have not paid rent since 1973. They are still living in their flats, having obtained possessory titles in 1993. Advise Mrs Woo of the necessary planning, lands and building plan application procedures for realizing the following redevelopment proposals: (a) a modern cinema; (b) a hotel; (c) an office block; (d) an office block with shops on the first three floors; and (e) an office block with a motor vehicle showroom on the ground floor.

21. Miss Lee owns a piece of vacant land on Hong Kong Island under lease conditions which restrict the user to 'residential only', which is zoned 'Residential 1' in the Outline Development Plan and 'Residential (Group A)' in the Outline Zoning Plan. The Occupation Permit is for residential use. Miss Lee wants to develop the site into an office block. Advise Miss Lee of the procedural requirements for the proposed change in use and the most valuable temporary use that is permitted on the site.

22. Miss Chen owns a piece of vacant land in Cheung Chau which is zoned 'Village' in the Outline Development Plan. She wants to lease her land to her friend at market rent for open storage use, but is concerned that the use may attract enforcement by government departments. Advise Miss Chen.

23. Mr Tang owns a piece of land in the New Territories which is subject to resumption. The land is zoned 'Residential (Group C)' in the Outline Zoning Plan, and 'Residential 3' in the Outline Development Plan which

shows an improved road that would provide vehicular access to the land. Explain the relevance and irrelevance of each type of town plan for negotiating compensation for resumption with the Lands Department.

24. Mr Cheng owns a piece of 'agricultural land' under Block Government Lease in the New Territories with a STW for the erection of a storehouse for agricultural products. The land is zoned Residential (Group D) in the Outline Development Plan which has a history of an Interim Development Permission Area Plan. Mr Cheng wants to use the storehouse for storing seeds and flowerpots. Advise Mr Cheng of the legal issues involved.

25. Work out the maximum achievable plot ratio and explain the necessary planning, lands and building applications for each scenario (across the row) in the table below:

| Scenario | Maximum Plot Ratio in OZP | Maximum Plot Ratio in lease/conditions | Maximum Plot Ratio under the Buildings (Planning) Regulations | De facto Plot Ratio in the adjoining development |
|---|---|---|---|---|
| A | 3 | 5 | 10 | 8 |
| B | 3 | 5 | 10 | 3 |
| C | 10 | 5 | 8 | 10 |
| D | 10 | 5 | 3 | 0.5 |
| E | 5 | 5 | 5 | 8 |

26. Work out the implications of the following 'change in use of buildings' scenarios for a multi-storey building under unitary ownership:

| Scenario | Lease/user | OZP | Occupation Permit | Original use | Structural changes involved? | Current use |
|---|---|---|---|---|---|---|
| A | 999-year | C/R | Non-domestic | Office | No | Service Apartment |
| B | 999-year | C/R | Non-domestic | Office | Yes | Service Apartment |
| C | Office | C/R | Non-domestic | Office | No | Residential |
| D | Office | C | Non-domestic | Office | Yes | Residential |

27. X Limited submitted through an Authorized Person (AP) a set of building plans for an office building with a plot ratio of 15 on 1 June 2000 (the date on which the plans were 'chopped') on a site for which the plot ratio restriction in the Outline Zoning Plan (OZP) was 10 maximum. The Building Authority wrote and informed the AP on 5 August 2000 that they refused to approve the plans for contravening the plot ratio limitations on the OZP. Advise X Limited on the next proper course of action in order to realize the development of an office block, given that the proposal is permitted by the lease and there is no other restriction affecting plot ratios.

28. Y Limited submitted through an Authorized Person (AP) a set of building plans for an residential building with a plot ratio 10 on 1 June on a site for which there was no plot ratio restriction for any zone in the relevant Outline Zoning Plan (OZP). The Building Authority wrote to the AP within 60 calendar days notifying him that they refused to approve the plans for contravening the zoning control in the OZP. The grounds of refusal were all related to access considerations and did not involve plot ratio calculation. X Limited lodged in a notice of appeal to the Appeal Tribunal within a week after receiving the notification from the Building Authority. A preliminary hearing for the appeal was heard on 1 September. The date for the full hearing was scheduled on 21 and 22 September. Meanwhile, on 31 August, an amendment to the OZP had been 'gazetted' such that there was a maximum plot ratio of 8 for all zones. Today is 2 September. Advise Y Limited of the effects of the amendment to the OZP on the original building plans submitted on 1 June if (a) the Tribunal allowed the appeal; and (b) the Tribunal dismissed the appeal.

29. Mr Q wishes to buy a piece of 'agricultural land' in the New Territories for storing building materials. He identifies a site that meets his requirements, but knows that an Outline Zoning Plan (OZP) has been recently imposed on the land, replacing an Development Permission Area (DPA) Plan. Mr Q has heard that there are enforcement provisions for a DPA plan. His friend, Mr W, advises Mr Q to go ahead and buy the property as there is no need to worry about the DPA Plan. It is because, as Mr W advises, the effects of the DPA should cease once it is replaced by the OZP, which permits temporary uses in all zones. How sound is Mr W's advice?

30. Based on the images from aerial photos, the matters on a piece of 'DD lot' under diver days are as shown in the following table.

| Date | Matters on the Lot | Remarks |
|---|---|---|
| 14.07.1981 | Vegetation, 1 hut | |
| 23.12.1983 | 1 Pond, 1 hut | |
| 04.06.1989 | 100 container boxes<br>3 trucks<br>2 huts (1 additional) | |
| 13.07.1990 | 150 container boxes<br>1 truck<br>2 huts | Date before notice of an IDPA Plan published in the gazette |
| 14.07.1990 | 120 container boxes<br>3 trucks<br>2 huts | Notice of an IDPA Plan published in the gazette designating the lot as part of an 'unspecified use' area |
| 13.07.1992 | 300 container boxes<br>8 trucks<br>3 huts (1 additional) | Date before notice of an DPA Plan published in the gazette |
| 14.07.1991 | 120 container boxes<br>5 trucks<br>3 huts | Notice of an DPA Plan published in the gazette designating the lot as part of an 'Agriculture Zone' |
| 15.09.1991 | 120 container boxes<br>3 trucks<br>4 huts | |
| 18.01.1994 | 120 container boxes<br>3 trucks<br>4 huts | Date before notice of an OZP Plan published in the gazette |
| 19.01.1994 | 120 container boxes<br>3 trucks<br>4 huts | Notice of an DPA Plan published in the gazette re-designating the lot as part of an 'Residential (Group D) Zone' |
| 01.07.1997 | 129 container boxes<br>0 truck<br>4 huts | |
| Today | 180 container boxes<br>1 truck<br>4 huts | |

Assuming that the facts shown in the table above are correct, and that there is no other aerial photo of the lot, advise whether the matters found on the lot today constitute 'unauthorized development'.

31. Mr Chan is a rich architect. He is also a hobby farmer who wishes to develop an indigenous farm inherited from his father for free public visits. This farm, fronting on a local road, is on several 'DD Lots' that

*104 Change in Use of Land*

amount to three hectares in area. He knows that his property was designated as an Interim Development Permission Area and is now under agriculture zoning in an Outline Zoning Plan. He has not read the Notes to the Plan, because a Registered Professional Planner whom he trusts has advised him that 'agriculture is a Column 1 use'. Mr Chan then fills up a lily pond by the boundary of the road and excavates another in the centre of his property. He also excavates a lot (half a hectare in area) that was used for dry cultivation, and plans to use it as two separate fish-ponds for breeding and cultivating Hong Kong snakeheads. Earth is removed; an artificial well is dug to get incoming water because the local rivers are either too dirty or channelized such that water extraction is difficult. A concrete filtration pond is built to age the water from underground. Since the land is very close to Mai Po Marshes, Mr Chan also erects a nylon bird net, which is supported by eight steel planks to protect the fish from bird attacks. Mr Chan uses the excavated earth to create an artificial hill and plants sunflowers on the slopes. On the hilltop he builds a rain-shelter, which is permitted under a Government Land licence. The remaining earth is used to form a boundary bund on which banana trees and roses are planted. Mr Chan also compacts earth on one DD lot which was under cultivation one season ago but has become fallow since then. The lot will provide parking space for two tourist buses and five private cars. He parks his own car here. All works are done according to a landscape plan he designs and the materials used are all environmentally friendly. Mr Wrong, a well-educated indigenous villager and a neighbour of Mr Chan's, has some private dispute with Mr Chan. Mr Chan has said to Mr Wrong that he should not build a small house on his private lot as it is in an Agriculture Zone and is against 'planning intention'. Mr Wrong writes to the Planning Department and complains against unauthorized development. He also writes to the Building Authority against unauthorized building works on Mr Chan's property. Mr Wrong copies all correspondence with the government bodies to Mr Chan. Advise Mr Chan.

32. X Company Limited brought a piece of land under a Crown (Government Lease) with a term of 999 years. The lease was modified by a deed of variation that surrenders all marine rights but not other rights. The land is zoned 'Commercial' in the Outline Zoning Plan and the existing use is a vehicle repair centre. The development adviser of X Company Limited suggests that the land be surrendered to the government in exchange for conditions that allow the erection of office building(s) only. This surrender and exchange proposal is necessary in order that the road

access to the site can be so improved that, under the Buildings Ordinance, there can be a gain in GFA of about 900 square metres. Assuming that this suggestion is made after 1984, advise X Company Limited of the implications of this proposal.

33. Mr So owns a vacant 'old schedule house lot' in a village that is located inside a village ('V') zone. He wants to build a house as a home for the aged. Must Mr So obtain planning permission and/or lease modification before building the house?

34. Mr A has a piece of land in Wanchai that abuts Hennessy Road zoned 'Commercial/Residential' (C/R) in the Outline Zoning Plan. On the carving-out plan, a strip of land now being part of a scavenging lane is indicated to be a 'right of way'. Should the area of this right of way be included in calculating the total gross floor area when making a building application?

35. A flatted factory building is situated on a piece of land zoned 'industrial' in Cheung Sha Wan. It is restricted to 'general industrial use' in the Crown Lease. A proprietor, Mr B, wishes to use the ground floor of the factory unit as a shopping arcade for selling apparels and garment fashions (instead of using it as a metal workshop). What are the relevant facts that must be ascertained before one can advise Mr B of the necessary land and planning procedures for the change-of-use application?

36. ABC Limited is the developer of a commercial/residential building, which the company built about twenty years ago. It owns the shares of the ground floor of the property, and has recently also taken up part of the entrance lobby as a shop space. The said entrance lobby has been used as a common area, but this is not clearly specified in the Deed of Mutual Covenant. A flat-owner objects to the enclosure action of ABC Limited. Under what circumstances would the flat-owner have a case?

37. A Deed of Mutual Covenant stipulates that a commercial/residential building is designed with 20 shops on the ground floor, 20 offices on the first floor which is surmounted by a 20-storey residential tower. It further stipulates that nobody can make any structural change to the building without the consent of the building manager appointed by the owners' corporation. The developer, still holding the whole of the ground and first floors, has obtained approval from the Building Authority to convert both floors into a shopping arcade by connecting them with staircases and escalators. The developer is about to commence work. Can the building manager stop the work?

*106 Change in Use of Land*

38. The Deed of Mutual Covenant stipulates that the cinema portion of a commercial/residential complex shall be used for 'cinema only'. The cinema-owner wishes to convert the cinema into a shopping arcade. What kind of approvals should the owner seek?

39. A developer has assembled over 90 per cent of the 'old schedule house lots' in a village in the New Territories, which is included in a 'village' zone in the Outline Zoning Plan. He wishes to develop this land into a large and high-rise commercial/residential complex. How feasible is his idea?

40. A cinema, being in existence for a long period of time, is zoned 'Government/Institution/Community' under the Outline Zoning Plan. The Crown Lease is virtually 'unrestricted'. Can this cinema be redeveloped into a commercial/residential building without any lease modification or planning application?

41. Mr A owns a piece of 'old schedule agriculture lot' in a remote area in the New Territories, which has not been covered by any Outline Zoning Plan yet. He is using the lot for open storage of containers and construction materials. Under what conditions is he entitled to do so? And under what circumstances is he not allowed to do so?

42. A two-storey house was built on a piece of land many years ago with a total gross floor area of 2,500 square feet. It is situated on a somewhat isolated building lot of 3,000 square feet. The lot is reached by a vehicular access, being a right of way, from the main road. The land is held under a New Grant with the proviso of compliance with special condition (2) of G.N. 364 of 1934. The land is now zoned 'Residential (Group C)' in the Outline Zoning Plan, which allows a maximum plot ratio of 0.4 or the plot ratio of the existing building, whichever is the greater. Mr G wishes to redevelop the property. What is the maximum gross floor area that he can attain?

43. Mr A is the owner of a house. Mr B builds a squatter hut on government land with one of its sides leaning and fixed to an external wall of Mr A's house. Mr C, an enemy of Mr A, complains to the Building Department about unauthorized work done to Mr A's house. Advise Mr A of the worst consequences that he, as a house-owner, may have to face. Advise him also of possible remedies.

44. Mr Chan owns two adjoining pieces of land in the New Territories. One (Site A) is half as large as the other (Site B). The user of the lease of Site A

is 'virtually unrestricted', and is zoned 'Residential' with a plot ratio of 8. The user and zoning of Site B is 'agriculture'. Mr Chan wishes to merge and develop the two pieces of land together. How should he proceed? Does he need to modify the lease of the two pieces of land in order to develop? Can he just erect a building on Site A and calculate the plot ratio based on the sum of the areas of Sites A and B?

45. Mr Leung has made several 'section 16 planning applications'. Each application involves some minor amendments to the earlier one. All these applications have been approved. However, Mr Leung does not like the last approved proposal or its amendments. What can he do so that he can go back to the previously approved scheme which he favours?

46. Mr Cheng has bought a flat in a building, which stands on a piece of land zoned for 'commercial' purposes with a residential user under the lease. Mr Cheng wishes to change the use of his flat into office use. What should he do?

47. B Limited has acquired all other flats in Mr Cheng's building (referred to in the question 46) and subsequently also acquired Mr Cheng's flat after its use has been converted to an office use. B Limited intends to redevelop the site. Will the change in use made by Mr Cheng affect the redevelopment? What should B Limited do to facilitate the redevelopment?

48. C Company has developed a new business strategy to promote the sale of their products. One of its plans is to erect vending machines in the streets over Hong Kong. How can C Company achieve this plan? Does the company need to obtain any permission? What are the procedures? Which government department(s) can help achieve or regulate this plan?

49. What are the procedures of applying for 'balcony green features'? Under what circumstances is premium necessary? What is the basis of premium assessment?

50. Mr Tang owns a piece of agricultural land in Kam Tin. This piece of land has been lying fallow. One day, a friend of Mr Tang's, Mr Tseng, finds that some strangers are dumping earth onto the land. Mr Tseng immediately rings the Planning Department's inquiry hotline and reports this activity. He also tells Mr Tang about this. Advise Mr Tang on the proper action to take so as to safeguard his interest.

51. Mr A has newly bought a flat in a 20-year-old high-rise building. He intends to remove the kitchen wall to form an 'open kitchen' that will

adjoin the dinning area. Advise Mr A of the factors to be considered under the Buildings Ordinance.

52. Mr A in Question 51 above would also like to enclose the balcony and remove the glazed separation with the living room. Advise Mr A of the feasibility and precautions that he needs to take.

53. Mr A in Question 51 above also wishes to build a new toilet in the master bedroom and convert it into a suite. The existing drainage system is a one-pipe system made of cast iron. Explain to Mr A about the procedures that he should follow and the implications under the Buildings Ordinance.

54. The owners' incorporation of a development has decided to carry out large-scale renovation to the electrical system, drainage system, as well as the external walls of the building. Explain the government requirements and assistance available under the current policy.

55. During a tenancy inspection, a prospective tenant asked the owner's agent whether he could add two new staircases within the ground-floor shop, and connect them with the cockloft above and the basement below. Elaborate on the points to be considered and advise the tenant accordingly.

56. The owner of the top-floor in a high-rise office building wishes to build a fish-pond with some creative rock ornaments and a jogging track on the roof for his own leisure activities. Advise him of the feasibility and points to consider in order to make his plan happen lawfully.

57. It is quite common for sites in the Mid-Levels and Western District of the Hong Kong Island to have stepped access in front of, or adjacent to them. Will these sites be regarded as facing 'streets'? How can emergency vehicles get access to these sites or their future development?

58. An office building has recently been converted into a 'guesthouse'. Elaborate on the requirements for obtaining a licence to operate the guesthouse.

59. The Occupation Permit (OP) of a completed building specifies its use(s) and basic configurations. Throughout the whole life cycle of a building, numerous alterations may be carried out to its fabric as well as use(s). How can one rely on the descriptions on the OP, in particular during the transaction of the subject property?

60. The owner of a shopping centre shows Mr B, a prospective purchaser of a particular portion of the centre, a drawing approved by the Building Authority which indicates the alterations made to that portion. The works are found to be constructed in all respects in accordance with the contents of the drawing. Would you therefore advise Mr B to conclude the deal from the building law point of view?

61. The 'height' of a building proposal may affect the permissible plot ratio and site coverage of a development. How is the 'height' of a building determined? Are there any differences in the interpretations of the definition of 'height' among various government departments? If yes, how would you resolve the differences or conflicts?

62. A land lease often specifies a certain amount of gross floor area to be constructed by a specific date. Explain the rationale behind this kind of covenant. Also explain the consequences for non-compliance.

63. If a developer wishes to make an application for lease modification to increase the permissible plot ratio of a site, what issues would you (as a developer and as the Lands Department) consider and why?

64. How is environmental control involved in infrastructural and building development projects?

65. Elaborate on the relationship (if any) between the size of a **site** and the building **height**.

66. What is the implication to a developer if there is a cap on plot ratio and site coverage beyond building height of 61 m?

67. Discuss the reasons why a developer sometimes does not use up the permissible plot ratio and/or site coverage under the First Schedule of the Building (Planning) Regulations.

68. Examine the contention of an *optimal* ratio between the residential and commercial area components in a C/R composite development. *'Optimal'* here may refer to *profit* (or return to investment) or *maximum floor areas* achieved.

69. If there are conflicts between the provisions for certain items (such as the permissible plot ratio) under the lease document, the OZP and the Buildings Ordinance, what would you, as a developer, do?

70. The construction and provision of 'green' features such as balconies and 'sky-gardens' in buildings seems to be a bonus to the developers, and

may open up channels of misuse and/or abuse of the 'green' features during the occupancy phase of a building. Explain the potential weaknesses of the concession and discuss how the government may curb these weaknesses.

71. What is the definition of a 'street'? Can a developer set out 'internal streets' within a development to enable more site area being classified as 'Class C' under the Buildings Ordinance?

72. Can a 'street' be covered? Can private shops be opened on footbridges across public roads?

73. Is it necessary for a 'street' to be of a minimum of 4.5 m in width for whole length in order to be regarded as a 'street' under the Buildings Ordinance? If yes, what is the meaning of 'adjacent' under section 2 of the Buildings Ordinance?

74. A trust managing wetlands in the *'Deep Bay Buffer Zones'* subject to a statutory town plan intends to dredge a few channels in a *gei wai* and reclaim part of another as a viewing and feeding platform for migratory birds. It also intends to erect a few bird viewing sheds on the bund of a fish pond it manages. Is there a need for it to obtain planning permission for these intended work to avoid violation of the Town Planning Ordinance? Discuss.

75. A developer acquires all shares of ownership of a building in the Mid-Levels governed by a '999-year lease'. The Occupation Permit (OP) for the property specifies the ground floor to be 'parking spaces' and floors above 'for domestic purpose'. Pending redevelopment, the developer leases two garages to an estate agent. Does the business of the estate agent violate the provision of the OP?

76. An estate agent advises Mr A to sell his flat urgently because 'according to the Outline Zoning Plan, a funeral parlour may be built' on a vacant site in front of the building in which A's flat is found. Advise A.

77. Normally, neither the purchaser nor the solicitor acting on his behalf would seek assistance of an AP or a RPP in conveyancing of 'second-hand' property units. Discuss potential problems regarding title.

78. The Highways Department proposes to close the road to traffic to implement a pedestrianization scheme in front of one of the long sides of a rectangular 'island site' under a Crown Lease for commerical use, which is accessible by vehicles on all sides. The closed road is the only

access to the carpark of the site. Advise the owner of the site the implications of the proposed pedestrianization scheme and the proper course of action to take.

79. Photos 1 to 3 show the sequence of development (outlined in Photo 2) of a new residential property approved by the Town Planning Board. It appears from the vantage point of where the photos were taken that the development constitutes 'visual intrusion' as it creates a great discontinuity of the pre-existing roof-line. Discuss why the new development can possibly exceed the height of the buildings in the immediate neighbourhood. Is there any legal or policy protection of views in general in Hong Kong?

80. How can we ascertain the 'planning intention' for a zone in a statutory town plan?

Photo 1  Before development

112 *Change in Use of Land*

Photo 2   Profile of proposed development

Photo 3   Development in progress

# APPENDIX 1
## TOWN PLANNING BOARD GUIDELINES (AS AT 8 APRIL 2004)

No. 2B    Town Planning Board Guidelines for Interim Planning Control on Service Apartment[s]*

No. 5    Town Planning Board Guidelines for Application[s] for Office Development in Residential (Group A) Zone[s] under Section 16 of the Town Planning Ordinance

No. 8    Town Planning Board Guidelines for Application[s] for Underground Development of Commercial/Car Parking Facilities Beneath Open Space, Government/Institution/ Community Zones and Road[s] under Section 16 of the Town Planning Ordinance

No. 10    Town Planning Board Guidelines for Application[s] for Development within Green Belt Zone[s] under Section 16 of the Town Planning Ordinance

No. 11    Town Planning Board Guidelines for Application[s] for Factory/ Workshop/Warehouse Use[s] within Unspecified Use Area[s] on Development Permission Area Plans under Section 16 of the Town Planning Ordinance

No. 12B    Town Planning Board Guidelines for Application[s] for Developments within Deep Bay Area under Section 16 of the Town Planning Ordinance

No. 13C    Town Planning Board Guidelines for Application[s] for Open Storage and Port Back-up Uses under Section 16 of the Town Planning Ordinance

No. 14B    Town Planning Board Guidelines for Application[s] for Commercial Bathhouse[s] and Massage Establishment[s] under Section 16 of the Town Planning Ordinance

---

\*    Square brackets added

No. 15A Town Planning Board Guidelines for Application[s] for Eating Place[s] within 'Village Type Development' Zone[s] in Rural Areas under Section 16 of the Town Planning Ordinance

No. 16 Town Planning Board Guidelines for Application[s] for Development/Redevelopment within 'Government, Institution or Community' Zone[s] for Uses other than Government, Institution or Community Uses under Section 16 of the Town Planning Ordinance

No. 17 Town Planning Board Guidelines for Designation of 'Comprehensive Development Area' ('CDA') Zones and Monitoring the Progress of 'CDA' Developments

No. 18A Town Planning Board Guidelines for Submission of Master Layout Plan[s] under Section 4A(2) of the Town Planning Ordinance

No. 19B Town Planning Board Guidelines on Minor Amendments to Approved Development Proposals

No. 20 Town Planning Board Guidelines on Compliance of[with] Approval Conditions

No. 21A Town Planning Board Guidelines for Renewal of Planning Permission[s] and Extension of Time for Compliance with Planning Conditions

No. 22A Town Planning Board Guidelines for Development within 'Other Specified Uses (Business)' Zone[s]

No. 23 Town Planning Board Guidelines for Application[s] for Kindergarten[s]/Child Care Centre[s] in Kowloon Tong Garden Estate under Section 16 of the Town Planning Ordinance

No. 24B Town Planning Board Guidelines for Interpretation of Existing Use[s] in the Urban and New Town Areas

No. 25B Town Planning Board Guidelines for Use/Development within 'Industrial' Zone[s]

No. 26 Town Planning Board Guidelines on Lapsing of Planning Permissions

No. 27 Town Planning Board Guidelines for Submission of Concept Plan[s] in Support of Section 16 Application[s]

# APPENDIX 2
## AGGREGATE STATISTICS REGARDING PLANNING APPLICATIONS 1975–2002

### Agriculture (AGR) Zones

Table A.1.1　Number of total and successful applications by year by stage of application for uses in AGR Zones

| Year | Planning Applications Approvals | Total | Success Rates % | Planning Reviews Approvals | Total | Success Rates % |
|---|---|---|---|---|---|---|
| 1994 | 44 | 56 | 78.6% | 0 | 0 | – |
| 1995 | 117 | 171 | 68.4% | 12 | 18 | 66.7% |
| 1996 | 149 | 207 | 72.0% | 1 | 22 | 4.5% |
| 1997 | 149 | 238 | 62.6% | 7 | 20 | 35.0% |
| 1998 | 118 | 181 | 65.2% | 6 | 42 | 14.3% |
| 1999 | 104 | 135 | 77.0% | 1 | 9 | 11.1% |
| 2000 | 123 | 163 | 75.5% | 0 | 5 | 0.0% |
| 2001 | 106 | 161 | 65.8% | 7 | 20 | 35.0% |
| 2002 | 98 | 133 | 73.7% | 1 | 24 | 4.2% |
| Total | 1,008 | 1,445 | 69.8% | 35 | 160 | 21.9% |

| Year | Planning Appeals Approvals | Total | Success Rates % | Extension of Time Limit Approvals | Total | Success Rates % |
|---|---|---|---|---|---|---|
| 1994 | 0 | 0 | – | 0 | 0 | – |
| 1995 | 0 | 0 | – | 0 | 0 | – |
| 1996 | 0 | 0 | – | 27 | 27 | 100.0% |
| 1997 | 0 | 0 | – | 29 | 29 | 100.0% |
| 1998 | 0 | 0 | – | 67 | 67 | 100.0% |
| 1999 | 0 | 0 | – | 23 | 23 | 100.0% |
| 2000 | 0 | 0 | – | 37 | 37 | 100.0% |
| 2001 | 0 | 3 | 0.0% | 51 | 52 | 98.1% |
| 2002 | 0 | 2 | 0.0% | 51 | 51 | 100.0% |
| Total | 0 | 5 | 0.0% | 285 | 286 | 99.7% |

## Appendix 2

Table A.1.2  Number of successful applications by location for uses in AGR Zones

| Location | Approvals | Total | Success Rates % |
|---|---|---|---|
| Hong Kong | 0 | 0 | – |
| Kowloon | 0 | 0 | – |
| Development Permission Area | 2 | 3 | 66.7% |
| New Towns | 0 | 0 | – |
| Rural | 1,039 | 1,442 | 72.1% |
| Total | 1,041 | 1,445 | 72.0% |

Table A.1.3  Number of successful applications by site area for uses in AGR Zones

| Site Area | Approvals | Total | Success Rates % |
|---|---|---|---|
| Smaller than 0.1 ha | 844 | 1,067 | 79.1% |
| 0.1 ha to 1 ha | 180 | 349 | 51.6% |
| Larger than 1 ha | 16 | 27 | 59.3% |
| N/A | 1 | 2 | 50.0% |
| Total | 1,041 | 1,445 | 72.0% |

Table A.1.4  Number of successful applications by Gross Floor Area for uses in AGR Zones

| GFA | Approvals | Total | Success Rates % |
|---|---|---|---|
| Smaller than 0.5 ha | 863 | 1,081 | 79.8% |
| 0.5 ha to 5 ha | 6 | 9 | 66.7% |
| Larger than 5 ha | 0 | 0 | – |
| N/A | 172 | 355 | 48.3% |
| Total | 1,041 | 1,445 | 72.0% |

Table A.1.5  Number of successful applications by applied use for AGR Zones

| Applied Use | Approvals | Total | Success Rates % |
|---|---|---|---|
| Open Storage | 129 | 293 | 44.0% |
| Village Type House | 824 | 1,016 | 81.1% |
| Other | 88 | 136 | 64.7% |
| Total | 1,041 | 1,445 | 72.0% |

# Conservation Area (CA) Zones

Table A.2.1  Number of total and successful applications by year by stage of application for uses in CA zones

| Year | Planning Applications | | | Planning Reviews | | |
|---|---|---|---|---|---|---|
| | Approvals | Total | Success Rates % | Approvals | Total | Success Rates % |
| 1994 | 2 | 2 | 100.0% | 0 | 0 | – |
| 1995 | 2 | 3 | 66.7% | 0 | 0 | – |
| 1996 | 0 | 2 | 0.0% | 0 | 0 | – |
| 1997 | 5 | 11 | 45.5% | 0 | 3 | 0.0% |
| 1998 | 2 | 4 | 50.0% | 0 | 3 | 0.0% |
| 1999 | 9 | 11 | 81.8% | 0 | 1 | 0.0% |
| 2000 | 3 | 5 | 60.0% | 0 | 0 | – |
| 2001 | 5 | 8 | 62.5% | 0 | 0 | – |
| 2002 | 2 | 3 | 66.7% | 0 | 0 | – |
| Total | 30 | 49 | 61.2% | 0 | 7 | 0.0% |

| Year | Planning Appeals | | | Extension of Time Limit | | |
|---|---|---|---|---|---|---|
| | Approvals | Total | Success Rates % | Approvals | Total | Success Rates % |
| 1994 | 0 | 0 | – | 0 | 0 | – |
| 1995 | 0 | 0 | – | 0 | 0 | – |
| 1996 | 0 | 0 | – | 0 | 0 | – |
| 1997 | 0 | 0 | – | 0 | 0 | – |
| 1998 | 0 | 0 | – | 0 | 0 | – |
| 1999 | 0 | 0 | – | 2 | 2 | 100.0% |
| 2000 | 0 | 0 | – | 0 | 0 | – |
| 2001 | 0 | 0 | – | 1 | 1 | 100.0% |
| 2002 | 0 | 0 | – | 0 | 0 | – |
| Total | 0 | 0 | – | 3 | 3 | 100.0% |

## 118  Appendix 2

Table A.2.2   Number of successful applications by location for uses in CA zones

| Location | Approvals | Total | Success Rates % |
|---|---|---|---|
| Hong Kong | 0 | 0 | – |
| Kowloon | 0 | 0 | – |
| Development Permission Area | 1 | 1 | 100.0% |
| New Towns | 0 | 0 | – |
| Rural | 29 | 48 | 60.4% |
| Total | 30 | 49 | 61.2% |

Table A.2.3   Number of successful applications by site area for uses in CA zones

| Site Area | Approvals | Total | Success Rates % |
|---|---|---|---|
| Smaller than 0.1 ha | 17 | 20 | 85.0% |
| 0.1 ha to 1 ha | 3 | 9 | 33.3% |
| Larger than 1 ha | 7 | 16 | 43.8% |
| N/A | 3 | 4 | 75.0% |
| Total | 30 | 49 | 61.2% |

Table A.2.4   Number of successful applications by Gross Floor Area for uses in CA zones

| GFA | Approvals | Total | Success Rates % |
|---|---|---|---|
| Smaller than 0.5 ha | 12 | 15 | 80.0% |
| 0.5 ha to 5 ha | 1 | 2 | 50.0% |
| Larger than 5 ha | 0 | 1 | 0.0% |
| N/A | 17 | 31 | 54.8% |
| Total | 30 | 49 | 61.2% |

Table A.2.5 Number of successful applications by applied use for CA zones

| Applied Use | Approvals | Total | Success Rates % |
|---|---|---|---|
| Utility | 16 | 17 | 94.1% |
| Other | 14 | 32 | 43.8% |
| Total | 30 | 49 | 61.2% |

## Comprehensive Development Area (CDA) Zones

Table A.3.1  Number of total and successful applications by year by stage of application for uses in CDA Zones

| Year | Planning Applications Approvals | Total | Success Rates % | Planning Reviews Approvals | Total | Success Rates % |
|---|---|---|---|---|---|---|
| 1980 | 1 | 1 | 100.0% | 0 | 0 | – |
| 1981 | 2 | 2 | 100.0% | 0 | 0 | – |
| 1982 | 1 | 3 | 33.3% | 0 | 0 | – |
| 1983 | 1 | 5 | 20.0% | 1 | 1 | 100.0% |
| 1984 | 6 | 7 | 85.7% | 0 | 0 | – |
| 1985 | 7 | 7 | 100.0% | 0 | 0 | – |
| 1986 | 7 | 8 | 87.5% | 0 | 0 | – |
| 1987 | 7 | 10 | 70.0% | 1 | 1 | 100.0% |
| 1988 | 10 | 14 | 71.4% | 2 | 2 | 100.0% |
| 1989 | 9 | 12 | 75.0% | 0 | 1 | 0.0% |
| 1990 | 16 | 18 | 88.9% | 0 | 0 | – |
| 1991 | 6 | 19 | 31.6% | 0 | 3 | 0.0% |
| 1992 | 12 | 26 | 46.2% | 3 | 4 | 75.0% |
| 1993 | 12 | 17 | 70.6% | 1 | 4 | 25.0% |
| 1994 | 31 | 40 | 77.5% | 3 | 5 | 60.0% |
| 1995 | 22 | 26 | 84.6% | 3 | 3 | 100.0% |
| 1996 | 34 | 45 | 75.6% | 2 | 5 | 40.0% |
| 1997 | 46 | 60 | 76.7% | 2 | 5 | 40.0% |
| 1998 | 60 | 78 | 76.9% | 7 | 13 | 53.8% |
| 1999 | 78 | 83 | 94.0% | 1 | 1 | 100.0% |
| 2000 | 99 | 104 | 95.2% | 1 | 1 | 100.0% |
| 2001 | 56 | 74 | 75.7% | 7 | 8 | 87.5% |
| 2002 | 97 | 106 | 91.5% | 1 | 3 | 33.3% |
| Total | 620 | 765 | 81.0% | 35 | 60 | 58.3% |

Table A.3.1 Number of total and successful applications by year by stage of application for uses in CDA Zones (Cont'd)

| Year | Petitions to Governor-in-Council/ Planning Appeals Approvals | Total | Success Rates % | Extension of Time Limit Approvals | Total | Success Rates % |
|---|---|---|---|---|---|---|
| 1980 | 0 | 0 | – | 0 | 0 | – |
| 1981 | 0 | 0 | – | 0 | 0 | – |
| 1982 | 0 | 0 | – | 0 | 0 | – |
| 1983 | 0 | 0 | – | 0 | 0 | – |
| 1984 | 0 | 0 | – | 0 | 0 | – |
| 1985 | 0 | 0 | – | 0 | 0 | – |
| 1986 | 0 | 0 | – | 0 | 0 | – |
| 1987 | 0 | 0 | – | 0 | 0 | – |
| 1988 | 0 | 0 | – | 0 | 0 | – |
| 1989 | 0 | 0 | – | 0 | 0 | – |
| 1990 | 0 | 0 | – | 0 | 0 | – |
| 1991 | 0 | 0 | – | 0 | 0 | – |
| 1992 | 0 | 2 | 0.0% | 3 | 3 | 100.0% |
| 1993 | 0 | 0 | – | 1 | 1 | 100.0% |
| 1994 | 0 | 1 | 0.0% | 4 | 4 | 100.0% |
| 1995 | 0 | 0 | – | 0 | 0 | – |
| 1996 | 0 | 0 | – | 4 | 4 | 100.0% |
| 1997 | 0 | 0 | – | 4 | 4 | 100.0% |
| 1998 | 0 | 0 | – | 5 | 6 | 83.3% |
| 1999 | 0 | 0 | – | 4 | 4 | 100.0% |
| 2000 | 0 | 0 | – | 7 | 7 | 100.0% |
| 2001 | 0 | 0 | – | 27 | 29 | 93.1% |
| 2002 | 0 | 0 | – | 17 | 17 | 100.0% |
| Total | 0 | 3 | 0.0% | 76 | 79 | 96.2% |

Table A.3.2 Number of successful applications by location for uses in CDA Zones

| Location | Approvals | Total | Success Rates % |
|---|---|---|---|
| Hong Kong | 135 | 159 | 84.9% |
| Kowloon | 143 | 162 | 88.3% |
| Development Permission Area | 1 | 1 | 100.0% |
| New Towns | 219 | 257 | 85.2% |
| Rural | 143 | 186 | 76.9% |
| Total | 641 | 765 | 83.8% |

Table A.3.3  Number of successful applications by site area for uses in CDA Zones

| Site Area | Approvals | Total | Success Rates % |
|---|---|---|---|
| Smaller than 0.1 ha | 33 | 51 | 64.7% |
| 0.1 ha to 1 ha | 223 | 275 | 81.1% |
| Larger than 1 ha | 349 | 400 | 87.3% |
| N/A | 36 | 39 | 92.3% |
| Total | 641 | 765 | 83.8% |

Table A.3.4  Number of successful applications by Gross Floor Area for uses in CDA Zones

| GFA | Approvals | Total | Success Rates % |
|---|---|---|---|
| Smaller than 0.5 ha | 78 | 106 | 73.6% |
| 0.5 ha to 5 ha | 125 | 146 | 85.6% |
| Larger than 5 ha | 322 | 361 | 89.2% |
| N/A | 116 | 152 | 76.3% |
| Total | 641 | 765 | 83.8% |

Table A.3.5  Number of successful applications by applied use for CDA Zones

| Applied Use | Approvals | Total | Success Rates % |
|---|---|---|---|
| Office | 125 | 145 | 86.2% |
| Commercial | 270 | 315 | 85.7% |
| Residential | 326 | 374 | 87.2% |
| Hotel | 109 | 122 | 89.3% |
| Open Storage | 57 | 67 | 85.1% |
| Container | 33 | 49 | 67.3% |
| Village Type House | 8 | 16 | 50.0% |
| School | 82 | 92 | 89.1% |
| Other | 73 | 91 | 80.2% |
| Total | 1,083 | 1,271 | 85.2% |

## Commercial (COM) Zones

Table A.4.1  Number of total and successful applications by year by stage of application for uses in COM Zones

| Year | Planning Applications Approvals | Total | Success Rates % | Planning Reviews Approvals | Total | Success Rates % |
|---|---|---|---|---|---|---|
| 1983 | 1 | 1 | 100.0% | 0 | 0 | – |
| 1984 | 1 | 1 | 100.0% | 0 | 0 | – |
| 1985 | 5 | 6 | 83.3% | 0 | 0 | – |
| 1986 | 1 | 1 | 100.0% | 0 | 0 | – |
| 1987 | 2 | 2 | 100.0% | 0 | 0 | – |
| 1988 | 2 | 3 | 66.7% | 0 | 1 | 0.0% |
| 1989 | 1 | 1 | 100.0% | 0 | 0 | – |
| 1990 | 1 | 2 | 50.0% | 0 | 0 | – |
| 1991 | 1 | 1 | 100.0% | 0 | 0 | – |
| 1992 | 0 | 0 | – | 0 | 0 | – |
| 1993 | 1 | 1 | 100.0% | 0 | 0 | – |
| 1994 | 2 | 3 | 66.7% | 0 | 0 | – |
| 1995 | 4 | 4 | 100.0% | 0 | 0 | – |
| 1996 | 11 | 12 | 91.7% | 0 | 0 | – |
| 1997 | 28 | 30 | 93.3% | 1 | 1 | 100.0% |
| 1998 | 8 | 9 | 88.9% | 0 | 0 | – |
| 1999 | 11 | 14 | 78.6% | 0 | 0 | – |
| 2000 | 12 | 14 | 85.7% | 1 | 1 | 100.0% |
| 2001 | 9 | 10 | 90.0% | 0 | 0 | – |
| 2002 | 16 | 18 | 88.9% | 0 | 0 | – |
| Total | 117 | 133 | 88.0% | 2 | 3 | 66.7% |

Table A.4.1  Number of total and successful applications by year by stage of application for uses in COM Zones (Cont'd)

| Year | Petitions to Governor-in-Council/ Planning Appeals Approvals | Total | Success Rates % | Extension of Time Limit Approvals | Total | Success Rates % |
|---|---|---|---|---|---|---|
| 1983 | 0 | 0 | – | 0 | 0 | – |
| 1984 | 0 | 0 | – | 0 | 0 | – |
| 1985 | 0 | 0 | – | 0 | 0 | – |
| 1986 | 0 | 0 | – | 0 | 0 | – |
| 1987 | 0 | 0 | – | 0 | 0 | – |
| 1988 | 0 | 0 | – | 0 | 0 | – |
| 1989 | 0 | 0 | – | 0 | 0 | – |
| 1990 | 0 | 0 | – | 0 | 0 | – |
| 1991 | 0 | 0 | – | 0 | 0 | – |
| 1992 | 0 | 0 | – | 0 | 0 | – |
| 1993 | 0 | 0 | – | 0 | 0 | – |
| 1994 | 0 | 0 | – | 0 | 0 | – |
| 1995 | 0 | 0 | – | 0 | 0 | – |
| 1996 | 0 | 0 | – | 0 | 0 | – |
| 1997 | 0 | 0 | – | 1 | 1 | 100.0% |
| 1998 | 0 | 0 | – | 0 | 0 | – |
| 1999 | 0 | 0 | – | 3 | 3 | 100.0% |
| 2000 | 0 | 0 | – | 0 | 0 | – |
| 2001 | 0 | 0 | – | 1 | 1 | 100.0% |
| 2002 | 0 | 0 | – | 0 | 0 | – |
| Total | 0 | 0 | – | 5 | 5 | 100.0% |

Table A.4.2  Number of successful applications by location for uses in COM Zones

| Location | Approvals | Total | Success Rates % |
|---|---|---|---|
| Hong Kong | 34 | 38 | 89.5% |
| Kowloon | 72 | 77 | 93.5% |
| Development Permission Area | 1 | 2 | 50.0% |
| New Towns | 10 | 12 | 83.3% |
| Rural | 2 | 4 | 50.0% |
| Total | 119 | 133 | 89.5% |

## Appendix 2

Table A.4.3 Number of successful applications by site area for uses in COM Zones

| Site Area | Approvals | Total | Success Rates % |
|---|---|---|---|
| Smaller than 0.1 ha | 17 | 22 | 77.3% |
| 0.1 ha to 1 ha | 21 | 28 | 75.0% |
| Larger than 1 ha | 10 | 10 | 100.0% |
| N/A | 71 | 73 | 97.3% |
| Total | 119 | 133 | 89.5% |

Table A.4.4 Number of successful applications by Gross Floor Area for uses in COM Zones

| GFA | Approvals | Total | Success Rates % |
|---|---|---|---|
| Smaller than 0.5 ha | 83 | 90 | 92.2% |
| 0.5 ha to 5 ha | 14 | 20 | 70.0% |
| Larger than 5 ha | 17 | 17 | 100.0% |
| N/A | 5 | 6 | 83.3% |
| Total | 119 | 133 | 89.5% |

Table A.4.5 Number of successful applications by applied use for COM Zones

| Applied Use | Approvals | Total | Success Rates % |
|---|---|---|---|
| Massage Parlour | 66 | 68 | 97.1% |
| Residential | 20 | 28 | 71.4% |
| Other | 33 | 37 | 89.2% |
| Total | 119 | 133 | 89.5% |

## Commercial/Residential (C/R) Zones

Table A.5.1   Number of total and successful applications by year by stage of application for uses in C/R Zones

| Year | Planning Applications Approvals | Total | Success Rates % | Planning Reviews Approvals | Total | Success Rates % |
|---|---|---|---|---|---|---|
| 1975 | 1 | 1 | 100.0% | 0 | 0 | – |
| 1976 | 4 | 4 | 100.0% | 0 | 0 | – |
| 1977 | 5 | 6 | 83.3% | 0 | 0 | – |
| 1978 | 15 | 16 | 93.8% | 0 | 0 | – |
| 1979 | 18 | 20 | 90.0% | 0 | 1 | 0.0% |
| 1980 | 12 | 13 | 92.3% | 1 | 2 | 50.0% |
| 1981 | 6 | 7 | 85.7% | 0 | 0 | – |
| 1982 | 18 | 22 | 81.8% | 2 | 2 | 100.0% |
| 1983 | 22 | 25 | 88.0% | 1 | 1 | 100.0% |
| 1984 | 32 | 33 | 97.0% | 0 | 0 | – |
| 1985 | 38 | 38 | 100.0% | 0 | 0 | – |
| 1986 | 17 | 17 | 100.0% | 0 | 0 | – |
| 1987 | 6 | 7 | 85.7% | 0 | 0 | – |
| 1988 | 9 | 10 | 90.0% | 1 | 1 | 100.0% |
| 1989 | 5 | 5 | 100.0% | 0 | 1 | 0.0% |
| 1990 | 5 | 6 | 83.3% | 0 | 0 | – |
| 1991 | 8 | 9 | 88.9% | 1 | 2 | 50.0% |
| 1992 | 4 | 5 | 80.0% | 0 | 0 | – |
| 1993 | 5 | 6 | 83.3% | 1 | 1 | 100.0% |
| 1994 | 2 | 2 | 100.0% | 0 | 0 | – |
| 1995 | 13 | 14 | 92.9% | 0 | 0 | – |
| 1996 | 17 | 18 | 94.4% | 0 | 1 | 0.0% |
| 1997 | 16 | 17 | 94.1% | 0 | 1 | 0.0% |
| 1998 | 8 | 10 | 80.0% | 1 | 1 | 100.0% |
| 1999 | 18 | 19 | 94.7% | 0 | 0 | – |
| 2000 | 14 | 15 | 93.3% | 0 | 0 | – |
| 2001 | 12 | 16 | 75.0% | 1 | 1 | 100.0% |
| 2002 | 13 | 15 | 86.7% | 0 | 1 | 0.0% |
| Total | 343 | 376 | 91.2% | 9 | 16 | 56.3% |

## Appendix 2

Table A.5.1  Number of total successful applications by year by stage of application for uses in C/R Zones (Cont'd)

| Year | Petitions to Governor-in-Council/ Planning Appeals ||| Extension of Time Limit |||
|---|---|---|---|---|---|---|
| | Approvals | Total | Success Rates % | Approvals | Total | Success Rates % |
| 1975 | 0 | 0 | – | 0 | 0 | – |
| 1976 | 0 | 0 | – | 0 | 0 | – |
| 1977 | 0 | 0 | – | 0 | 0 | – |
| 1978 | 0 | 0 | – | 0 | 0 | – |
| 1979 | 0 | 0 | – | 0 | 0 | – |
| 1980 | 0 | 0 | – | 0 | 0 | – |
| 1981 | 0 | 0 | – | 0 | 0 | – |
| 1982 | 0 | 0 | – | 0 | 0 | – |
| 1983 | 0 | 0 | – | 0 | 0 | – |
| 1984 | 0 | 0 | – | 0 | 0 | – |
| 1985 | 0 | 0 | – | 0 | 0 | – |
| 1986 | 0 | 0 | – | 0 | 0 | – |
| 1987 | 0 | 0 | – | 0 | 0 | – |
| 1988 | 0 | 0 | – | 0 | 0 | – |
| 1989 | 0 | 0 | – | 0 | 0 | – |
| 1990 | 0 | 0 | – | 0 | 0 | – |
| 1991 | 0 | 0 | – | 0 | 0 | – |
| 1992 | 0 | 0 | – | 0 | 0 | – |
| 1993 | 0 | 0 | – | 0 | 0 | – |
| 1994 | 0 | 0 | – | 0 | 0 | – |
| 1995 | 0 | 0 | – | 0 | 0 | – |
| 1996 | 0 | 0 | – | 0 | 0 | – |
| 1997 | 0 | 0 | – | 0 | 0 | – |
| 1998 | 0 | 0 | – | 0 | 0 | – |
| 1999 | 0 | 0 | – | 0 | 0 | – |
| 2000 | 0 | 0 | – | 0 | 0 | – |
| 2001 | 0 | 0 | – | 0 | 0 | – |
| 2002 | 0 | 0 | – | 0 | 0 | – |
| Total | 0 | 0 | – | 0 | 0 | – |

Table A.5.2  Number of successful applications by location for uses in C/R Zones

| Location | Approvals | Total | Success Rates % |
|---|---|---|---|
| Hong Kong | 223 | 237 | 94.1% |
| Kowloon | 70 | 75 | 93.3% |
| Development Permission Area | 0 | 0 | – |
| New Towns | 55 | 58 | 94.8% |
| Rural | 3 | 6 | 50.0% |
| Total | 351 | 376 | 93.4% |

Table A.5.3  Number of successful applications by site area for uses in C/R Zones

| Site Area | Approvals | Total | Success Rates % |
|---|---|---|---|
| Smaller than 0.1 ha | 127 | 138 | 92.0% |
| 0.1 ha to 1 ha | 49 | 53 | 92.5% |
| Larger than 1 ha | 9 | 9 | 100.0% |
| N/A | 166 | 176 | 94.3% |
| Total | 351 | 376 | 93.4% |

Table A.5.4  Number of successful applications by Gross Floor Area for uses in C/R Zones

| GFA | Approvals | Total | Success Rates % |
|---|---|---|---|
| Smaller than 0.5 ha | 285 | 302 | 94.4% |
| 0.5 ha to 5 ha | 20 | 21 | 95.2% |
| Larger than 5 ha | 3 | 3 | 100.0% |
| N/A | 43 | 50 | 86.0% |
| Total | 351 | 376 | 93.4% |

Table A.5.5  Number of successful applications by applied use for C/R Zones

| Applied Use | Approvals | Total | Success Rates % |
|---|---|---|---|
| School | 157 | 161 | 97.5% |
| Massage Parlour | 92 | 99 | 92.9% |
| Mass Transit Railway | 21 | 22 | 95.5% |
| Religious | 35 | 35 | 100.0% |
| Other | 48 | 61 | 78.7% |
| Total | 353 | 378 | 93.4% |

## Coastal Protection Area (CPA) Zones

Table A.6.1  Number of total and successful applications by year by stage of application for uses in CPA Zones

| Year | Planning Applications Approvals | Total | Success Rates % | Planning Reviews Approvals | Total | Success Rates % |
|---|---|---|---|---|---|---|
| 1981 | 2 | 2 | 100.0% | 0 | 0 | – |
| 1982 | 3 | 3 | 100.0% | 0 | 0 | – |
| 1983 | 2 | 2 | 100.0% | 0 | 0 | – |
| 1984 | 0 | 0 | – | 0 | 0 | – |
| 1985 | 1 | 1 | 100.0% | 0 | 0 | – |
| 1986 | 1 | 1 | 100.0% | 0 | 0 | – |
| 1987 | 0 | 0 | – | 0 | 0 | – |
| 1988 | 0 | 0 | – | 0 | 0 | – |
| 1989 | 1 | 1 | 100.0% | 0 | 0 | – |
| 1990 | 0 | 0 | – | 0 | 0 | – |
| 1991 | 0 | 0 | – | 0 | 0 | – |
| 1992 | 1 | 2 | 50.0% | 0 | 0 | – |
| 1993 | 1 | 3 | 33.3% | 0 | 0 | – |
| 1994 | 2 | 2 | 100.0% | 1 | 1 | 100.0% |
| 1995 | 2 | 2 | 100.0% | 0 | 0 | – |
| 1996 | 2 | 3 | 66.7% | 0 | 0 | – |
| 1997 | 2 | 2 | 100.0% | 0 | 1 | 0.0% |
| 1998 | 1 | 2 | 50.0% | 0 | 0 | – |
| 1999 | 2 | 2 | 100.0% | 0 | 0 | – |
| 2000 | 3 | 6 | 50.0% | 0 | 0 | – |
| 2001 | 2 | 3 | 66.7% | 0 | 0 | – |
| 2002 | 2 | 6 | 33.3% | 0 | 0 | – |
| Total | 30 | 43 | 69.8% | 1 | 2 | 50.0% |

Table A.6.1   Number of total and successful applications by year by stage of application for uses in CPA Zones (Cont'd)

| Year | Petitions to Governor-in-Council/ Planning Appeals ||| Extension of Time Limit |||
|---|---|---|---|---|---|---|
| | Approvals | Total | Success Rates % | Approvals | Total | Success Rates % |
| 1981 | 0 | 0 | – | 0 | 0 | – |
| 1982 | 0 | 0 | – | 0 | 0 | – |
| 1983 | 0 | 0 | – | 0 | 0 | – |
| 1984 | 0 | 0 | – | 0 | 0 | – |
| 1985 | 0 | 0 | – | 0 | 0 | – |
| 1986 | 0 | 0 | – | 0 | 0 | – |
| 1987 | 0 | 0 | – | 0 | 0 | – |
| 1988 | 0 | 0 | – | 0 | 0 | – |
| 1989 | 0 | 0 | – | 0 | 0 | – |
| 1990 | 0 | 0 | – | 0 | 0 | – |
| 1991 | 0 | 0 | – | 0 | 0 | – |
| 1992 | 0 | 0 | – | 0 | 0 | – |
| 1993 | 0 | 0 | – | 0 | 0 | – |
| 1994 | 0 | 0 | – | 1 | 1 | 100.0% |
| 1995 | 0 | 0 | – | 0 | 0 | – |
| 1996 | 0 | 0 | – | 2 | 2 | 100.0% |
| 1997 | 0 | 0 | – | 0 | 0 | – |
| 1998 | 0 | 0 | – | 2 | 2 | 100.0% |
| 1999 | 0 | 0 | – | 0 | 0 | – |
| 2000 | 0 | 0 | – | 2 | 2 | 100.0% |
| 2001 | 0 | 0 | – | 0 | 0 | – |
| 2002 | 0 | 0 | – | 1 | 1 | 100.0% |
| Total | 0 | 0 | – | 8 | 8 | 100.0% |

Table A.6.2   Number of successful applications by location for uses in CPA Zones

| Location | Approvals | Total | Success Rates % |
|---|---|---|---|
| Hong Kong | 2 | 2 | 100.0% |
| Kowloon | 0 | 0 | – |
| Development Permission Area | 0 | 0 | – |
| New Towns | 22 | 26 | 84.6% |
| Rural | 7 | 15 | 46.7% |
| Total | 31 | 43 | 72.1% |

Table A.6.3  Number of successful applications by site area for uses in CPA Zones

| Site Area | Approvals | Total | Success Rates % |
|---|---|---|---|
| Smaller than 0.1 ha | 12 | 17 | 70.6% |
| 0.1 ha to 1 ha | 10 | 14 | 71.4% |
| Larger than 1 ha | 6 | 8 | 75.0% |
| N/A | 3 | 4 | 75.0% |
| Total | 31 | 43 | 72.1% |

Table A.6.4  Number of successful applications by Gross Floor Area for uses in CPA Zones

| GFA | Approvals | Total | Success Rates |
|---|---|---|---|
| Smaller than 0.5 ha | 14 | 18 | 77.8% |
| 0.5 ha to 5 ha | 0 | 0 | – |
| Larger than 5 ha | 0 | 0 | – |
| N/A | 17 | 25 | 68.0% |
| Total | 31 | 43 | 72.1% |

Table A.6.5  Number of successful applications by applied use for CPA Zones

| Applied Use | Approvals | Total | Success Rates % |
|---|---|---|---|
| Utility | 14 | 15 | 93.3% |
| Other | 17 | 28 | 60.7% |
| Total | 31 | 43 | 72.1% |

# Green Belt (GB) Zones

Table A.7.1 Number of total and successful applications by year by stage of application for uses in GB Zones

| Year | Planning Applications |  |  | Planning Reviews |  |  |
|---|---|---|---|---|---|---|
|  | Approvals | Total | Success Rates % | Approvals | Total | Success Rates % |
| 1975 | 1 | 1 | 100.0% | 0 | 0 | – |
| 1976 | 2 | 2 | 100.0% | 0 | 0 | – |
| 1977 | 2 | 2 | 100.0% | 0 | 0 | – |
| 1978 | 1 | 1 | 100.0% | 0 | 0 | – |
| 1979 | 4 | 6 | 66.7% | 2 | 2 | 100.0% |
| 1980 | 1 | 1 | 100.0% | 0 | 0 | – |
| 1981 | 3 | 6 | 50.0% | 1 | 2 | 50.0% |
| 1982 | 4 | 6 | 66.7% | 0 | 0 | – |
| 1983 | 11 | 12 | 91.7% | 0 | 1 | 0.0% |
| 1984 | 9 | 9 | 100.0% | 1 | 1 | 100.0% |
| 1985 | 8 | 8 | 100.0% | 0 | 0 | – |
| 1986 | 8 | 9 | 88.9% | 0 | 0 | – |
| 1987 | 8 | 12 | 66.7% | 2 | 2 | 100.0% |
| 1988 | 12 | 19 | 63.2% | 0 | 3 | 0.0% |
| 1989 | 10 | 14 | 71.4% | 0 | 4 | 0.0% |
| 1990 | 16 | 28 | 57.1% | 0 | 4 | 0.0% |
| 1991 | 29 | 55 | 52.7% | 3 | 5 | 60.0% |
| 1992 | 27 | 52 | 51.9% | 2 | 7 | 28.6% |
| 1993 | 40 | 61 | 65.6% | 0 | 5 | 0.0% |
| 1994 | 48 | 81 | 59.3% | 0 | 17 | 0.0% |
| 1995 | 44 | 72 | 61.1% | 6 | 17 | 35.3% |
| 1996 | 66 | 105 | 62.9% | 3 | 11 | 27.3% |
| 1997 | 52 | 102 | 51.0% | 8 | 24 | 33.3% |
| 1998 | 48 | 101 | 47.5% | 4 | 23 | 17.4% |
| 1999 | 70 | 85 | 82.4% | 0 | 5 | 0.0% |
| 2000 | 49 | 84 | 58.3% | 0 | 12 | 0.0% |
| 2001 | 43 | 64 | 67.2% | 2 | 10 | 20.0% |
| 2002 | 49 | 80 | 61.3% | 4 | 12 | 33.3% |
| Total | 665 | 1,078 | 61.7% | 38 | 167 | 22.8% |

## 132  Appendix 2

Table A.7.1  Number of total and successful applications by year by stage of application for uses in GB Zones (Cont'd)

| Year | Petitions to Governor-in-Council/ Planning Appeals |  |  | Extension of Time Limit |  |  |
|---|---|---|---|---|---|---|
|  | Approvals | Total | Success Rates % | Approvals | Total | Success Rates % |
| 1975 | 0 | 0 | – | 0 | 0 | – |
| 1976 | 0 | 0 | – | 0 | 0 | – |
| 1977 | 0 | 0 | – | 0 | 0 | – |
| 1978 | 0 | 0 | – | 0 | 0 | – |
| 1979 | 0 | 0 | – | 0 | 0 | – |
| 1980 | 0 | 0 | – | 0 | 0 | – |
| 1981 | 0 | 0 | – | 0 | 0 | – |
| 1982 | 1 | 1 | 100.0% | 0 | 0 | – |
| 1983 | 0 | 0 | – | 0 | 0 | – |
| 1984 | 0 | 0 | – | 0 | 0 | – |
| 1985 | 0 | 0 | – | 0 | 0 | – |
| 1986 | 0 | 0 | – | 0 | 0 | – |
| 1987 | 0 | 0 | – | 0 | 0 | – |
| 1988 | 0 | 0 | – | 0 | 0 | – |
| 1989 | 0 | 0 | – | 0 | 0 | – |
| 1990 | 0 | 0 | – | 0 | 0 | – |
| 1991 | 0 | 0 | – | 0 | 0 | – |
| 1992 | 0 | 0 | – | 4 | 4 | 100.0% |
| 1993 | 0 | 1 | 0.0% | 4 | 4 | 100.0% |
| 1994 | 0 | 0 | – | 9 | 9 | 100.0% |
| 1995 | 0 | 5 | 0.0% | 3 | 3 | 100.0% |
| 1996 | 0 | 0 | – | 8 | 8 | 100.0% |
| 1997 | 0 | 0 | – | 11 | 11 | 100.0% |
| 1998 | 0 | 0 | – | 29 | 29 | 100.0% |
| 1999 | 0 | 0 | – | 9 | 9 | 100.0% |
| 2000 | 0 | 0 | – | 13 | 13 | 100.0% |
| 2001 | 0 | 1 | 0.0% | 27 | 28 | 96.4% |
| 2002 | 0 | 1 | 0.0% | 26 | 27 | 96.3% |
| Total | 1 | 9 | 11.1% | 143 | 145 | 98.6% |

Table A.7.2  Number of successful applications by location for uses in GB Zones

| Location | Approvals | Total | Success Rates % |
|---|---|---|---|
| Hong Kong | 113 | 145 | 77.9% |
| Kowloon | 33 | 37 | 89.2% |
| Development Permission Area | 34 | 82 | 41.5% |
| New Territories | 268 | 403 | 66.5% |
| Rural | 249 | 411 | 60.6% |
| Total | 697 | 1,078 | 64.7% |

Table A.7.3  Number of successful applications by site area for uses in GB Zone

| Site Area | Approvals | Total | Success Rates % |
|---|---|---|---|
| Smaller than 0.1 ha | 384 | 554 | 69.3% |
| 0.1 ha to 1 ha | 186 | 331 | 56.2% |
| Larger than 1 ha | 119 | 182 | 65.4% |
| N/A | 8 | 11 | 72.7% |
| Total | 697 | 1,078 | 64.7% |

Table A.7.4  Number of successful applications by Gross Floor Area for uses in GB Zones

| GFA | Approvals | Total | Success Rates % |
|---|---|---|---|
| Smaller than 0.5 ha | 457 | 688 | 66.4% |
| 0.5 ha to 5 ha | 63 | 113 | 55.8% |
| Larger than 5 ha | 22 | 31 | 71.0% |
| N/A | 155 | 246 | 63.0% |
| Total | 697 | 1,078 | 64.7% |

Table A.7.5  Number of successful applications by applied use for GB Zones

| Applied Use | Approvals | Total | Success Rates % |
|---|---|---|---|
| Container | 17 | 34 | 50.0% |
| OS | 29 | 66 | 43.9% |
| Utility | 107 | 113 | 94.7% |
| Religious | 31 | 39 | 79.5% |
| Residential | 81 | 183 | 44.3% |
| VTH | 249 | 387 | 64.3% |
| Other | 184 | 259 | 71.0% |
| Total | 698 | 1,081 | 64.6% |

## Government/Institution/Community (GIC) Zones

Table A.8.1  Number of total and successful applications by year by stage of application for uses in GIC Zones

| Year | Planning Applications Approvals | Total | Success Rates % | Planning Reviews Approvals | Total | Success Rates % |
|---|---|---|---|---|---|---|
| 1975 | 1 | 1 | 100.0% | 0 | 0 | – |
| 1976 | 1 | 10 | 10.0% | 1 | 4 | 25.0% |
| 1977 | 4 | 11 | 36.4% | 0 | 3 | 0.0% |
| 1978 | 6 | 14 | 42.9% | 1 | 5 | 20.0% |
| 1979 | 8 | 15 | 53.3% | 0 | 4 | 0.0% |
| 1980 | 5 | 12 | 41.7% | 2 | 5 | 40.0% |
| 1981 | 10 | 17 | 58.8% | 1 | 3 | 33.3% |
| 1982 | 12 | 18 | 66.7% | 1 | 3 | 33.3% |
| 1983 | 5 | 10 | 50.0% | 0 | 3 | 0.0% |
| 1984 | 13 | 17 | 76.5% | 0 | 2 | 0.0% |
| 1985 | 14 | 15 | 93.3% | 0 | 1 | 0.0% |
| 1986 | 17 | 21 | 81.0% | 0 | 1 | 0.0% |
| 1987 | 27 | 34 | 79.4% | 3 | 8 | 37.5% |
| 1988 | 23 | 28 | 82.1% | 1 | 2 | 50.0% |
| 1989 | 21 | 23 | 91.3% | 0 | 0 | – |
| 1990 | 16 | 22 | 72.7% | 0 | 1 | 0.0% |
| 1991 | 29 | 43 | 67.4% | 2 | 4 | 50.0% |
| 1992 | 28 | 44 | 63.6% | 1 | 7 | 14.3% |
| 1993 | 27 | 48 | 56.3% | 2 | 7 | 28.6% |
| 1994 | 36 | 56 | 64.3% | 3 | 5 | 60.0% |
| 1995 | 28 | 45 | 62.2% | 6 | 12 | 50.0% |
| 1996 | 31 | 42 | 73.8% | 2 | 6 | 33.3% |
| 1997 | 47 | 61 | 77.0% | 0 | 7 | 0.0% |
| 1998 | 29 | 43 | 67.4% | 1 | 7 | 14.3% |
| 1999 | 28 | 33 | 84.8% | 0 | 0 | – |
| 2000 | 57 | 62 | 91.9% | 2 | 5 | 40.0% |
| 2001 | 48 | 54 | 88.9% | 0 | 0 | – |
| 2002 | 34 | 40 | 85.0% | 2 | 4 | 50.0% |
| Total | 605 | 839 | 72.1% | 31 | 109 | 28.4% |

Table A.8.1  Number of total and successful applications by year by stage of application for uses in GIC Zones (Cont'd)

| Year | Petitions to Governor-in-Council/ Planning Appeals ||| Extension of Time Limit |||
| --- | --- | --- | --- | --- | --- | --- |
| | Approvals | Total | Success Rates % | Approvals | Total | Success Rates % |
| 1975 | 0 | 0 | – | 0 | 0 | – |
| 1976 | 0 | 0 | – | 0 | 0 | – |
| 1977 | 0 | 0 | – | 0 | 0 | – |
| 1978 | 0 | 0 | – | 0 | 0 | – |
| 1979 | 0 | 2 | 0.0% | 0 | 0 | – |
| 1980 | 0 | 1 | 0.0% | 0 | 0 | – |
| 1981 | 0 | 0 | – | 0 | 0 | – |
| 1982 | 0 | 0 | – | 0 | 0 | – |
| 1983 | 0 | 0 | – | 0 | 0 | – |
| 1984 | 0 | 0 | – | 0 | 0 | – |
| 1985 | 0 | 2 | 0.0% | 0 | 0 | – |
| 1986 | 0 | 1 | 0.0% | 0 | 0 | – |
| 1987 | 0 | 0 | – | 0 | 0 | – |
| 1988 | 0 | 2 | 0.0% | 0 | 0 | – |
| 1989 | 0 | 0 | – | 0 | 0 | – |
| 1990 | 0 | 0 | – | 0 | 0 | – |
| 1991 | 0 | 0 | – | 0 | 0 | – |
| 1992 | 0 | 1 | 0.0% | 1 | 1 | 100.0% |
| 1993 | 0 | 0 | – | 2 | 2 | 100.0% |
| 1994 | 0 | 1 | 0.0% | 2 | 2 | 100.0% |
| 1995 | 0 | 2 | 0.0% | 3 | 3 | 100.0% |
| 1996 | 0 | 0 | – | 5 | 5 | 100.0% |
| 1997 | 0 | 0 | – | 6 | 6 | 100.0% |
| 1998 | 0 | 0 | – | 4 | 4 | 100.0% |
| 1999 | 0 | 0 | – | 2 | 2 | 100.0% |
| 2000 | 0 | 0 | – | 1 | 1 | 100.0% |
| 2001 | 0 | 0 | – | 4 | 5 | 80.0% |
| 2002 | 0 | 0 | – | 5 | 5 | 100.0% |
| Total | 0 | 12 | 0.0% | 35 | 36 | 97.2% |

## 136  Appendix 2

Table A.8.2  Number of successful applications by location for uses in GIC Zones

| Location | Approvals | Total | Success Rates % |
|---|---|---|---|
| Hong Kong | 258 | 362 | 71.3% |
| Kowloon | 189 | 249 | 75.9% |
| Development Permission Area | 12 | 15 | 80.0% |
| New Towns | 109 | 143 | 76.2% |
| Rural | 61 | 70 | 87.1% |
| Total | 629 | 839 | 75.0% |

Table A.8.3  Number of successful applications by site area for uses in GIC Zones

| Site Area | Approvals | Total | Success Rates % |
|---|---|---|---|
| Smaller than 0.1 ha | 179 | 263 | 68.1% |
| 0.1 ha to 1 ha | 281 | 365 | 77.0% |
| Larger than 1 ha | 102 | 141 | 72.3% |
| N/A | 67 | 70 | 95.7% |
| Total | 629 | 839 | 75.0% |

Table A.8.4  Number of successful applications by Gross Floor Area for uses in GIC Zones

| GFA | Approvals | Total | Success Rates % |
|---|---|---|---|
| Smaller than 0.5 ha | 263 | 350 | 75.1% |
| 0.5 ha to 5 ha | 225 | 297 | 75.8% |
| Larger than 5 ha | 64 | 101 | 63.4% |
| N/A | 77 | 91 | 84.6% |
| Total | 629 | 839 | 75.0% |

Table A.8.5  Number of successful applications by applied use for GIC Zones

| Applied Use | Approvals | Total | Success Rates % |
|---|---|---|---|
| Commercial | 148 | 227 | 65.2% |
| Office | 81 | 133 | 60.9% |
| Residential | 216 | 326 | 66.3% |
| Residential Institution | 45 | 55 | 81.8% |
| Hotel | 20 | 37 | 54.1% |
| School | 101 | 124 | 81.5% |
| VTH | 28 | 40 | 70.0% |
| Utility | 31 | 33 | 93.9% |
| Other | 140 | 160 | 87.5% |
| Total | 810 | 1,135 | 71.4% |

# Hotel Zones

Table A.9.1  Number of total and successful applications by year by stage of application for uses in Hotel Zones

|      | Planning Applications ||| Planning Reviews |||
| Year | Approvals | Total | Success Rates % | Approvals | Total | Success Rates % |
|---|---|---|---|---|---|---|
| 1977 | 1 | 1 | 100.0% | 0 | 0 | – |
| 1978 | 0 | 0 | – | 0 | 0 | – |
| 1979 | 0 | 2 | 0.0% | 0 | 1 | 0.0% |
| 1980 | 1 | 2 | 50.0% | 0 | 1 | 0.0% |
| 1981 | 0 | 1 | 0.0% | 0 | 0 | – |
| 1982 | 0 | 0 | – | 0 | 0 | – |
| 1983 | 1 | 3 | 33.3% | 0 | 1 | 0.0% |
| 1984 | 1 | 1 | 100.0% | 0 | 0 | – |
| 1985 | 2 | 3 | 66.7% | 0 | 0 | – |
| 1986 | 2 | 2 | 100.0% | 0 | 0 | – |
| 1987 | 3 | 4 | 75.0% | 0 | 0 | – |
| 1988 | 16 | 23 | 69.6% | 0 | 0 | – |
| 1989 | 13 | 20 | 65.0% | 3 | 4 | 75.0% |
| 1990 | 3 | 8 | 37.5% | 0 | 0 | – |
| 1991 | 2 | 6 | 33.3% | 0 | 0 | – |
| 1992 | 0 | 1 | 0.0% | 0 | 0 | – |
| 1993 | 0 | 0 | – | 0 | 0 | – |
| 1994 | 5 | 7 | 71.4% | 0 | 0 | – |
| 1995 | 12 | 16 | 75.0% | 0 | 0 | – |
| 1996 | 13 | 20 | 65.0% | 0 | 2 | 0.0% |
| 1997 | 17 | 21 | 81.0% | 2 | 3 | 66.7% |
| 1998 | 17 | 17 | 100.0% | 2 | 4 | 50.0% |
| 1999 | 10 | 14 | 71.4% | 0 | 0 | – |
| 2000 | 17 | 17 | 100.0% | 0 | 1 | 0.0% |
| 2001 | 21 | 23 | 91.3% | 0 | 1 | 0.0% |
| 2002 | 18 | 18 | 100.0% | 0 | 0 | – |
| Total | 175 | 230 | 76.1% | 7 | 18 | 38.9% |

Table A.9.1 Number of total and successful applications by year by stage of application for uses in Hotel Zones (Cont'd)

| Year | Petitions to Governor–in–Council / Planning Appeals |||  Extension of Time Limit |||
|---|---|---|---|---|---|---|
|  | Approvals | Total | Success Rates % | Approvals | Total | Success Rates % |
| 1977 | 0 | 0 | – | 0 | 0 | – |
| 1978 | 0 | 0 | – | 0 | 0 | – |
| 1979 | 0 | 0 | – | 0 | 0 | – |
| 1980 | 0 | 0 | – | 0 | 0 | – |
| 1981 | 0 | 0 | – | 0 | 0 | – |
| 1982 | 0 | 0 | – | 0 | 0 | – |
| 1983 | 0 | 0 | – | 0 | 0 | – |
| 1984 | 0 | 0 | – | 0 | 0 | – |
| 1985 | 0 | 0 | – | 0 | 0 | – |
| 1986 | 0 | 0 | – | 0 | 0 | – |
| 1987 | 0 | 0 | – | 0 | 0 | – |
| 1988 | 0 | 0 | – | 0 | 0 | – |
| 1989 | 0 | 0 | – | 0 | 0 | – |
| 1990 | 0 | 0 | – | 0 | 0 | – |
| 1991 | 0 | 0 | – | 0 | 0 | – |
| 1992 | 0 | 0 | – | 0 | 0 | – |
| 1993 | 0 | 0 | – | 1 | 1 | 100.0% |
| 1994 | 0 | 0 | – | 0 | 0 | – |
| 1995 | 0 | 0 | – | 0 | 0 | – |
| 1996 | 0 | 0 | – | 0 | 0 | – |
| 1997 | 0 | 0 | – | 1 | 1 | 100.0% |
| 1998 | 0 | 0 | – | 2 | 2 | 100.0% |
| 1999 | 0 | 0 | – | 0 | 0 | – |
| 2000 | 0 | 0 | – | 0 | 0 | – |
| 2001 | 0 | 0 | – | 0 | 0 | – |
| 2002 | 0 | 0 | – | 0 | 0 | – |
| Total | 0 | 0 | – | 4 | 4 | 100.0% |

Table A.9.2  Number of successful applications by location for uses in Hotel Zones

| Location | Approvals | Total | Success Rates % |
|---|---|---|---|
| Hong Kong | 60 | 85 | 70.6% |
| Kowloon | 86 | 108 | 79.6% |
| Development Permission Area | 0 | 0 | – |
| New Towns | 29 | 36 | 80.6% |
| Rural | 0 | 1 | 0.0% |
| Total | 175 | 230 | 76.1% |

Table A.9.3  Number of successful applications by site area for uses in Hotel Zones

| Site Area | Approvals | Total | Success Rates % |
|---|---|---|---|
| Smaller than 0.1 ha | 45 | 61 | 73.8% |
| 0.1 ha to 1 ha | 43 | 69 | 62.3% |
| Larger than 1 ha | 84 | 94 | 89.4% |
| N/A | 3 | 6 | 50.0% |
| Total | 175 | 230 | 76.1% |

Table A.9.4  Number of successful applications by Gross Floor Area for uses in Hotel Zones

| GFA | Approvals | Total | Success Rates % |
|---|---|---|---|
| Smaller than 0.5 ha | 19 | 30 | 63.3% |
| 0.5 ha to 5 ha | 67 | 96 | 69.8% |
| Larger than 5 ha | 85 | 95 | 89.5% |
| N/A | 4 | 9 | 44.4% |
| Total | 175 | 230 | 76.1% |

Table A.9.5  Number of successful applications by zoning for Hotel Uses

| Applied Use | Approvals | Total | Success Rates % |
|---|---|---|---|
| CDA | 89 | 99 | 89.9% |
| RA | 57 | 79 | 72.2% |
| Other | 29 | 52 | 55.8% |
| Total | 175 | 230 | 76.1% |

## Industrial (I) Zones

Table A.10.1 Number of total and successful applications by year by stage of application for uses in I Zones

| Year | Planning Applications ||| Planning Reviews |||
|---|---|---|---|---|---|---|
| | Approvals | Total | Success Rates % | Approvals | Total | Success Rates % |
| 1975 | 1 | 1 | 100.0% | 0 | 0 | – |
| 1976 | 4 | 7 | 57.1% | 1 | 1 | 100.0% |
| 1977 | 7 | 10 | 70.0% | 1 | 2 | 50.0% |
| 1978 | 17 | 21 | 81.0% | 4 | 4 | 100.0% |
| 1979 | 10 | 21 | 47.6% | 4 | 8 | 50.0% |
| 1980 | 12 | 24 | 50.0% | 4 | 7 | 57.1% |
| 1981 | 14 | 22 | 63.6% | 3 | 5 | 60.0% |
| 1982 | 22 | 27 | 81.5% | 1 | 2 | 50.0% |
| 1983 | 20 | 28 | 71.4% | 1 | 5 | 20.0% |
| 1984 | 18 | 22 | 81.8% | 2 | 2 | 100.0% |
| 1985 | 27 | 32 | 84.4% | 0 | 0 | – |
| 1986 | 17 | 27 | 63.0% | 0 | 0 | – |
| 1987 | 39 | 77 | 50.6% | 4 | 7 | 57.1% |
| 1988 | 51 | 72 | 70.8% | 12 | 18 | 66.7% |
| 1989 | 62 | 109 | 56.9% | 0 | 8 | 0.0% |
| 1990 | 41 | 91 | 45.1% | 6 | 12 | 50.0% |
| 1991 | 51 | 82 | 62.2% | 3 | 16 | 18.8% |
| 1992 | 73 | 105 | 69.5% | 1 | 4 | 25.0% |
| 1993 | 102 | 132 | 77.3% | 2 | 5 | 40.0% |
| 1994 | 242 | 296 | 81.8% | 6 | 13 | 46.2% |
| 1995 | 116 | 138 | 84.1% | 8 | 17 | 47.1% |
| 1996 | 124 | 149 | 83.2% | 3 | 9 | 33.3% |
| 1997 | 139 | 164 | 84.8% | 2 | 10 | 20.0% |
| 1998 | 39 | 62 | 62.9% | 2 | 7 | 28.6% |
| 1999 | 34 | 48 | 70.8% | 1 | 4 | 25.0% |
| 2000 | 80 | 91 | 87.9% | 1 | 1 | 100.0% |
| 2001 | 45 | 53 | 84.9% | 1 | 3 | 33.3% |
| 2002 | 11 | 11 | 100.0% | 0 | 0 | – |
| Total | 1,418 | 1,922 | 73.8% | 73 | 170 | 42.9% |

Table A.10.1  Number of total and successful applications by year by stage of application for uses in I Zones (Cont'd)

| Year | Petitions to Governor–in–Council / Planning Appeals Approvals | Total | Success Rates % | Extension of Time Limit Approvals | Total | Success Rates % |
|---|---|---|---|---|---|---|
| 1975 | 0 | 0 | – | 0 | 0 | – |
| 1976 | 0 | 0 | – | 0 | 0 | – |
| 1977 | 0 | 0 | – | 0 | 0 | – |
| 1978 | 0 | 0 | – | 0 | 0 | – |
| 1979 | 0 | 0 | – | 0 | 0 | – |
| 1980 | 0 | 0 | – | 0 | 0 | – |
| 1981 | 0 | 0 | – | 0 | 0 | – |
| 1982 | 0 | 1 | 0.0% | 0 | 0 | – |
| 1983 | 0 | 0 | – | 0 | 0 | – |
| 1984 | 0 | 0 | – | 0 | 0 | – |
| 1985 | 0 | 0 | – | 0 | 0 | – |
| 1986 | 0 | 0 | – | 0 | 0 | – |
| 1987 | 0 | 0 | – | 0 | 0 | – |
| 1988 | 0 | 0 | – | 0 | 0 | – |
| 1989 | 0 | 0 | – | 0 | 0 | – |
| 1990 | 0 | 1 | 0.0% | 0 | 0 | – |
| 1991 | 0 | 0 | – | 0 | 0 | – |
| 1992 | 0 | 3 | 0.0% | 1 | 1 | 100.0% |
| 1993 | 0 | 0 | – | 1 | 1 | 100.0% |
| 1994 | 1 | 1 | 100.0% | 4 | 4 | 100.0% |
| 1995 | 0 | 4 | 0.0% | 2 | 2 | 100.0% |
| 1996 | 0 | 0 | – | 13 | 13 | 100.0% |
| 1997 | 0 | 0 | – | 7 | 8 | 87.5% |
| 1998 | 0 | 0 | – | 7 | 8 | 87.5% |
| 1999 | 0 | 0 | – | 1 | 1 | 100.0% |
| 2000 | 0 | 0 | – | 0 | 0 | – |
| 2001 | 0 | 0 | – | 1 | 1 | 100.0% |
| 2002 | 0 | 0 | – | 0 | 0 | – |
| Total | 1 | 10 | 10.0% | 37 | 39 | 94.9% |

## Appendix 2

**Table A.10.2  Number of successful applications by location for uses in I Zones**

| Location | Approvals | Total | Success Rates % |
| --- | --- | --- | --- |
| Hong Kong | 232 | 288 | 80.6% |
| Kowloon | 692 | 950 | 72.8% |
| Development Permission Area | 0 | 0 | – |
| New Towns | 554 | 679 | 81.6% |
| Rural | 3 | 5 | 60.0% |
| Total | 1,481 | 1,922 | 77.1% |

**Table A.10.3 Number of successful applications by site area for uses in I Zones**

| Site Area | Approvals | Total | Success Rates % |
| --- | --- | --- | --- |
| Smaller than 0.1 ha | 182 | 244 | 74.6% |
| 0.1 ha to 1 ha | 536 | 715 | 75.0% |
| Larger than 1 ha | 52 | 64 | 81.3% |
| N/A | 711 | 899 | 79.1% |
| Total | 1,481 | 1,922 | 77.1% |

**Table A.10.4  Number of successful applications by Gross Floor Area for uses in I Zones**

| GFA | Approvals | Total | Success Rates % |
| --- | --- | --- | --- |
| Smaller than 0.5 ha | 960 | 1,248 | 76.9% |
| 0.5 ha to 5 ha | 378 | 493 | 76.7% |
| Larger than 5 ha | 74 | 102 | 72.0% |
| N/A | 69 | 79 | 87.3% |
| Total | 1,481 | 1,922 | 77.1% |

**Table A.10.5  Number of successful applications by applied use for I Zones**

| Applied Use | Approvals | Total | Success Rates % |
| --- | --- | --- | --- |
| Commercial | 534 | 754 | 70.8% |
| Office | 521 | 668 | 78.0% |
| Residential | 34 | 39 | 87.2% |
| IND/OFF | 262 | 317 | 82.6% |
| IND(Offensive) | 36 | 36 | 100.0% |
| LPS | 71 | 76 | 93.4% |
| Hardware Shop | 51 | 51 | 100.0% |
| Restaurant | 66 | 108 | 61.1% |
| Other | 112 | 172 | 65.1% |
| Total | 1,687 | 2,221 | 76.0% |

## Industrial (Group D) Zones

Table A.11.1  Number of total and successful applications by year by stage of application for uses in I(D) Zones

| Year | Planning Applications |||  Planning Reviews |||
|---|---|---|---|---|---|---|
| | Approvals | Total | Success Rates % | Approvals | Total | Success Rates % |
| 1994 | 1 | 1 | 100.0% | 0 | 0 | – |
| 1995 | 5 | 5 | 100.0% | 0 | 0 | – |
| 1996 | 17 | 17 | 100.0% | 0 | 0 | – |
| 1997 | 12 | 13 | 92.3% | 0 | 0 | – |
| 1998 | 13 | 14 | 92.9% | 0 | 0 | – |
| 1999 | 12 | 13 | 92.3% | 0 | 0 | – |
| 2000 | 9 | 10 | 90.0% | 0 | 1 | 0.0% |
| 2001 | 7 | 8 | 87.5% | 1 | 1 | 100.0% |
| 2002 | 8 | 8 | 100.0% | 0 | 0 | – |
| Total | 84 | 89 | 94.4% | 1 | 2 | 50.0% |

| Year | Planning Appeals ||| Extension of Time Limit |||
|---|---|---|---|---|---|---|
| | Approvals | Total | Success Rates % | Approvals | Total | Success Rates % |
| 1994 | 0 | 0 | – | 0 | 0 | – |
| 1995 | 0 | 0 | – | 0 | 0 | – |
| 1996 | 0 | 0 | – | 1 | 1 | 100.0% |
| 1997 | 0 | 0 | – | 1 | 1 | 100.0% |
| 1998 | 0 | 0 | – | 0 | 0 | – |
| 1999 | 0 | 0 | – | 0 | 0 | – |
| 2000 | 0 | 0 | – | 1 | 1 | 100.0% |
| 2001 | 0 | 0 | – | 3 | 3 | 100.0% |
| 2002 | 0 | 0 | – | 2 | 2 | 100.0% |
| Total | 0 | 0 | – | 8 | 8 | 100.0% |

Table A.11.2 Number of successful applications by location for uses in I(D) Zones

| Location | Approvals | Total | Success Rates % |
|---|---|---|---|
| Hong Kong | 0 | 0 | – |
| Kowloon | 0 | 0 | – |
| Development Permission Area | 0 | 0 | – |
| New Towns | 0 | 0 | – |
| Rural | 86 | 89 | 96.6% |
| Total | 86 | 89 | 96.6% |

Table A.11.3 Number of successful applications by site area for uses in I(D) Zones

| Site Area | Approvals | Total | Success Rates % |
|---|---|---|---|
| Smaller than 0.1 ha | 13 | 13 | 100.0% |
| 0.1 ha to 1 ha | 73 | 75 | 97.3% |
| Larger than 1 ha | 0 | 1 | 0.0% |
| N/A | 0 | 0 | – |
| Total | 86 | 89 | 96.6% |

Table A.11.4 Number of successful applications by Gross Floor Area for uses in I(D) Zones

| GFA | Approvals | Total | Success Rates % |
|---|---|---|---|
| Smaller than 0.5 ha | 51 | 52 | 98.1% |
| 0.5 ha to 5 ha | 0 | 0 | – |
| Larger than 5 ha | 0 | 0 | – |
| N/A | 35 | 37 | 94.6% |
| Total | 86 | 89 | 96.6% |

Table A.11.5 Number of successful applications by applied use for I(D) Zones

| Applied Use | Approvals | Total | Success Rates % |
|---|---|---|---|
| CBP | 7 | 8 | 87.5% |
| Container | 6 | 7 | 85.7% |
| Garage | 25 | 25 | 100.0% |
| Industrial | 22 | 22 | 100.0% |
| Open Storage | 21 | 22 | 95.5% |
| Other | 14 | 14 | 100.0% |
| Total | 95 | 98 | 96.9% |

## Open Space (O) Zones

Table A.12.1  Number of total and successful applications by year by stage of application for uses in O Zones

| Year | Planning Applications |||Planning Reviews|||
|---|---|---|---|---|---|---|
| | Approvals | Total | Success Rates % | Approvals | Total | Success Rates % |
| 1975 | 2 | 7 | 28.6% | 0 | 1 | 0.0% |
| 1976 | 5 | 6 | 83.3% | 2 | 3 | 66.7% |
| 1977 | 4 | 7 | 57.1% | 1 | 2 | 50.0% |
| 1978 | 9 | 10 | 90.0% | 0 | 1 | 0.0% |
| 1979 | 9 | 10 | 90.0% | 1 | 2 | 50.0% |
| 1980 | 1 | 3 | 33.3% | 0 | 2 | 0.0% |
| 1981 | 2 | 4 | 50.0% | 0 | 0 | – |
| 1982 | 7 | 9 | 77.8% | 1 | 2 | 50.0% |
| 1983 | 15 | 18 | 83.3% | 0 | 2 | 0.0% |
| 1984 | 8 | 9 | 88.9% | 0 | 1 | 0.0% |
| 1985 | 8 | 13 | 61.5% | 0 | 0 | – |
| 1986 | 12 | 17 | 70.6% | 0 | 1 | 0.0% |
| 1987 | 11 | 12 | 91.7% | 0 | 3 | 0.0% |
| 1988 | 9 | 12 | 75.0% | 0 | 0 | – |
| 1989 | 9 | 10 | 90.0% | 0 | 0 | – |
| 1990 | 12 | 13 | 92.3% | 0 | 0 | – |
| 1991 | 15 | 21 | 71.4% | 1 | 2 | 50.0% |
| 1992 | 14 | 18 | 77.8% | 0 | 0 | – |
| 1993 | 14 | 20 | 70.0% | 1 | 2 | 50.0% |
| 1994 | 10 | 16 | 62.5% | 1 | 2 | 50.0% |
| 1995 | 7 | 12 | 58.3% | 1 | 1 | 100.0% |
| 1996 | 13 | 20 | 65.0% | 1 | 5 | 20.0% |
| 1997 | 18 | 19 | 94.7% | 0 | 2 | 0.0% |
| 1998 | 11 | 14 | 78.6% | 1 | 2 | 50.0% |
| 1999 | 9 | 14 | 64.3% | 0 | 1 | 0.0% |
| 2000 | 16 | 17 | 94.1% | 0 | 0 | – |
| 2001 | 22 | 25 | 88.0% | 1 | 2 | 50.0% |
| 2002 | 20 | 23 | 87.0% | 1 | 2 | 50.0% |
| Total | 292 | 379 | 77.0% | 13 | 41 | 31.7% |

## 146  Appendix 2

Table A.12.1  Number of total and successful applications by year by stage of application for uses in O Zones (Cont'd)

| Year | Petitions to Governor-in-Council/ Planning Appeals ||| Extension of Time Limit |||
|---|---|---|---|---|---|---|
| | Approvals | Total | Success Rates % | Approvals | Total | Success Rates % |
| 1975 | 0 | 0 | – | 0 | 0 | – |
| 1976 | 0 | 1 | 0.0% | 0 | 0 | – |
| 1977 | 0 | 0 | – | 0 | 0 | – |
| 1978 | 0 | 0 | – | 0 | 0 | – |
| 1979 | 0 | 1 | 0.0% | 0 | 0 | – |
| 1980 | 0 | 0 | – | 0 | 0 | – |
| 1981 | 0 | 0 | – | 0 | 0 | – |
| 1982 | 0 | 0 | – | 0 | 0 | – |
| 1983 | 0 | 0 | – | 0 | 0 | – |
| 1984 | 0 | 1 | 0.0% | 0 | 0 | – |
| 1985 | 0 | 0 | – | 0 | 0 | – |
| 1986 | 0 | 1 | 0.0% | 0 | 0 | – |
| 1987 | 0 | 0 | – | 0 | 0 | – |
| 1988 | 0 | 1 | 0.0% | 0 | 0 | – |
| 1989 | 0 | 0 | – | 0 | 0 | – |
| 1990 | 0 | 0 | – | 0 | 0 | – |
| 1991 | 0 | 0 | – | 0 | 0 | – |
| 1992 | 0 | 0 | – | 0 | 0 | – |
| 1993 | 0 | 0 | – | 0 | 0 | – |
| 1994 | 0 | 0 | – | 1 | 1 | 100.0% |
| 1995 | 0 | 0 | – | 2 | 2 | 100.0% |
| 1996 | 0 | 0 | – | 2 | 2 | 100.0% |
| 1997 | 0 | 0 | – | 0 | 0 | – |
| 1998 | 0 | 0 | – | 3 | 3 | 100.0% |
| 1999 | 0 | 0 | – | 1 | 1 | 100.0% |
| 2000 | 0 | 1 | 0.0% | 2 | 2 | 100.0% |
| 2001 | 0 | 0 | – | 5 | 5 | 100.0% |
| 2002 | 0 | 0 | – | 4 | 4 | 100.0% |
| Total | 0 | 6 | 0.0% | 20 | 20 | 100.0% |

Table A.12.2  Number of successful applications by location for uses in O Zones

| Location | Approvals | Total | Success Rates % |
| --- | --- | --- | --- |
| Hong Kong | 120 | 168 | 71.4% |
| Kowloon | 68 | 81 | 84.0% |
| Development Permission Area | 0 | 0 | – |
| New Towns | 73 | 79 | 92.4% |
| Rural | 43 | 51 | 84.3% |
| Total | 304 | 379 | 80.2% |

Table A.12.3  Number of successful applications by site area for uses in O Zones

| Site Area | Approvals | Total | Success Rates % |
| --- | --- | --- | --- |
| Smaller than 0.1 ha | 131 | 171 | 76.6% |
| 0.1 ha to 1 ha | 104 | 126 | 82.5% |
| Larger than 1 ha | 57 | 68 | 83.8% |
| N/A | 12 | 14 | 85.7% |
| Total | 304 | 379 | 80.2% |

Table A.12.4  Number of successful applications by Gross Floor Area for uses in O Zones

| GFA | Approvals | Total | Success Rates % |
| --- | --- | --- | --- |
| Smaller than 0.5 ha | 122 | 148 | 82.4% |
| 0.5 ha to 5 ha | 46 | 73 | 63.0% |
| Larger than 5 ha | 22 | 29 | 75.9% |
| N/A | 114 | 129 | 88.4% |
| Total | 304 | 379 | 80.2% |

Table A.12.5  Number of successful applications by applied use for O Zones

| Applied Use | Approvals | Total | Success Rates % |
| --- | --- | --- | --- |
| Commercial | 31 | 63 | 49.2% |
| Residential | 53 | 99 | 53.5% |
| Recreation | 47 | 57 | 82.5% |
| Utility | 65 | 66 | 98.5% |
| Restaurant | 16 | 21 | 76.2% |
| Open Storage | 10 | 14 | 71.4% |
| Other | 113 | 123 | 91.9% |
| Total | 335 | 443 | 75.6% |

## Open Storage (OS) Zones

Table A.13.1  Number of total and successful applications by year by stage of application for uses in OS Zones

| Year | Planning Applications ||| Planning Reviews |||
|---|---|---|---|---|---|---|
| | Approvals | Total | Success Rates % | Approvals | Total | Success Rates % |
| 1991 | 0 | 1 | 0.0% | 0 | 0 | – |
| 1992 | 5 | 10 | 50.0% | 0 | 0 | – |
| 1993 | 3 | 6 | 50.0% | 0 | 0 | – |
| 1994 | 11 | 16 | 68.8% | 2 | 3 | 66.7% |
| 1995 | 23 | 26 | 88.5% | 1 | 1 | 100.0% |
| 1996 | 30 | 32 | 93.8% | 0 | 1 | 0.0% |
| 1997 | 49 | 52 | 94.2% | 1 | 2 | 50.0% |
| 1998 | 49 | 50 | 98.0% | 1 | 1 | 100.0% |
| 1999 | 39 | 39 | 100.0% | 0 | 0 | – |
| 2000 | 57 | 57 | 100.0% | 0 | 0 | – |
| 2001 | 24 | 29 | 82.8% | 1 | 1 | 100.0% |
| 2002 | 24 | 36 | 66.7% | 1 | 6 | 16.7% |
| Total | 314 | 354 | 88.7% | 7 | 15 | 46.7% |

| Year | Planning Appeals ||| Extension of Time Limit |||
|---|---|---|---|---|---|---|
| | Approvals | Total | Success Rates % | Approvals | Total | Success Rates % |
| 1991 | 0 | 0 | – | 0 | 0 | – |
| 1992 | 0 | 0 | – | 0 | 0 | – |
| 1993 | 0 | 0 | – | 0 | 0 | – |
| 1994 | 0 | 0 | – | 2 | 2 | 100.0% |
| 1995 | 0 | 0 | – | 2 | 2 | 100.0% |
| 1996 | 0 | 0 | – | 1 | 1 | 100.0% |
| 1997 | 0 | 0 | – | 3 | 3 | 100.0% |
| 1998 | 0 | 0 | – | 2 | 2 | 100.0% |
| 1999 | 0 | 0 | – | 1 | 1 | 100.0% |
| 2000 | 0 | 0 | – | 4 | 4 | 100.0% |
| 2001 | 0 | 0 | – | 28 | 28 | 100.0% |
| 2002 | 0 | 0 | – | 15 | 15 | 100.0% |
| Total | 0 | 0 | – | 58 | 58 | 100.0% |

Table A.13.2 Number of successful applications by location for uses in OS Zones

| Location | Approvals | Total | Success Rates % |
|---|---|---|---|
| Hong Kong | 0 | 0 | – |
| Kowloon | 0 | 0 | – |
| Development Permission Area | 15 | 26 | 57.7% |
| New Towns | 0 | 0 | – |
| Rural | 298 | 328 | 90.9% |
| Total | 313 | 354 | 88.4% |

Table A.13.3 Number of successful applications by site area for uses in OS Zones

| Site Area | Approvals | Total | Success Rates % |
|---|---|---|---|
| Smaller than 0.1 ha | 97 | 104 | 93.3% |
| 0.1 ha to 1 ha | 187 | 212 | 88.2% |
| Larger than 1 ha | 29 | 38 | 76.3% |
| N/A | 0 | 0 | – |
| Total | 313 | 354 | 88.4% |

Table A.13.4 Number of successful applications by Gross Floor Area for uses in OS Zones

| GFA | Approvals | Total | Success Rates % |
|---|---|---|---|
| Smaller than 0.5 ha | 67 | 81 | 82.7% |
| 0.5 ha to 5 ha | 4 | 6 | 66.7% |
| Larger than 5 ha | 1 | 1 | 100.0% |
| N/A | 241 | 266 | 90.6% |
| Total | 313 | 354 | 88.4% |

Table A.13.5 Number of successful applications by applied use for OS Zones

| Applied Use | Approvals | Total | Success Rates % |
|---|---|---|---|
| Container | 44 | 50 | 88.0% |
| Garage | 47 | 50 | 94.0% |
| OS | 165 | 181 | 91.2% |
| Industrial | 39 | 45 | 86.7% |
| Warehouse | 59 | 64 | 92.2% |
| Other | 22 | 32 | 68.8% |
| Total | 376 | 422 | 89.1% |

## Other Use (OU) Zones

Table A.14.1 Number of total and successful applications by year by stage of application for uses in OU Zones

| Year | Planning Applications |||  Planning Reviews |||
|---|---|---|---|---|---|---|
| | Approvals | Total | Success Rates % | Approvals | Total | Success Rates % |
| 1978 | 1 | 1 | 100.0% | 0 | 0 | – |
| 1979 | 0 | 1 | 0.0% | 0 | 1 | 0.0% |
| 1980 | 1 | 1 | 100.0% | 0 | 0 | – |
| 1981 | 0 | 0 | – | 0 | 0 | – |
| 1982 | 0 | 0 | – | 0 | 0 | – |
| 1983 | 2 | 2 | 100.0% | 0 | 0 | – |
| 1984 | 1 | 1 | 100.0% | 0 | 0 | – |
| 1985 | 0 | 0 | – | 0 | 0 | – |
| 1986 | 5 | 5 | 100.0% | 0 | 0 | – |
| 1987 | 5 | 5 | 100.0% | 0 | 0 | – |
| 1988 | 3 | 4 | 75.0% | 0 | 0 | – |
| 1989 | 7 | 8 | 87.5% | 0 | 0 | – |
| 1990 | 9 | 10 | 90.0% | 1 | 1 | 100.0% |
| 1991 | 10 | 15 | 66.7% | 0 | 0 | – |
| 1992 | 3 | 3 | 100.0% | 0 | 0 | – |
| 1993 | 2 | 3 | 66.7% | 1 | 1 | 100.0% |
| 1994 | 7 | 8 | 87.5% | 0 | 0 | – |
| 1995 | 6 | 11 | 54.5% | 0 | 0 | – |
| 1996 | 5 | 7 | 71.4% | 1 | 4 | 25.0% |
| 1997 | 18 | 21 | 85.7% | 0 | 1 | 0.0% |
| 1998 | 17 | 19 | 89.5% | 2 | 2 | 100.0% |
| 1999 | 15 | 19 | 78.9% | 0 | 0 | – |
| 2000 | 19 | 21 | 90.5% | 0 | 4 | 0.0% |
| 2001 | 22 | 36 | 61.1% | 1 | 1 | 100.0% |
| 2002 | 52 | 67 | 77.6% | 2 | 5 | 40.0% |
| Total | 210 | 268 | 78.4% | 8 | 20 | 40.0% |

Table A.14.1  Number of total and successful applications by year by stage of application for uses in OU Zones (Cont'd)

| Year | Petitions to Governor-in-Council/ Planning Appeals Approvals | Total | Success Rates % | Extension of Time Limit Approvals | Total | Success Rates % |
|---|---|---|---|---|---|---|
| 1978 | 0 | 0 | – | 0 | 0 | – |
| 1979 | 0 | 0 | – | 0 | 0 | – |
| 1980 | 0 | 0 | – | 0 | 0 | – |
| 1981 | 0 | 0 | – | 0 | 0 | – |
| 1982 | 0 | 0 | – | 0 | 0 | – |
| 1983 | 0 | 0 | – | 0 | 0 | – |
| 1984 | 0 | 0 | – | 0 | 0 | – |
| 1985 | 0 | 0 | – | 0 | 0 | – |
| 1986 | 0 | 0 | – | 0 | 0 | – |
| 1987 | 0 | 0 | – | 0 | 0 | – |
| 1988 | 0 | 0 | – | 0 | 0 | – |
| 1989 | 0 | 0 | – | 0 | 0 | – |
| 1990 | 0 | 0 | – | 0 | 0 | – |
| 1991 | 0 | 0 | – | 0 | 0 | – |
| 1992 | 0 | 0 | – | 0 | 0 | – |
| 1993 | 0 | 0 | – | 1 | 1 | 100.0% |
| 1994 | 0 | 0 | – | 0 | 0 | – |
| 1995 | 0 | 0 | – | 1 | 1 | 100.0% |
| 1996 | 0 | 0 | – | 0 | 0 | – |
| 1997 | 0 | 0 | – | 1 | 1 | 100.0% |
| 1998 | 0 | 0 | – | 2 | 2 | 100.0% |
| 1999 | 0 | 0 | – | 2 | 2 | 100.0% |
| 2000 | 0 | 0 | – | 3 | 3 | 100.0% |
| 2001 | 0 | 0 | – | 9 | 9 | 100.0% |
| 2002 | 1 | 3 | 33.3% | 6 | 6 | 100.0% |
| Total | 1 | 3 | 33.3% | 25 | 25 | 100.0% |

Table A.14.2  Number of successful applications by location for uses in OU Zones

| Location | Approvals | Total | Success Rates % |
|---|---|---|---|
| Hong Kong | 75 | 84 | 89.3% |
| Kowloon | 60 | 69 | 87.0% |
| Development Permission Area | 0 | 0 | – |
| New Towns | 57 | 63 | 90.5% |
| Rural | 28 | 52 | 53.8% |
| Total | 220 | 268 | 82.1% |

## 152  Appendix 2

Table A.14.3  Number of successful applications by site area for uses in OU Zones

| Site Area | Approvals | Total | Success Rates % |
|---|---|---|---|
| Smaller than 0.1 ha | 22 | 26 | 84.6% |
| 0.1 ha to 1 ha | 62 | 86 | 72.1% |
| Larger than 1 ha | 54 | 65 | 83.1% |
| N/A | 82 | 91 | 90.1% |
| Total | 220 | 268 | 82.1% |

Table A.14.4  Number of successful applications by Gross Floor Area for uses in OU Zones

| GFA | Approvals | Total | Success Rates % |
|---|---|---|---|
| Smaller than 0.5 ha | 100 | 116 | 86.2% |
| 0.5 ha to 5 ha | 25 | 31 | 80.6% |
| Larger than 5 ha | 33 | 36 | 91.7% |
| N/A | 62 | 85 | 72.9% |
| Total | 220 | 268 | 82.1% |

Table A.14.5  Number of successful applications by applied use for OU Zones

| Applied Use | Approvals | Total | Success Rates % |
|---|---|---|---|
| Commercial | 67 | 76 | 88.2% |
| Residential | 33 | 37 | 89.2% |
| Container | 12 | 26 | 46.2% |
| Utility | 34 | 34 | 100.0% |
| Office | 43 | 48 | 89.6% |
| Other | 78 | 97 | 80.4% |
| Total | 267 | 318 | 84.0% |

Table A.14.6  Number of successful applications by zoning for OU Zones

| Zoning | Approvals | Total | Success Rates % |
|---|---|---|---|
| OU* | 31 | 36 | 86.1% |
| OU–BUSS | 21 | 26 | 80.8% |
| OU–CDWR | 13 | 30 | 43.3% |
| OU–PIER | 20 | 24 | 83.3% |
| Other | 135 | 152 | 88.8% |
| Total | 220 | 268 | 82.1% |

## Pedestrian Street (PS) Zones

Table A.15.1 Number of total and successful applications by year by stage of application for uses in PS Zones

| Year | Planning Applications Approvals | Total | Success Rates % | Planning Reviews Approvals | Total | Success Rates % |
|---|---|---|---|---|---|---|
| 1976 | 0 | 1 | 0.0% | 0 | 0 | – |
| 1977 | 0 | 0 | – | 0 | 0 | – |
| 1978 | 0 | 0 | – | 0 | 0 | – |
| 1979 | 0 | 0 | – | 0 | 0 | – |
| 1980 | 0 | 0 | – | 0 | 0 | – |
| 1981 | 0 | 0 | – | 0 | 0 | – |
| 1982 | 0 | 0 | – | 0 | 0 | – |
| 1983 | 0 | 1 | 0.0% | 0 | 0 | – |
| 1984 | 0 | 1 | 0.0% | 0 | 0 | – |
| 1985 | 0 | 0 | – | 0 | 0 | – |
| 1986 | 1 | 1 | 100.0% | 0 | 0 | – |
| 1987 | 0 | 0 | – | 0 | 0 | – |
| 1988 | 1 | 1 | 100.0% | 0 | 0 | – |
| 1989 | 0 | 0 | – | 0 | 0 | – |
| 1990 | 0 | 1 | 0.0% | 0 | 0 | – |
| 1991 | 2 | 2 | 100.0% | 1 | 1 | 100.0% |
| 1992 | 0 | 0 | – | 0 | 0 | – |
| 1993 | 1 | 1 | 100.0% | 0 | 0 | – |
| 1994 | 0 | 0 | – | 0 | 0 | – |
| 1995 | 0 | 1 | 0.0% | 1 | 1 | 100.0% |
| 1996 | 0 | 0 | – | 0 | 0 | – |
| 1997 | 0 | 0 | – | 0 | 0 | – |
| 1998 | 0 | 1 | 0.0% | 0 | 1 | 0.0% |
| 1999 | 0 | 1 | 0.0% | 0 | 0 | – |
| 2000 | 0 | 0 | – | 0 | 1 | 0.0% |
| 2001 | 0 | 0 | – | 0 | 0 | – |
| 2002 | 0 | 0 | – | 0 | 0 | – |
| Total | 5 | 12 | 41.7% | 2 | 4 | 50.0% |

## Appendix 2

Table A.15.1 Number of total and successful applications by year by stage of application for uses in PED ST Zones (Cont'd)

| Year | Petitions to Governor-in-Council/ Planning Appeals ||| Extension of Time Limit |||
|---|---|---|---|---|---|---|
|  | Approvals | Total | Success Rates % | Approvals | Total | Success Rates % |
| 1976 | 0 | 0 | – | 0 | 0 | – |
| 1977 | 0 | 0 | – | 0 | 0 | – |
| 1978 | 0 | 0 | – | 0 | 0 | – |
| 1979 | 0 | 0 | – | 0 | 0 | – |
| 1980 | 0 | 0 | – | 0 | 0 | – |
| 1981 | 0 | 0 | – | 0 | 0 | – |
| 1982 | 0 | 0 | – | 0 | 0 | – |
| 1983 | 0 | 0 | – | 0 | 0 | – |
| 1984 | 0 | 0 | – | 0 | 0 | – |
| 1985 | 0 | 0 | – | 0 | 0 | – |
| 1986 | 0 | 0 | – | 0 | 0 | – |
| 1987 | 0 | 0 | – | 0 | 0 | – |
| 1988 | 0 | 0 | – | 0 | 0 | – |
| 1989 | 0 | 0 | – | 0 | 0 | – |
| 1990 | 0 | 0 | – | 0 | 0 | – |
| 1991 | 0 | 0 | – | 0 | 0 | – |
| 1992 | 0 | 0 | – | 0 | 0 | – |
| 1993 | 0 | 0 | – | 0 | 0 | – |
| 1994 | 0 | 0 | – | 0 | 0 | – |
| 1995 | 0 | 0 | – | 0 | 0 | – |
| 1996 | 0 | 0 | – | 0 | 0 | – |
| 1997 | 0 | 0 | – | 0 | 0 | – |
| 1998 | 0 | 0 | – | 0 | 0 | – |
| 1999 | 0 | 0 | – | 0 | 0 | – |
| 2000 | 0 | 0 | – | 0 | 0 | – |
| 2001 | 0 | 0 | – | 0 | 0 | – |
| 2002 | 0 | 0 | – | 0 | 0 | – |
| Total | 0 | 0 | – | 0 | 0 | – |

Table A.15.2 Number of successful applications by location for uses in PED ST Zones

| Location | Approvals | Total | Success Rates % |
|---|---|---|---|
| Hong Kong | 7 | 12 | 58.3% |
| Kowloon | 0 | 0 | – |
| Development Permission Area | 0 | 0 | – |
| New Towns | 0 | 0 | – |
| Rural | 0 | 0 | – |
| Total | 7 | 12 | 58.3% |

Table A.15.3 Number of successful applications by site area for uses in PED ST Zones

| Site Area | Approvals | Total | Success Rates % |
|---|---|---|---|
| Smaller than 0.1 ha | 7 | 12 | 58.3% |
| 0.1 ha to 1 ha | 0 | 0 | – |
| Larger than 1 ha | 0 | 0 | – |
| N/A | 0 | 0 | – |
| Total | 7 | 12 | 58.3% |

Table A.15.4 Number of successful applications by Gross Floor Area for uses in PED ST Zones

| GFA | Approvals | Total | Success Rates % |
|---|---|---|---|
| Smaller than 0.5 ha | 5 | 10 | 50.0% |
| 0.5 ha to 5 ha | 1 | 1 | 100.0% |
| Larger than 5 ha | 0 | 0 | – |
| N/A | 1 | 1 | 100.0% |
| Total | 7 | 12 | 58.3% |

Table A.15.5 Number of successful applications by applied use for PED ST Zones

| Applied Use | Approvals | Total | Success Rates % |
|---|---|---|---|
| Office | 4 | 7 | 57.1% |
| Other | 3 | 5 | 60.0% |
| Total | 7 | 12 | 58.3% |

## Residential Zones

Table A.16.1  Number of total and successful applications by year by stage of application for uses in R Zones

| Year | Planning Applications |||Planning Reviews|||
|---|---|---|---|---|---|---|
| | Approvals | Total | Success Rates % | Approvals | Total | Success Rates % |
| 1975 | 8 | 13 | 61.5% | 4 | 4 | 100.0% |
| 1976 | 17 | 18 | 94.4% | 2 | 2 | 100.0% |
| 1977 | 17 | 24 | 70.8% | 3 | 4 | 75.0% |
| 1978 | 13 | 21 | 61.9% | 4 | 8 | 50.0% |
| 1979 | 6 | 18 | 33.3% | 1 | 5 | 20.0% |
| 1980 | 14 | 26 | 53.8% | 4 | 11 | 36.4% |
| 1981 | 4 | 12 | 33.3% | 1 | 3 | 33.3% |
| 1982 | 5 | 6 | 83.3% | 0 | 2 | 0.0% |
| 1983 | 2 | 2 | 100.0% | 0 | 0 | – |
| 1984 | 3 | 4 | 75.0% | 0 | 0 | – |
| 1985 | 5 | 5 | 100.0% | 0 | 1 | 0.0% |
| 1986 | 3 | 3 | 100.0% | 0 | 0 | – |
| 1987 | 2 | 2 | 100.0% | 0 | 0 | – |
| Total | 99 | 154 | 64.3% | 19 | 40 | 47.5% |

| Year | Petitions to Governor-in-Council/ Planning Appeals |||Extension of Time Limit|||
|---|---|---|---|---|---|---|
| | Approvals | Total | Success Rates % | Approvals | Total | Success Rates % |
| 1975 | 0 | 0 | – | 0 | 0 | – |
| 1976 | 0 | 0 | – | 0 | 0 | – |
| 1977 | 0 | 0 | – | 0 | 0 | – |
| 1978 | 0 | 0 | – | 0 | 0 | – |
| 1979 | 0 | 1 | 0.0% | 0 | 0 | – |
| 1980 | 0 | 0 | – | 0 | 0 | – |
| 1981 | 0 | 0 | – | 0 | 0 | – |
| 1982 | 0 | 0 | – | 0 | 0 | – |
| 1983 | 0 | 0 | – | 0 | 0 | – |
| 1984 | 0 | 0 | – | 0 | 0 | – |
| 1985 | 0 | 0 | – | 0 | 0 | – |
| 1986 | 0 | 0 | – | 0 | 0 | – |
| 1987 | 0 | 0 | – | 0 | 0 | – |
| Total | 0 | 1 | 0.0% | 0 | 0 | – |

Table A.16.2  Number of successful applications by location for uses in R Zones

| Location | Approvals | Total | Success Rates % |
|---|---|---|---|
| Hong Kong | 41 | 51 | 80.4% |
| Kowloon | 71 | 103 | 68.9% |
| Development Permission Area | 0 | 0 | – |
| New Towns | 0 | 0 | – |
| Rural | 0 | 0 | – |
| Total | 112 | 154 | 72.7% |

Table A.16.3  Number of successful applications by site area for uses in R Zones

| Site Area | Approvals | Total | Success Rates % |
|---|---|---|---|
| Smaller than 0.1 ha | 83 | 119 | 69.7% |
| 0.1 ha to 1 ha | 19 | 22 | 86.4% |
| Larger than 1 ha | 2 | 2 | 100.0% |
| N/A | 8 | 11 | 72.7% |
| Total | 112 | 154 | 72.7% |

Table A.16.4  Number of successful applications by Gross Floor Area for uses in R Zones

| GFA | Approvals | Total | Success Rates % |
|---|---|---|---|
| Smaller than 0.5 ha | 62 | 77 | 80.5% |
| 0.5 ha to 5 ha | 10 | 14 | 71.4% |
| Larger than 5 ha | 1 | 1 | 100.0% |
| N/A | 39 | 62 | 62.9% |
| Total | 112 | 154 | 72.7% |

Table A.16.5  Number of successful applications by applied use for R Zones

| Applied Use | Approvals | Total | Success Rates % |
|---|---|---|---|
| Commercial | 40 | 48 | 83.3% |
| Office | 47 | 82 | 57.3% |
| School | 35 | 36 | 97.2% |
| Other | 6 | 8 | 75.0% |
| Total | 128 | 174 | 73.6% |

## Residential (Group A) Zones

Table A.17.1 Number of total and successful applications by year by stage of application for uses in R(A) Zones

| Year | Planning Applications | | | Planning Reviews | | |
|---|---|---|---|---|---|---|
| | Approvals | Total | Success Rates % | Approvals | Total | Success Rates % |
| 1977 | 3 | 4 | 75.0% | 0 | 0 | – |
| 1978 | 10 | 15 | 66.7% | 0 | 2 | 0.0% |
| 1979 | 15 | 22 | 68.2% | 3 | 3 | 100.0% |
| 1980 | 14 | 18 | 77.8% | 2 | 4 | 50.0% |
| 1981 | 17 | 26 | 65.4% | 1 | 3 | 33.3% |
| 1982 | 16 | 28 | 57.1% | 2 | 6 | 33.3% |
| 1983 | 24 | 28 | 85.7% | 2 | 4 | 50.0% |
| 1984 | 14 | 16 | 87.5% | 0 | 0 | – |
| 1985 | 38 | 39 | 97.4% | 0 | 1 | 0.0% |
| 1986 | 14 | 14 | 100.0% | 0 | 0 | – |
| 1987 | 17 | 19 | 89.5% | 1 | 1 | 100.0% |
| 1988 | 38 | 42 | 90.5% | 1 | 2 | 50.0% |
| 1989 | 70 | 88 | 79.5% | 3 | 5 | 60.0% |
| 1990 | 28 | 52 | 53.8% | 0 | 6 | 0.0% |
| 1991 | 24 | 38 | 63.2% | 2 | 3 | 66.7% |
| 1992 | 19 | 45 | 42.2% | 3 | 7 | 42.9% |
| 1993 | 47 | 79 | 59.5% | 4 | 13 | 30.8% |
| 1994 | 25 | 58 | 43.1% | 2 | 11 | 18.2% |
| 1995 | 43 | 63 | 68.3% | 7 | 10 | 70.0% |
| 1996 | 37 | 48 | 77.1% | 0 | 6 | 0.0% |
| 1997 | 34 | 41 | 82.9% | 3 | 5 | 60.0% |
| 1998 | 39 | 44 | 88.6% | 1 | 2 | 50.0% |
| 1999 | 98 | 100 | 98.0% | 0 | 0 | – |
| 2000 | 41 | 42 | 97.6% | 0 | 1 | 0.0% |
| 2001 | 57 | 59 | 96.6% | 0 | 0 | – |
| 2002 | 43 | 45 | 95.6% | 1 | 2 | 50.0% |
| Total | 825 | 1,073 | 76.9% | 38 | 97 | 39.2% |

Table A.17.1 Number of total and successful applications by year by stage of application for uses in R(A) Zones (Cont'd)

| Year | Petitions to Governor-in-Council/ Planning Appeals Approvals | Total | Success Rates % | Extension of Time Limit Approvals | Total | Success Rates % |
|---|---|---|---|---|---|---|
| 1977 | 0 | 0 | – | 0 | 0 | – |
| 1978 | 0 | 0 | – | 0 | 0 | – |
| 1979 | 0 | 0 | – | 0 | 0 | – |
| 1980 | 0 | 0 | – | 0 | 0 | – |
| 1981 | 0 | 0 | – | 0 | 0 | – |
| 1982 | 0 | 0 | – | 0 | 0 | – |
| 1983 | 0 | 0 | – | 0 | 0 | – |
| 1984 | 0 | 0 | – | 0 | 0 | – |
| 1985 | 0 | 0 | – | 0 | 0 | – |
| 1986 | 0 | 0 | – | 0 | 0 | – |
| 1987 | 0 | 0 | – | 0 | 0 | – |
| 1988 | 0 | 0 | – | 0 | 0 | – |
| 1989 | 0 | 0 | – | 0 | 0 | – |
| 1990 | 0 | 0 | – | 0 | 0 | – |
| 1991 | 0 | 0 | – | 0 | 0 | – |
| 1992 | 0 | 0 | – | 0 | 0 | – |
| 1993 | 0 | 1 | 0.0% | 2 | 2 | 100.0% |
| 1994 | 0 | 1 | 0.0% | 0 | 0 | – |
| 1995 | 0 | 0 | – | 3 | 3 | 100.0% |
| 1996 | 1 | 1 | 100.0% | 2 | 2 | 100.0% |
| 1997 | 0 | 0 | – | 4 | 4 | 100.0% |
| 1998 | 0 | 0 | – | 4 | 4 | 100.0% |
| 1999 | 0 | 0 | – | 0 | 0 | – |
| 2000 | 0 | 0 | – | 0 | 0 | – |
| 2001 | 0 | 0 | – | 1 | 1 | 100.0% |
| 2002 | 0 | 0 | – | 2 | 2 | 100.0% |
| Total | 1 | 3 | 33.3% | 18 | 18 | 100.0% |

Table A.17.2 Number of successful applications by location for uses in R(A) Zones

| Location | Approvals | Total | Success Rates % |
|---|---|---|---|
| Hong Kong | 257 | 349 | 73.6% |
| Kowloon | 413 | 527 | 78.4% |
| Development Permission Area | 0 | 0 | – |
| New Towns | 192 | 196 | 98.0% |
| Rural | 3 | 3 | 100.0% |
| Total | 865 | 1,075 | 80.5% |

Table A.17.3 Number of successful applications by site area for uses in R(A) Zones

| Site Area | Approvals | Total | Success Rates % |
|---|---|---|---|
| Smaller than 0.1 ha | 381 | 540 | 70.6% |
| 0.1 ha to 1 ha | 176 | 208 | 84.6% |
| Larger than 1 ha | 57 | 60 | 95.0% |
| N/A | 251 | 267 | 94.0% |
| Total | 865 | 1,075 | 80.5% |

Table A.17.4 Number of successful applications by Gross Floor Area for uses in R(A) Zones

| GFA | Approvals | Total | Success Rates % |
|---|---|---|---|
| Smaller than 0.5 ha | 460 | 590 | 78.0% |
| 0.5 ha to 5 ha | 238 | 308 | 77.3% |
| Larger than 5 ha | 28 | 32 | 87.5% |
| N/A | 139 | 145 | 95.9% |
| Total | 865 | 1,075 | 80.5% |

Table A.17.5 Number of successful applications by applied use for R(A) Zones

| Applied Use | Approvals | Total | Success Rates % |
|---|---|---|---|
| Commercial | 157 | 202 | 77.7% |
| Office | 237 | 389 | 60.9% |
| Residential | 55 | 65 | 84.6% |
| School | 210 | 212 | 99.1% |
| Massage | 55 | 64 | 85.9% |
| Utility | 111 | 112 | 99.1% |
| Car park | 28 | 31 | 90.3% |
| Religious | 40 | 42 | 95.2% |
| Hotel | 60 | 85 | 70.6% |
| Restaurant | 16 | 18 | 88.9% |
| Other | 45 | 50 | 90.0% |
| Total | 1,014 | 1,270 | 79.8% |

## Residential (Group B) Zones

Table A.18.1 Number of total and successful applications by year by stage of application for uses in R(B) Zones

| Year | Planning Applications Approvals | Total | Success Rates % | Planning Reviews Approvals | Total | Success Rates % |
|---|---|---|---|---|---|---|
| 1977 | 1 | 1 | 100.0% | 0 | 0 | – |
| 1978 | 1 | 1 | 100.0% | 0 | 0 | – |
| 1979 | 1 | 2 | 50.0% | 0 | 0 | – |
| 1980 | 0 | 5 | 0.0% | 1 | 6 | 16.7% |
| 1981 | 3 | 4 | 75.0% | 0 | 0 | – |
| 1982 | 4 | 8 | 50.0% | 0 | 1 | 0.0% |
| 1983 | 0 | 2 | 0.0% | 1 | 2 | 50.0% |
| 1984 | 8 | 16 | 50.0% | 2 | 3 | 66.7% |
| 1985 | 8 | 10 | 80.0% | 1 | 1 | 100.0% |
| 1986 | 10 | 13 | 76.9% | 2 | 2 | 100.0% |
| 1987 | 10 | 16 | 62.5% | 0 | 0 | – |
| 1988 | 10 | 22 | 45.5% | 1 | 6 | 16.7% |
| 1989 | 4 | 9 | 44.4% | 3 | 4 | 75.0% |
| 1990 | 10 | 19 | 52.6% | 0 | 1 | 0.0% |
| 1991 | 18 | 35 | 51.4% | 1 | 9 | 11.1% |
| 1992 | 10 | 16 | 62.5% | 0 | 4 | 0.0% |
| 1993 | 5 | 9 | 55.6% | 0 | 0 | – |
| 1994 | 10 | 16 | 62.5% | 1 | 3 | 33.3% |
| 1995 | 11 | 14 | 78.6% | 1 | 2 | 50.0% |
| 1996 | 3 | 4 | 75.0% | 0 | 0 | – |
| 1997 | 10 | 11 | 90.9% | 0 | 0 | – |
| 1998 | 16 | 18 | 88.9% | 0 | 0 | – |
| 1999 | 11 | 13 | 84.6% | 0 | 0 | – |
| 2000 | 27 | 32 | 84.4% | 0 | 1 | 0.0% |
| 2001 | 23 | 25 | 92.0% | 0 | 1 | 0.0% |
| 2002 | 23 | 32 | 71.9% | 1 | 2 | 50.0% |
| Total | 237 | 353 | 67.1% | 15 | 48 | 31.3% |

## 162  Appendix 2

**Table A.18.1  Number of total and successful applications by year by stage of application for uses in R(B) Zones (Cont'd)**

| Year | Petitions to Governor-in-Council/ Planning Appeals Approvals | Total | Success Rates % | Extension of Time Limit Approvals | Total | Success Rates % |
|---|---|---|---|---|---|---|
| 1977 | 0 | 0 | – | 0 | 0 | – |
| 1978 | 0 | 0 | – | 0 | 0 | – |
| 1979 | 0 | 0 | – | 0 | 0 | – |
| 1980 | 0 | 0 | – | 0 | 0 | – |
| 1981 | 0 | 0 | – | 0 | 0 | – |
| 1982 | 0 | 0 | – | 0 | 0 | – |
| 1983 | 1 | 1 | 100.0% | 0 | 0 | – |
| 1984 | 0 | 0 | – | 0 | 0 | – |
| 1985 | 0 | 0 | – | 0 | 0 | – |
| 1986 | 0 | 0 | – | 0 | 0 | – |
| 1987 | 0 | 0 | – | 0 | 0 | – |
| 1988 | 0 | 0 | – | 0 | 0 | – |
| 1989 | 0 | 0 | – | 0 | 0 | – |
| 1990 | 0 | 0 | – | 0 | 0 | – |
| 1991 | 0 | 0 | – | 0 | 0 | – |
| 1992 | 0 | 2 | 0.0% | 0 | 0 | – |
| 1993 | 0 | 0 | – | 1 | 1 | 100.0% |
| 1994 | 0 | 0 | – | 2 | 2 | 100.0% |
| 1995 | 0 | 0 | – | 0 | 0 | – |
| 1996 | 0 | 0 | – | 2 | 2 | 100.0% |
| 1997 | 0 | 0 | – | 1 | 1 | 100.0% |
| 1998 | 0 | 0 | – | 1 | 1 | 100.0% |
| 1999 | 0 | 0 | – | 0 | 0 | – |
| 2000 | 0 | 0 | – | 0 | 0 | – |
| 2001 | 0 | 0 | – | 3 | 3 | 100.0% |
| 2002 | 0 | 0 | – | 1 | 1 | 100.0% |
| Total | 1 | 3 | 33.3% | 11 | 11 | 100.0% |

Table A.18.2 Number of successful applications by location for uses in R(B) Zones

| Location | Approvals | Total | Success Rates % |
|---|---|---|---|
| Hong Kong | 80 | 119 | 67.2% |
| Kowloon | 50 | 78 | 64.1% |
| Development Permission Area | 4 | 6 | 66.7% |
| New Towns | 101 | 121 | 83.5% |
| Rural | 18 | 30 | 60.0% |
| Total | 253 | 354 | 71.5% |

Table A.18.3 Number of successful applications by site area for uses in R(B) Zones

| Site Area | Approvals | Total | Success Rates % |
|---|---|---|---|
| Smaller than 0.1 ha | 69 | 97 | 71.1% |
| 0.1 ha to 1 ha | 69 | 109 | 63.3% |
| Larger than 1 ha | 54 | 67 | 80.6% |
| N/A | 61 | 81 | 75.3% |
| Total | 253 | 354 | 71.5% |

Table A.18.4 Number of successful applications by Gross Floor Area for uses in R(B) Zones

| GFA | Approvals | Total | Success Rates % |
|---|---|---|---|
| Smaller than 0.5 ha | 164 | 217 | 75.6% |
| 0.5 ha to 5 ha | 43 | 71 | 60.6% |
| Larger than 5 ha | 20 | 25 | 80.0% |
| N/A | 26 | 41 | 63.4% |
| Total | 253 | 354 | 71.5% |

Table A.18.5 Number of successful applications by applied use for R(B) Zones

| Applied Use | Approvals | Total | Success Rates % |
|---|---|---|---|
| Commercial | 28 | 56 | 50.0% |
| Residential | 40 | 56 | 71.4% |
| School | 74 | 80 | 92.5% |
| Petrol-filling Station | 8 | 13 | 61.5% |
| Restaurant | 8 | 15 | 53.3% |
| Community | 24 | 25 | 96.0% |
| Hotel | 13 | 29 | 44.8% |
| Other | 83 | 109 | 76.1% |
| Total | 278 | 383 | 72.6% |

## Residential (Group C) Zones

Table A.19.1 Number of total and successful applications by year by stage of application for uses in R(C) Zones

| Year | Planning Applications Approvals | Total | Success Rates % | Planning Reviews Approvals | Total | Success Rates % |
|---|---|---|---|---|---|---|
| 1979 | 0 | 3 | 0.0% | 1 | 1 | 100.0% |
| 1980 | 1 | 2 | 50.0% | 1 | 1 | 100.0% |
| 1981 | 0 | 1 | 0.0% | 1 | 1 | 100.0% |
| 1982 | 1 | 4 | 25.0% | 1 | 2 | 50.0% |
| 1983 | 0 | 0 | – | 0 | 1 | 0.0% |
| 1984 | 4 | 5 | 80.0% | 0 | 0 | – |
| 1985 | 7 | 7 | 100.0% | 0 | 1 | 0.0% |
| 1986 | 8 | 9 | 88.9% | 0 | 0 | – |
| 1987 | 6 | 10 | 60.0% | 1 | 2 | 50.0% |
| 1988 | 8 | 15 | 53.3% | 1 | 3 | 33.3% |
| 1989 | 6 | 15 | 40.0% | 2 | 2 | 100.0% |
| 1990 | 8 | 20 | 40.0% | 2 | 7 | 28.6% |
| 1991 | 10 | 25 | 40.0% | 1 | 3 | 33.3% |
| 1992 | 14 | 29 | 48.3% | 3 | 4 | 75.0% |
| 1993 | 6 | 10 | 60.0% | 1 | 3 | 33.3% |
| 1994 | 8 | 21 | 38.1% | 0 | 1 | 0.0% |
| 1995 | 8 | 24 | 33.3% | 2 | 6 | 33.3% |
| 1996 | 15 | 27 | 55.6% | 1 | 5 | 20.0% |
| 1997 | 8 | 20 | 40.0% | 2 | 5 | 40.0% |
| 1998 | 14 | 22 | 63.6% | 0 | 3 | 0.0% |
| 1999 | 21 | 31 | 67.7% | 1 | 4 | 25.0% |
| 2000 | 26 | 48 | 54.2% | 0 | 3 | 0.0% |
| 2001 | 38 | 50 | 76.0% | 1 | 6 | 16.7% |
| 2002 | 30 | 49 | 61.2% | 4 | 8 | 50.0% |
| Total | 247 | 447 | 55.3% | 26 | 72 | 36.1% |

Table A.19.1 Number of total and successful applications by year by stage of application for uses in R(C) Zones (Cont'd)

| Year | Petitions to Governor-in-Council/ Planning Appeals ||| Extension of Time Limit |||
| --- | --- | --- | --- | --- | --- | --- |
|  | Approvals | Total | Success Rates % | Approvals | Total | Success Rates % |
| 1979 | 0 | 0 | – | 0 | 0 | – |
| 1980 | 0 | 0 | – | 0 | 0 | – |
| 1981 | 0 | 0 | – | 0 | 0 | – |
| 1982 | 0 | 0 | – | 0 | 0 | – |
| 1983 | 0 | 0 | – | 0 | 0 | – |
| 1984 | 0 | 0 | – | 0 | 0 | – |
| 1985 | 0 | 0 | – | 0 | 0 | – |
| 1986 | 0 | 0 | – | 0 | 0 | – |
| 1987 | 0 | 0 | – | 0 | 0 | – |
| 1988 | 0 | 0 | – | 0 | 0 | – |
| 1989 | 0 | 0 | – | 0 | 0 | – |
| 1990 | 0 | 0 | – | 0 | 0 | – |
| 1991 | 0 | 0 | – | 0 | 0 | – |
| 1992 | 0 | 0 | – | 0 | 0 | – |
| 1993 | 0 | 0 | – | 0 | 0 | – |
| 1994 | 1 | 1 | 100.0% | 0 | 0 | – |
| 1995 | 0 | 0 | – | 1 | 1 | 100.0% |
| 1996 | 0 | 0 | – | 2 | 2 | 100.0% |
| 1997 | 0 | 0 | – | 0 | 0 | – |
| 1998 | 0 | 0 | – | 2 | 2 | 100.0% |
| 1999 | 0 | 0 | – | 0 | 0 | – |
| 2000 | 0 | 0 | – | 0 | 0 | – |
| 2001 | 0 | 0 | – | 4 | 4 | 100.0% |
| 2002 | 0 | 0 | – | 0 | 0 | – |
| Total | 1 | 1 | 100.0% | 9 | 9 | 100.0% |

Table A.19.2  Number of successful applications by location for uses in R(C) Zones

| Location | Approvals | Total | Success Rates % |
|---|---|---|---|
| Hong Kong | 120 | 171 | 70.2% |
| Kowloon | 67 | 128 | 52.3% |
| Development Permission Area | 10 | 17 | 58.8% |
| New Towns | 26 | 44 | 59.1% |
| Rural | 50 | 87 | 57.5% |
| Total | 273 | 447 | 61.1% |

Table A.19.3  Number of successful applications by site area for uses in R(C) Zones

| Site Area | Approvals | Total | Success Rates % |
|---|---|---|---|
| Smaller than 0.1 ha | 69 | 128 | 53.9% |
| 0.1 ha to 1 ha | 148 | 239 | 61.9% |
| Larger than 1 ha | 30 | 48 | 62.5% |
| N/A | 26 | 32 | 81.3% |
| Total | 273 | 447 | 61.1% |

Table A.19.4  Number of successful applications by Gross Floor Area for uses in R(C) Zones

| GFA | Approvals | Total | Success Rates % |
|---|---|---|---|
| Smaller than 0.5 ha | 168 | 279 | 60.2% |
| 0.5 ha to 5 ha | 48 | 78 | 61.5% |
| Larger than 5 ha | 7 | 8 | 87.5% |
| N/A | 50 | 82 | 61.0% |
| Total | 273 | 447 | 61.1% |

Table A.19.5  Number of successful applications by applied use for R(C) Zones

| Applied Use | Approvals | Total | Success Rates % |
|---|---|---|---|
| Residential | 115 | 181 | 63.5% |
| School | 52 | 83 | 62.7% |
| Petrol-filling Station | 6 | 22 | 27.3% |
| Religious | 13 | 17 | 76.5% |
| Car Park | 9 | 16 | 56.3% |
| Nursery | 7 | 11 | 63.6% |
| Container / Open Storage | 10 | 25 | 40.0% |
| Other | 61 | 92 | 66.3% |
| Total | 273 | 447 | 61.1% |

## Residential (Group D) Zones

Table A.20.1  Number of total and successful applications by year by stage of application for uses in R(C) Zones

|  | Planning Applications ||| Planning Reviews |||
| --- | --- | --- | --- | --- | --- | --- |
| Year | Approvals | Total | Success Rates % | Approvals | Total | Success Rates % |
| 1994 | 1 | 5 | 20.0% | 0 | 0 | – |
| 1995 | 2 | 9 | 22.2% | 0 | 3 | 0.0% |
| 1996 | 11 | 23 | 47.8% | 0 | 1 | 0.0% |
| 1997 | 19 | 41 | 46.3% | 4 | 13 | 30.8% |
| 1998 | 22 | 40 | 55.0% | 1 | 10 | 10.0% |
| 1999 | 57 | 69 | 82.6% | 0 | 4 | 0.0% |
| 2000 | 38 | 62 | 61.3% | 0 | 4 | 0.0% |
| 2001 | 12 | 44 | 27.3% | 6 | 10 | 60.0% |
| 2002 | 23 | 49 | 46.9% | 5 | 8 | 62.5% |
| Total | 185 | 342 | 54.1% | 16 | 53 | 30.2% |

|  | Planning Appeals ||| Extension of Time Limit |||
| --- | --- | --- | --- | --- | --- | --- |
| Year | Approvals | Total | Success Rates % | Approvals | Total | Success Rates % |
| 1994 | 0 | 0 | – | 0 | 0 | – |
| 1995 | 0 | 0 | – | 0 | 0 | – |
| 1996 | 0 | 2 | 0.0% | 0 | 0 | – |
| 1997 | 0 | 0 | – | 0 | 0 | – |
| 1998 | 0 | 0 | – | 2 | 2 | 100.0% |
| 1999 | 0 | 0 | – | 0 | 0 | – |
| 2000 | 0 | 0 | – | 10 | 10 | 100.0% |
| 2001 | 0 | 0 | – | 39 | 42 | 92.9% |
| 2002 | 0 | 1 | 0.0% | 19 | 19 | 100.0% |
| Total | 0 | 3 | 0.0% | 70 | 73 | 95.9% |

*168  Appendix 2*

Table A.20.2  Number of successful applications by location for uses in R(D) Zones

| Location | Approvals | Total | Success Rates % |
|---|---|---|---|
| Hong Kong | 0 | 0 | – |
| Kowloon | 0 | 0 | – |
| Development Permission Area | 0 | 0 | – |
| New Towns | 2 | 4 | 50.0% |
| Rural | 196 | 338 | 58.0% |
| Total | 198 | 342 | 57.9% |

Table A.20.3  Number of successful applications by site area for uses in R(D) Zones

| Site Area | Approvals | Total | Success Rates % |
|---|---|---|---|
| Smaller than 0.1 ha | 43 | 88 | 48.9% |
| 0.1 ha to 1 ha | 135 | 224 | 60.3% |
| Larger than 1 ha | 20 | 30 | 66.7% |
| N/A | 0 | 0 | – |
| Total | 198 | 342 | 57.9% |

Table A.20.4  Number of successful applications by Gross Floor Area for uses in R(D) Zones

| GFA | Approvals | Total | Success Rates % |
|---|---|---|---|
| Smaller than 0.5 ha | 38 | 81 | 46.9% |
| 0.5 ha to 5 ha | 1 | 2 | 50.0% |
| Larger than 5 ha | 0 | 0 | – |
| N/A | 159 | 259 | 61.4% |
| Total | 198 | 342 | 57.9% |

Table A.20.5  Number of successful applications by applied use for R(D) Zones

| Applied Use | Approvals | Total | Success Rates % |
|---|---|---|---|
| Car park | 26 | 46 | 56.5% |
| Container | 40 | 61 | 65.6% |
| Open Storage | 98 | 158 | 62.0% |
| Residential | 11 | 22 | 50.0% |
| Village Type House | 13 | 42 | 31.0% |
| Other | 23 | 38 | 60.5% |
| Total | 211 | 367 | 57.5% |

## Residential (Group E) Zones

Table A.21.1  Number of total and successful applications by year by stage of application for uses in R(E) Zones

| | Planning Applications ||| Planning Reviews |||
|---|---|---|---|---|---|---|
| Year | Approvals | Total | Success Rates % | Approvals | Total | Success Rates % |
| 1999 | 1 | 1 | 100.0% | 0 | 0 | – |
| 2000 | 12 | 14 | 85.7% | 0 | 1 | 0.0% |
| 2001 | 11 | 17 | 64.7% | 0 | 1 | 0.0% |
| 2002 | 18 | 26 | 69.2% | 2 | 5 | 40.0% |
| Total | 42 | 58 | 72.4% | 2 | 7 | 28.6% |

| | Planning Appeals ||| Extension of Time Limit |||
|---|---|---|---|---|---|---|
| Year | Approvals | Total | Success Rates % | Approvals | Total | Success Rates % |
| 1999 | 0 | 0 | – | 0 | 0 | – |
| 2000 | 0 | 0 | – | 0 | 0 | – |
| 2001 | 0 | 0 | – | 0 | 0 | – |
| 2002 | 0 | 0 | – | 1 | 1 | 100.0% |
| Total | 0 | 0 | – | 1 | 1 | 100.0% |

## 170  Appendix 2

Table A.21.2  Number of successful applications by location for uses in R(E) Zones

| Location | Approvals | Total | Success Rates % |
|---|---|---|---|
| Hong Kong | 4 | 5 | 80.0% |
| Kowloon | 25 | 27 | 92.6% |
| Development Permission Area | 0 | 0 | – |
| New Towns | 2 | 4 | 50.0% |
| Rural | 13 | 22 | 59.1% |
| Total | 44 | 58 | 75.9% |

Table A.21.3  Number of successful applications by site area for uses in R(E) Zones

| Site Area | Approvals | Total | Success Rates % |
|---|---|---|---|
| Smaller than 0.1 ha | 14 | 17 | 82.4% |
| 0.1 ha to 1 ha | 20 | 30 | 66.7% |
| Larger than 1 ha | 8 | 9 | 88.9% |
| N/A | 2 | 2 | 100.0% |
| Total | 44 | 58 | 75.9% |

Table A.21.4  Number of successful applications by Gross Floor Area for uses in R(E) Zones

| GFA | Approvals | Total | Success Rates % |
|---|---|---|---|
| Smaller than 0.5 ha | 11 | 15 | 73.3% |
| 0.5 ha to 5 ha | 19 | 21 | 90.5% |
| Larger than 5 ha | 5 | 6 | 83.3% |
| N/A | 9 | 16 | 56.3% |
| Total | 44 | 58 | 75.9% |

Table A.21.5  Number of successful applications by applied use for R(E) Zones

| Applied Use | Approvals | Total | Success Rates % |
|---|---|---|---|
| Residential | 26 | 32 | 81.3% |
| Other | 18 | 26 | 69.2% |
| Total | 44 | 58 | 75.9% |

## Recreation Zones

Table A.22.1  Number of total and successful applications by year by stage of application for uses in REC Zones

| Year | Planning Applications |||Planning Reviews|||
|---|---|---|---|---|---|---|
| | Approvals | Total | Success Rates % | Approvals | Total | Success Rates % |
| 1994 | 1 | 3 | 33.3% | 0 | 0 | – |
| 1995 | 12 | 18 | 66.7% | 0 | 3 | 0.0% |
| 1996 | 9 | 23 | 39.1% | 1 | 8 | 12.5% |
| 1997 | 18 | 37 | 48.6% | 2 | 3 | 66.7% |
| 1998 | 14 | 42 | 33.3% | 2 | 13 | 15.4% |
| 1999 | 33 | 46 | 71.7% | 2 | 7 | 28.6% |
| 2000 | 15 | 26 | 57.7% | 1 | 2 | 50.0% |
| 2001 | 15 | 34 | 44.1% | 4 | 7 | 57.1% |
| 2002 | 14 | 31 | 45.2% | 1 | 4 | 25.0% |
| Total | 131 | 260 | 50.4% | 13 | 47 | 27.7% |

| Year | Planning Appeals |||Extension of Time Limit|||
|---|---|---|---|---|---|---|
| | Approvals | Total | Success Rates % | Approvals | Total | Success Rates % |
| 1994 | 0 | 0 | – | 0 | 0 | – |
| 1995 | 0 | 0 | – | 0 | 0 | – |
| 1996 | 0 | 0 | – | 1 | 1 | 100.0% |
| 1997 | 0 | 0 | – | 4 | 4 | 100.0% |
| 1998 | 0 | 0 | – | 4 | 5 | 80.0% |
| 1999 | 0 | 1 | 0.0% | 5 | 5 | 100.0% |
| 2000 | 0 | 0 | – | 6 | 6 | 100.0% |
| 2001 | 0 | 0 | – | 5 | 5 | 100.0% |
| 2002 | 0 | 0 | – | 6 | 6 | 100.0% |
| Total | 0 | 1 | 0.0% | 31 | 32 | 96.9% |

## Appendix 2

Table A.22.2 Number of successful applications by location for uses in REC Zones

| Location | Approvals | Total | Success Rates % |
|---|---|---|---|
| Hong Kong | 0 | 0 | – |
| Kowloon | 0 | 0 | – |
| Development Permission Area | 0 | 0 | – |
| New Towns | 1 | 2 | 50.0% |
| Rural | 142 | 258 | 55.0% |
| Total | 143 | 260 | 55.0% |

Table A.22.3 Number of successful applications by site area for uses in REC Zones

| Site Area | Approvals | Total | Success Rates % |
|---|---|---|---|
| Smaller than 0.1 ha | 71 | 97 | 73.2% |
| 0.1 ha to 1 ha | 42 | 97 | 43.3% |
| Larger than 1 ha | 30 | 65 | 46.2% |
| N/A | 0 | 1 | 0.0% |
| Total | 143 | 260 | 55.0% |

Table A.22.4 Number of successful applications by Gross Floor Area for uses in REC Zones

| GFA | Approvals | Total | Success Rates % |
|---|---|---|---|
| Smaller than 0.5 ha | 70 | 88 | 79.5% |
| 0.5 ha to 5 ha | 4 | 11 | 36.4% |
| Larger than 5 ha | 0 | 2 | 0.0% |
| N/A | 69 | 159 | 43.4% |
| Total | 143 | 260 | 55.0% |

Table A.22.5 Number of successful applications by applied use for REC Zones

| Applied Use | Approvals | Total | Success Rates % |
|---|---|---|---|
| Car Park | 11 | 27 | 40.7% |
| Container | 9 | 36 | 25.0% |
| Open Storage | 43 | 92 | 46.7% |
| Residential | 6 | 20 | 30.0% |
| Village Type House | 39 | 46 | 84.8% |
| Warehouse | 9 | 17 | 52.9% |
| Other | 32 | 44 | 72.7% |
| Total | 149 | 282 | 52.8% |

# Road Zones

Table A.23.1 Number of total and successful applications by year by stage of application for uses in Road Zones

| Year | Planning Applications ||| Planning Reviews |||
|---|---|---|---|---|---|---|
| | Approvals | Total | Success Rates % | Approvals | Total | Success Rates % |
| 1978 | 1 | 1 | 100.0% | 0 | 0 | – |
| 1979 | 0 | 0 | – | 0 | 0 | – |
| 1980 | 0 | 0 | – | 0 | 0 | – |
| 1981 | 0 | 0 | – | 0 | 0 | – |
| 1982 | 0 | 0 | – | 0 | 0 | – |
| 1983 | 7 | 8 | 87.5% | 0 | 1 | 0.0% |
| 1984 | 1 | 1 | 100.0% | 0 | 0 | – |
| 1985 | 2 | 2 | 100.0% | 0 | 0 | – |
| 1986 | 3 | 3 | 100.0% | 0 | 0 | – |
| 1987 | 7 | 7 | 100.0% | 0 | 0 | – |
| 1988 | 4 | 6 | 66.7% | 0 | 0 | – |
| 1989 | 3 | 6 | 50.0% | 0 | 1 | 0.0% |
| 1990 | 6 | 7 | 85.7% | 1 | 1 | 100.0% |
| 1991 | 4 | 10 | 40.0% | 1 | 1 | 100.0% |
| 1992 | 7 | 13 | 53.8% | 0 | 1 | 0.0% |
| 1993 | 9 | 15 | 60.0% | 0 | 1 | 0.0% |
| 1994 | 10 | 16 | 62.5% | 1 | 3 | 33.3% |
| 1995 | 3 | 9 | 33.3% | 0 | 0 | – |
| 1996 | 7 | 10 | 70.0% | 1 | 3 | 33.3% |
| 1997 | 22 | 26 | 84.6% | 0 | 1 | 0.0% |
| 1998 | 14 | 19 | 73.7% | 1 | 1 | 100.0% |
| 1999 | 19 | 19 | 100.0% | 0 | 1 | 0.0% |
| 2000 | 16 | 19 | 84.2% | 0 | 0 | – |
| 2001 | 25 | 28 | 89.3% | 0 | 0 | – |
| 2002 | 24 | 32 | 75.0% | 1 | 2 | 50.0% |
| Total | 194 | 257 | 75.5% | 6 | 17 | 35.3% |

## Appendix 2

Table A.23.1  Number of total and successful applications by year by stage of application for uses in Road Zones (Cont'd)

| Year | Petitions to Governor-in-Council/ Planning Appeals Approvals | Total | Success Rates % | Extension of Time Limit Approvals | Total | Success Rates % |
|---|---|---|---|---|---|---|
| 1978 | 0 | 0 | – | 0 | 0 | – |
| 1979 | 0 | 0 | – | 0 | 0 | – |
| 1980 | 0 | 0 | – | 0 | 0 | – |
| 1981 | 0 | 0 | – | 0 | 0 | – |
| 1982 | 0 | 0 | – | 0 | 0 | – |
| 1983 | 0 | 0 | – | 0 | 0 | – |
| 1984 | 0 | 0 | – | 0 | 0 | – |
| 1985 | 0 | 0 | – | 0 | 0 | – |
| 1986 | 0 | 0 | – | 0 | 0 | – |
| 1987 | 0 | 0 | – | 0 | 0 | – |
| 1988 | 0 | 0 | – | 0 | 0 | – |
| 1989 | 1 | 1 | 100.0% | 0 | 0 | – |
| 1990 | 0 | 0 | – | 0 | 0 | – |
| 1991 | 0 | 0 | – | 0 | 0 | – |
| 1992 | 0 | 0 | – | 0 | 0 | – |
| 1993 | 0 | 0 | – | 2 | 2 | 100.0% |
| 1994 | 0 | 1 | 0.0% | 0 | 0 | – |
| 1995 | 0 | 0 | – | 2 | 2 | 100.0% |
| 1996 | 0 | 0 | – | 4 | 5 | 80.0% |
| 1997 | 0 | 0 | – | 2 | 2 | 100.0% |
| 1998 | 0 | 0 | – | 3 | 4 | 75.0% |
| 1999 | 0 | 0 | – | 4 | 4 | 100.0% |
| 2000 | 0 | 0 | – | 2 | 2 | 100.0% |
| 2001 | 0 | 0 | – | 3 | 3 | 100.0% |
| 2002 | 0 | 0 | – | 10 | 10 | 100.0% |
| Total | 1 | 2 | 50.0% | 32 | 34 | 94.1% |

Table A.23.2  Number of successful applications by location for uses in Road Zones

| Location | Approvals | Total | Success Rates % |
|---|---|---|---|
| Hong Kong | 65 | 81 | 80.2% |
| Kowloon | 43 | 52 | 82.7% |
| Development Permission Area | 2 | 10 | 20.0% |
| New Towns | 35 | 42 | 83.3% |
| Rural | 54 | 72 | 75.0% |
| Total | 199 | 257 | 77.4% |

Table A.23.3  Number of successful applications by site area for uses in Road Zones

| Site Area | Approvals | Total | Success Rates % |
|---|---|---|---|
| Smaller than 0.1 ha | 64 | 90 | 71.1% |
| 0.1 ha to 1 ha | 77 | 97 | 79.4% |
| Larger than 1 ha | 45 | 55 | 81.8% |
| N/A | 13 | 15 | 86.7% |
| Total | 199 | 257 | 77.4% |

Table A.23.4  Number of successful applications by Gross Floor Area for uses in Road Zones

| GFA | Approvals | Total | Success Rates % |
|---|---|---|---|
| Smaller than 0.5 ha | 83 | 116 | 71.6% |
| 0.5 ha to 5 ha | 34 | 42 | 81.0% |
| Larger than 5 ha | 25 | 28 | 89.3% |
| N/A | 57 | 71 | 80.3% |
| Total | 199 | 257 | 77.4% |

Table A.23.5  Number of successful applications by applied use for Road Zones

| Applied Use | Approvals | Total | Success Rates % |
|---|---|---|---|
| Commercial | 41 | 47 | 87.2% |
| Residential | 37 | 50 | 74.0% |
| Utility | 38 | 41 | 92.7% |
| Petrol-filling Station | 7 | 14 | 50.0% |
| Village Type House | 6 | 13 | 46.2% |
| Other | 86 | 109 | 78.9% |
| Total | 215 | 274 | 78.5% |

## Recreation Priority Area (RPA) Zones

Table A.24.1  Number of total and successful applications by year by stage of application for uses in RPA Zones

| Year | Planning Applications Approvals | Total | Success Rates % | Planning Reviews Approvals | Total | Success Rates % |
|---|---|---|---|---|---|---|
| 1987 | 0 | 1 | 0.0% | 0 | 0 | – |
| 1988 | 0 | 0 | – | 0 | 1 | 0.0% |
| 1989 | 0 | 1 | 0.0% | 0 | 0 | – |
| 1990 | 1 | 1 | 100.0% | 0 | 0 | – |
| 1991 | 0 | 0 | – | 0 | 0 | – |
| 1992 | 0 | 0 | – | 0 | 0 | – |
| 1993 | 0 | 0 | – | 0 | 0 | – |
| 1994 | 0 | 0 | – | 0 | 0 | – |
| 1995 | 0 | 0 | – | 0 | 0 | – |
| 1996 | 0 | 0 | – | 0 | 0 | – |
| 1997 | 2 | 3 | 66.7% | 0 | 0 | – |
| 1998 | 1 | 2 | 50.0% | 0 | 1 | 0.0% |
| 1999 | 2 | 2 | 100.0% | 0 | 0 | – |
| 2000 | 1 | 2 | 50.0% | 1 | 1 | 100.0% |
| 2001 | 0 | 0 | – | 0 | 0 | – |
| 2002 | 1 | 1 | 100.0% | 0 | 0 | – |
| Total | 8 | 13 | 61.5% | 1 | 3 | 33.3% |

Table A.24.1 Number of total and successful applications by year by stage of application for uses in RPA Zones (Cont'd)

| Year | Petitions to Governor-in-Council/ Planning Appeals Approvals | Total | Success Rates % | Extension of Time Limit Approvals | Total | Success Rates % |
|---|---|---|---|---|---|---|
| 1987 | 0 | 0 | – | 0 | 0 | – |
| 1988 | 0 | 0 | – | 0 | 0 | – |
| 1989 | 0 | 0 | – | 0 | 0 | – |
| 1990 | 0 | 0 | – | 0 | 0 | – |
| 1991 | 0 | 0 | – | 0 | 0 | – |
| 1992 | 0 | 0 | – | 1 | 1 | 100.0% |
| 1993 | 0 | 0 | – | 0 | 0 | – |
| 1994 | 0 | 0 | – | 1 | 1 | 100.0% |
| 1995 | 0 | 0 | – | 0 | 0 | – |
| 1996 | 0 | 0 | – | 1 | 1 | 100.0% |
| 1997 | 0 | 0 | – | 0 | 0 | – |
| 1998 | 0 | 0 | – | 0 | 0 | – |
| 1999 | 0 | 0 | – | 0 | 0 | – |
| 2000 | 0 | 0 | – | 0 | 0 | – |
| 2001 | 0 | 0 | – | 0 | 0 | – |
| 2002 | 0 | 0 | – | 0 | 0 | – |
| Total | 0 | 0 | – | 3 | 3 | 100.0% |

Table A.24.2 Number of successful applications by location for uses in RPA Zones

| Location | Approvals | Total | Success Rates % |
|---|---|---|---|
| Hong Kong | 0 | 0 | – |
| Kowloon | 0 | 0 | – |
| Development Permission Area | 0 | 0 | – |
| New Towns | 8 | 13 | 61.5% |
| Rural | 0 | 0 | – |
| Total | 8 | 13 | 61.5% |

Table A.24.3  Number of successful applications by site area for uses in RPA Zones

| Site Area | Approvals | Total | Success Rates % |
|---|---|---|---|
| Smaller than 0.1 ha | 0 | 0 | – |
| 0.1 ha to 1 ha | 1 | 2 | 50.0% |
| Larger than 1 ha | 7 | 11 | 63.6% |
| N/A | 0 | 0 | – |
| Total | 8 | 13 | 61.5% |

Table A.24.4  Number of successful applications by Gross Floor Area for uses in RPA Zones

| GFA | Approvals | Total | Success Rates % |
|---|---|---|---|
| Smaller than 0.5 ha | 1 | 2 | 50.0% |
| 0.5 ha to 5 ha | 7 | 7 | 100.0% |
| Larger than 5 ha | 0 | 4 | 0.0% |
| N/A | 0 | 0 | – |
| Total | 8 | 13 | 61.5% |

Table A.24.5  Number of successful applications by applied use for RPA Zones

| Applied Use | Approvals | Total | Success Rates % |
|---|---|---|---|
| Residential | 3 | 6 | 50.0% |
| Other | 5 | 7 | 71.4% |
| Total | 8 | 13 | 61.5% |

Appendix 2  179

# Site of Special Scientific Interest (SSSI) Zones

Table A.25.1  Number of total and successful applications by year by stage of application for uses in SSSI Zones

|      | Planning Applications ||| Planning Reviews |||
|------|-----------|-------|------------------|-----------|-------|------------------|
| Year | Approvals | Total | Success Rates % | Approvals | Total | Success Rates % |
| 1992 | 0 | 1 | 0.0% | 0 | 0 | – |
| 1993 | 0 | 1 | 0.0% | 0 | 2 | 0.0% |
| 1994 | 1 | 2 | 50.0% | 0 | 0 | – |
| 1995 | 0 | 0 | – | 0 | 0 | – |
| 1996 | 0 | 0 | – | 0 | 0 | – |
| 1997 | 2 | 2 | 100.0% | 0 | 0 | – |
| 1998 | 0 | 0 | – | 0 | 0 | – |
| 1999 | 2 | 2 | 100.0% | 0 | 0 | – |
| 2000 | 0 | 0 | – | 0 | 0 | – |
| 2001 | 2 | 2 | 100.0% | 0 | 0 | – |
| 2002 | 1 | 1 | 100.0% | 0 | 0 | – |
| Total | 8 | 11 | 72.7% | 0 | 2 | 0.0% |

|      | Planning Appeals ||| Extension of Time Limit |||
|------|-----------|-------|------------------|-----------|-------|------------------|
| Year | Approvals | Total | Success Rates % | Approvals | Total | Success Rates % |
| 1992 | 0 | 0 | – | 0 | 0 | – |
| 1993 | 0 | 0 | – | 0 | 0 | – |
| 1994 | 1 | 1 | 100.0% | 0 | 0 | – |
| 1995 | 0 | 0 | – | 0 | 0 | – |
| 1996 | 0 | 0 | – | 0 | 0 | – |
| 1997 | 0 | 0 | – | 0 | 0 | – |
| 1998 | 0 | 0 | – | 0 | 0 | – |
| 1999 | 0 | 0 | – | 0 | 0 | – |
| 2000 | 0 | 0 | – | 0 | 0 | – |
| 2001 | 0 | 0 | – | 1 | 1 | 100.0% |
| 2002 | 0 | 0 | – | 0 | 0 | – |
| Total | 1 | 1 | 100.0% | 1 | 1 | 100.0% |

## Appendix 2

Table A.25.2 Number of successful applications by location for uses in SSSI Zones

| Location | Approvals | Total | Success Rates % |
| --- | --- | --- | --- |
| Hong Kong | 0 | 0 | – |
| Kowloon | 0 | 0 | – |
| Development Permission Area | 1 | 3 | 33.3% |
| New Towns | 1 | 1 | 100.0% |
| Rural | 6 | 7 | 85.7% |
| Total | 8 | 11 | 72.7% |

Table A.25.3 Number of successful applications by site area for uses in SSSI Zones

| Site Area | Approvals | Total | Success Rates % |
| --- | --- | --- | --- |
| Smaller than 0.1 ha | 4 | 5 | 80.0% |
| 0.1 ha to 1 ha | 0 | 1 | 0.0% |
| Larger than 1 ha | 2 | 3 | 66.7% |
| N/A | 2 | 2 | 100.0% |
| Total | 8 | 11 | 72.7% |

Table A.25.4 Number of successful applications by Gross Floor Area for uses in SSSI Zones

| GFA | Approvals | Total | Success Rates % |
| --- | --- | --- | --- |
| Smaller than 0.5 ha | 2 | 4 | 50.0% |
| 0.5 ha to 5 ha | 0 | 0 | – |
| Larger than 5 ha | 1 | 1 | 100.0% |
| N/A | 5 | 6 | 83.3% |
| Total | 8 | 11 | 72.7% |

## Undetermined (U) Zones

Table A.26.1  Number of total and successful applications by year by stage of application for uses in U Zones

| Year | Planning Applications Approvals | Total | Success Rates % | Planning Reviews Approvals | Total | Success Rates % |
|---|---|---|---|---|---|---|
| 1976 | 2 | 2 | 100.0% | 0 | 0 | – |
| 1977 | 2 | 2 | 100.0% | 0 | 0 | – |
| 1978 | 0 | 0 | – | 0 | 0 | – |
| 1979 | 0 | 0 | – | 0 | 0 | – |
| 1980 | 0 | 0 | – | 0 | 0 | – |
| 1981 | 1 | 1 | 100.0% | 1 | 1 | 100.0% |
| 1982 | 0 | 0 | – | 0 | 0 | – |
| 1983 | 0 | 0 | – | 0 | 0 | – |
| 1984 | 2 | 2 | 100.0% | 0 | 0 | – |
| 1985 | 0 | 0 | – | 0 | 0 | – |
| 1986 | 2 | 4 | 50.0% | 0 | 1 | 0.0% |
| 1987 | 2 | 2 | 100.0% | 0 | 0 | – |
| 1988 | 2 | 4 | 50.0% | 0 | 0 | – |
| 1989 | 1 | 1 | 100.0% | 0 | 0 | – |
| 1990 | 3 | 3 | 100.0% | 1 | 1 | 100.0% |
| 1991 | 1 | 2 | 50.0% | 0 | 0 | – |
| 1992 | 2 | 4 | 50.0% | 0 | 1 | 0.0% |
| 1993 | 1 | 4 | 25.0% | 0 | 1 | 0.0% |
| 1994 | 3 | 3 | 100.0% | 0 | 0 | – |
| 1995 | 3 | 11 | 27.3% | 0 | 0 | – |
| 1996 | 15 | 20 | 75.0% | 1 | 2 | 50.0% |
| 1997 | 16 | 17 | 94.1% | 2 | 2 | 100.0% |
| 1998 | 29 | 37 | 78.4% | 1 | 5 | 20.0% |
| 1999 | 27 | 29 | 93.1% | 0 | 2 | 0.0% |
| 2000 | 28 | 41 | 68.3% | 0 | 0 | – |
| 2001 | 14 | 44 | 31.8% | 0 | 6 | 0.0% |
| 2002 | 32 | 40 | 80.0% | 2 | 4 | 50.0% |
| Total | 188 | 273 | 68.9% | 8 | 26 | 30.8% |

Table A.26.1 Number of total and successful applications by year by stage of application for uses in U Zones (Cont'd)

| Year | Petitions to Governor-in-Council/ Planning Appeals Approvals | Total | Success Rates % | Extension of Time Limit Approvals | Total | Success Rates % |
|---|---|---|---|---|---|---|
| 1976 | 0 | 0 | – | 0 | 0 | – |
| 1977 | 0 | 0 | – | 0 | 0 | – |
| 1978 | 0 | 0 | – | 0 | 0 | – |
| 1979 | 0 | 0 | – | 0 | 0 | – |
| 1980 | 0 | 0 | – | 0 | 0 | – |
| 1981 | 0 | 0 | – | 0 | 0 | – |
| 1982 | 0 | 0 | – | 0 | 0 | – |
| 1983 | 0 | 0 | – | 0 | 0 | – |
| 1984 | 0 | 0 | – | 0 | 0 | – |
| 1985 | 0 | 0 | – | 0 | 0 | – |
| 1986 | 0 | 0 | – | 0 | 0 | – |
| 1987 | 0 | 0 | – | 0 | 0 | – |
| 1988 | 0 | 0 | – | 0 | 0 | – |
| 1989 | 0 | 0 | – | 0 | 0 | – |
| 1990 | 0 | 0 | – | 0 | 0 | – |
| 1991 | 0 | 0 | – | 0 | 0 | – |
| 1992 | 0 | 0 | – | 0 | 0 | – |
| 1993 | 0 | 0 | – | 0 | 0 | – |
| 1994 | 0 | 0 | – | 0 | 0 | – |
| 1995 | 0 | 0 | – | 0 | 0 | – |
| 1996 | 0 | 0 | – | 3 | 3 | 100.0% |
| 1997 | 0 | 0 | – | 0 | 0 | – |
| 1998 | 0 | 0 | – | 4 | 5 | 80.0% |
| 1999 | 0 | 0 | – | 1 | 1 | 100.0% |
| 2000 | 0 | 0 | – | 7 | 7 | 100.0% |
| 2001 | 0 | 0 | – | 27 | 30 | 90.0% |
| 2002 | 0 | 0 | – | 18 | 18 | 100.0% |
| Total | 0 | 0 | – | 60 | 64 | 93.8% |

Table A.26.2  Number of successful applications by location for uses in U Zones

| Location | Approvals | Total | Success Rates % |
|---|---|---|---|
| Hong Kong | 4 | 4 | 100.0% |
| Kowloon | 6 | 6 | 100.0% |
| Development Permission Area | 0 | 3 | 0.0% |
| New Towns | 29 | 43 | 67.4% |
| Rural | 152 | 217 | 70.0% |
| Total | 191 | 273 | 70.0% |

Table A.26.3  Number of successful applications by site area for uses in U Zones

| Site Area | Approvals | Total | Success Rates % |
|---|---|---|---|
| Smaller than 0.1 ha | 31 | 46 | 67.4% |
| 0.1 ha to 1 ha | 108 | 140 | 77.1% |
| Larger than 1 ha | 52 | 86 | 60.5% |
| N/A | 0 | 1 | 0.0% |
| Total | 191 | 273 | 70.0% |

Table A.26.4  Number of successful applications by Gross Floor Area for uses in U Zones

| GFA | Approvals | Total | Success Rates % |
|---|---|---|---|
| Smaller than 0.5 ha | 25 | 35 | 71.4% |
| 0.5 ha to 5 ha | 13 | 27 | 48.1% |
| Larger than 5 ha | 20 | 29 | 69.0% |
| N/A | 133 | 182 | 73.1% |
| Total | 191 | 273 | 70.0% |

Table A.26.5  Number of successful applications by applied use for U Zones

| Applied Use | Approvals | Total | Success Rates % |
|---|---|---|---|
| Residential | 23 | 45 | 51.1% |
| Commercial | 11 | 21 | 52.4% |
| Village Type House | 6 | 12 | 50.0% |
| Car Park | 20 | 29 | 69.0% |
| Container | 22 | 29 | 75.9% |
| Open Storage | 87 | 122 | 71.3% |
| Warehouse | 10 | 12 | 83.3% |
| Industrial | 12 | 17 | 70.6% |
| Other | 27 | 32 | 84.4% |
| Total | 218 | 319 | 68.3% |

## Unspecified Use (UNSP) Zones

Table A.27.1 Number of total and successful applications by year by stage of application for uses in UNSP Zones

| Year | Planning Applications | | | Planning Reviews | | |
|---|---|---|---|---|---|---|
| | Approvals | Total | Success Rates % | Approvals | Total | Success Rates % |
| 1991 | 31 | 58 | 53.4% | 0 | 0 | – |
| 1992 | 104 | 276 | 37.7% | 11 | 58 | 19.0% |
| 1993 | 177 | 336 | 52.7% | 22 | 54 | 40.7% |
| 1994 | 161 | 323 | 49.8% | 41 | 87 | 47.1% |
| 1995 | 29 | 72 | 40.3% | 18 | 34 | 52.9% |
| 1996 | 13 | 38 | 34.2% | 7 | 15 | 46.7% |
| 1997 | 0 | 0 | – | 1 | 2 | 50.0% |
| 1998 | 0 | 0 | – | 0 | 0 | – |
| 1999 | 0 | 0 | – | 0 | 0 | – |
| 2000 | 0 | 0 | – | 0 | 0 | – |
| 2001 | 0 | 0 | – | 0 | 0 | – |
| 2002 | 0 | 0 | – | 0 | 0 | – |
| Total | 515 | 1,103 | 46.7% | 100 | 250 | 40.0% |

| Year | Planning Appeals | | | Extension of Time Limit | | |
|---|---|---|---|---|---|---|
| | Approvals | Total | Success Rates % | Approvals | Total | Success Rates % |
| 1991 | 0 | 0 | – | 0 | 0 | – |
| 1992 | 0 | 2 | 0.0% | 1 | 1 | 100.0% |
| 1993 | 0 | 8 | 0.0% | 0 | 0 | – |
| 1994 | 2 | 5 | 40.0% | 14 | 14 | 100.0% |
| 1995 | 0 | 9 | 0.0% | 21 | 21 | 100.0% |
| 1996 | 1 | 2 | 50.0% | 24 | 25 | 96.0% |
| 1997 | 0 | 0 | – | 13 | 14 | 92.9% |
| 1998 | 0 | 0 | – | 9 | 9 | 100.0% |
| 1999 | 0 | 0 | – | 4 | 4 | 100.0% |
| 2000 | 0 | 0 | – | 4 | 4 | 100.0% |
| 2001 | 0 | 0 | – | 0 | 0 | – |
| 2002 | 0 | 0 | – | 1 | 1 | 100.0% |
| Total | 3 | 26 | 11.5% | 91 | 93 | 97.8% |

Table A.27.2  Number of successful applications by location for uses in UNSP Zones

| Location | Approvals | Total | Success Rates % |
|---|---|---|---|
| Hong Kong | 0 | 0 | – |
| Kowloon | 0 | 0 | – |
| Development Permission Area | 614 | 1,103 | 55.7% |
| New Towns | 0 | 0 | – |
| Rural | 0 | 0 | – |
| Total | 614 | 1,103 | 55.7% |

Table A.27.3  Number of successful applications by site area for uses in UNSP Zones

| Site Area | Approvals | Total | Success Rates % |
|---|---|---|---|
| Smaller than 0.1 ha | 451 | 660 | 68.3% |
| 0.1 ha to 1 ha | 109 | 286 | 38.1% |
| Larger than 1 ha | 54 | 157 | 34.4% |
| N/A | 0 | 0 | – |
| Total | 614 | 1,103 | 55.7% |

Table A.27.4  Number of successful applications by Gross Floor Area for uses in UNSP Zones

| GFA | Approvals | Total | Success Rates % |
|---|---|---|---|
| Smaller than 0.5 ha | 525 | 835 | 62.9% |
| 0.5 ha to 5 ha | 24 | 79 | 30.4% |
| Larger than 5 ha | 6 | 30 | 20.0% |
| N/A | 59 | 159 | 37.1% |
| Total | 614 | 1,103 | 55.7% |

Table A.27.5  Number of successful applications by applied use for UNSP Zones

| Applied Use | Approvals | Total | Success Rates % |
|---|---|---|---|
| Container | 16 | 60 | 26.7% |
| Industrial | 21 | 47 | 44.7% |
| Open Storage | 40 | 120 | 33.3% |
| Refuse Collection Point | 32 | 32 | 100.0% |
| Residential | 43 | 143 | 30.1% |
| Village Type House | 391 | 595 | 65.7% |
| Warehouse | 22 | 51 | 43.1% |
| Other | 62 | 89 | 69.7% |
| Total | 627 | 1,137 | 55.1% |

## Village Type House (V) Zones

Table A.28.1  Number of total and successful applications by year by stage of application for uses in V Zones

| Year | Planning Applications Approvals | Total | Success Rates % | Planning Reviews Approvals | Total | Success Rates % |
|---|---|---|---|---|---|---|
| 1977 | 1 | 1 | 100.0% | 0 | 0 | – |
| 1978 | 0 | 0 | – | 0 | 0 | – |
| 1979 | 0 | 0 | – | 0 | 0 | – |
| 1980 | 0 | 0 | – | 0 | 0 | – |
| 1981 | 1 | 2 | 50.0% | 0 | 0 | – |
| 1982 | 0 | 0 | – | 0 | 0 | – |
| 1983 | 1 | 1 | 100.0% | 0 | 0 | – |
| 1984 | 1 | 1 | 100.0% | 0 | 0 | – |
| 1985 | 1 | 1 | 100.0% | 0 | 0 | – |
| 1986 | 1 | 1 | 100.0% | 0 | 0 | – |
| 1987 | 1 | 2 | 50.0% | 0 | 0 | – |
| 1988 | 2 | 2 | 100.0% | 0 | 1 | 0.0% |
| 1989 | 1 | 2 | 50.0% | 0 | 0 | – |
| 1990 | 1 | 4 | 25.0% | 0 | 1 | 0.0% |
| 1991 | 14 | 23 | 60.9% | 0 | 0 | – |
| 1992 | 10 | 28 | 35.7% | 2 | 10 | 20.0% |
| 1993 | 15 | 23 | 65.2% | 0 | 5 | 0.0% |
| 1994 | 18 | 29 | 62.1% | 3 | 5 | 60.0% |
| 1995 | 21 | 37 | 56.8% | 4 | 6 | 66.7% |
| 1996 | 52 | 67 | 77.6% | 1 | 3 | 33.3% |
| 1997 | 55 | 97 | 56.7% | 7 | 11 | 63.6% |
| 1998 | 45 | 101 | 44.6% | 8 | 30 | 26.7% |
| 1999 | 77 | 111 | 69.4% | 2 | 10 | 20.0% |
| 2000 | 62 | 92 | 67.4% | 1 | 9 | 11.1% |
| 2001 | 55 | 96 | 57.3% | 5 | 9 | 55.6% |
| 2002 | 77 | 113 | 68.1% | 2 | 6 | 33.3% |
| Total | 512 | 834 | 61.4% | 35 | 106 | 33.0% |

Table A.28.1  Number of total and successful applications by year by stage of application for uses in V Zones (Cont'd)

| Year | Petitions to Governor-in-Council/ Planning Appeals ||| Extension of Time Limit |||
| --- | --- | --- | --- | --- | --- | --- |
|  | Approvals | Total | Success Rates % | Approvals | Total | Success Rates % |
| 1977 | 0 | 0 | – | 0 | 0 | – |
| 1978 | 0 | 0 | – | 0 | 0 | – |
| 1979 | 0 | 0 | – | 0 | 0 | – |
| 1980 | 0 | 0 | – | 0 | 0 | – |
| 1981 | 0 | 0 | – | 0 | 0 | – |
| 1982 | 0 | 0 | – | 0 | 0 | – |
| 1983 | 0 | 0 | – | 0 | 0 | – |
| 1984 | 0 | 0 | – | 0 | 0 | – |
| 1985 | 0 | 0 | – | 0 | 0 | – |
| 1986 | 0 | 0 | – | 0 | 0 | – |
| 1987 | 0 | 0 | – | 0 | 0 | – |
| 1988 | 0 | 0 | – | 0 | 0 | – |
| 1989 | 0 | 0 | – | 0 | 0 | – |
| 1990 | 0 | 0 | – | 0 | 0 | – |
| 1991 | 0 | 0 | – | 0 | 0 | – |
| 1992 | 0 | 0 | – | 0 | 0 | – |
| 1993 | 0 | 1 | 0.0% | 1 | 1 | 100.0% |
| 1994 | 0 | 1 | 0.0% | 1 | 1 | 100.0% |
| 1995 | 0 | 0 | – | 0 | 0 | – |
| 1996 | 0 | 0 | – | 8 | 8 | 100.0% |
| 1997 | 0 | 0 | – | 5 | 5 | 100.0% |
| 1998 | 0 | 0 | – | 14 | 14 | 100.0% |
| 1999 | 0 | 0 | – | 9 | 9 | 100.0% |
| 2000 | 0 | 0 | – | 5 | 5 | 100.0% |
| 2001 | 0 | 0 | – | 26 | 26 | 100.0% |
| 2002 | 0 | 0 | – | 22 | 22 | 100.0% |
| Total | 0 | 2 | 0.0% | 91 | 91 | 100.0% |

Table A.28.2  Number of successful applications by location for uses in V Zones

| Location | Approvals | Total | Success Rates % |
|---|---|---|---|
| Hong Kong | 0 | 0 | – |
| Kowloon | 2 | 3 | 66.7% |
| Development Permission Area | 64 | 102 | 62.7% |
| New Towns | 42 | 59 | 71.2% |
| Rural | 436 | 670 | 65.1% |
| Total | 544 | 834 | 65.2% |

Table A.28.3  Number of successful applications by site area for uses in V Zones

| Site Area | Approvals | Total | Success Rates % |
|---|---|---|---|
| Smaller than 0.1 ha | 348 | 444 | 78.4% |
| 0.1 ha to 1 ha | 153 | 301 | 50.8% |
| Larger than 1 ha | 31 | 76 | 40.8% |
| N/A | 12 | 13 | 92.3% |
| Total | 544 | 834 | 65.2% |

Table A.28.4  Number of successful applications by Gross Floor Area for uses in V Zones

| GFA | Approvals | Total | Success Rates % |
|---|---|---|---|
| Smaller than 0.5 ha | 325 | 394 | 82.5% |
| 0.5 ha to 5 ha | 11 | 27 | 40.7% |
| Larger than 5 ha | 6 | 16 | 37.5% |
| N/A | 202 | 397 | 50.9% |
| Total | 544 | 834 | 65.2% |

Table A.28.5  Number of successful applications by applied use for V Zones

| Applied Use | Approvals | Total | Success Rates % |
|---|---|---|---|
| Car Park | 43 | 74 | 58.1% |
| Container | 8 | 37 | 21.6% |
| Open Storage | 75 | 196 | 38.3% |
| Utility | 44 | 44 | 100.0% |
| Village Type House | 201 | 250 | 80.4% |
| Residential | 30 | 61 | 49.2% |
| Refuse Collection Point | 27 | 27 | 100.0% |
| School | 35 | 38 | 92.1% |
| Restaurant | 11 | 14 | 78.6% |
| Other | 77 | 117 | 65.8% |
| Total | 551 | 858 | 64.2% |

# All Zones

Table A.29.1 Number of total and successful applications by year by stage of application for uses for all zones

| Year | Planning Applications | | | Planning Reviews | | |
|---|---|---|---|---|---|---|
| | Approvals | Total | Success Rates % | Approvals | Total | Success Rates % |
| 1975 | 14 | 24 | 58.3% | 4 | 5 | 80.0% |
| 1976 | 35 | 50 | 70.0% | 6 | 10 | 60.0% |
| 1977 | 47 | 69 | 68.1% | 5 | 11 | 45.5% |
| 1978 | 74 | 101 | 73.3% | 9 | 20 | 45.0% |
| 1979 | 71 | 120 | 59.2% | 12 | 28 | 42.9% |
| 1980 | 63 | 108 | 58.3% | 15 | 39 | 38.5% |
| 1981 | 65 | 107 | 60.7% | 9 | 18 | 50.0% |
| 1982 | 93 | 134 | 69.4% | 8 | 20 | 40.0% |
| 1983 | 114 | 148 | 77.0% | 6 | 22 | 27.3% |
| 1984 | 122 | 146 | 83.6% | 5 | 9 | 55.6% |
| 1985 | 171 | 187 | 91.4% | 1 | 5 | 20.0% |
| 1986 | 129 | 156 | 82.7% | 2 | 5 | 40.0% |
| 1987 | 153 | 222 | 68.9% | 12 | 24 | 50.0% |
| 1988 | 200 | 277 | 72.2% | 19 | 40 | 47.5% |
| 1989 | 223 | 325 | 68.6% | 11 | 30 | 36.7% |
| 1990 | 176 | 305 | 57.7% | 11 | 35 | 31.4% |
| 1991 | 255 | 445 | 57.3% | 16 | 49 | 32.7% |
| 1992 | 333 | 678 | 49.1% | 26 | 107 | 24.3% |
| 1993 | 468 | 775 | 60.4% | 35 | 104 | 33.7% |
| 1994 | 681 | 1,062 | 64.1% | 64 | 156 | 41.0% |
| 1995 | 533 | 803 | 66.4% | 70 | 134 | 52.2% |
| 1996 | 674 | 939 | 71.8% | 25 | 109 | 22.9% |
| 1997 | 784 | 1,106 | 70.9% | 44 | 122 | 36.1% |
| 1998 | 614 | 930 | 66.0% | 41 | 171 | 24.0% |
| 1999 | 787 | 953 | 82.6% | 8 | 49 | 16.3% |
| 2000 | 824 | 1,044 | 78.9% | 8 | 54 | 14.8% |
| 2001 | 674 | 963 | 70.0% | 38 | 88 | 43.2% |
| 2002 | 730 | 983 | 74.3% | 31 | 98 | 31.6% |
| Total | 9,107 | 13,160 | 69.2% | 541 | 1,562 | 34.6% |

## Appendix 2

Table A.29.1 Number of total and successful applications by year by stage of application for uses for all zones (Cont'd)

| Year | Petitions to Governor-in-Council/ Planning Appeals ||| Extension of Time Limit |||
|---|---|---|---|---|---|---|
| | Approvals | Total | Success Rates % | Approvals | Total | Success Rates % |
| 1975 | 0 | 0 | – | 0 | 0 | – |
| 1976 | 0 | 1 | 0.0% | 0 | 0 | – |
| 1977 | 0 | 0 | – | 0 | 0 | – |
| 1978 | 0 | 0 | – | 0 | 0 | – |
| 1979 | 0 | 4 | 0.0% | 0 | 0 | – |
| 1980 | 0 | 1 | 0.0% | 0 | 0 | – |
| 1981 | 0 | 0 | – | 0 | 0 | – |
| 1982 | 1 | 2 | 50.0% | 0 | 0 | – |
| 1983 | 1 | 1 | 100.0% | 0 | 0 | – |
| 1984 | 0 | 1 | 0.0% | 0 | 0 | – |
| 1985 | 0 | 2 | 0.0% | 0 | 0 | – |
| 1986 | 0 | 2 | 0.0% | 0 | 0 | – |
| 1987 | 0 | 0 | – | 0 | 0 | – |
| 1988 | 0 | 3 | 0.0% | 0 | 0 | – |
| 1989 | 1 | 1 | 100.0% | 0 | 0 | – |
| 1990 | 0 | 1 | 0.0% | 0 | 0 | – |
| 1991 | 0 | 0 | – | 0 | 0 | – |
| 1992 | 0 | 10 | 0.0% | 11 | 11 | 100.0% |
| 1993 | 0 | 11 | 0.0% | 16 | 16 | 100.0% |
| 1994 | 5 | 13 | 38.5% | 41 | 41 | 100.0% |
| 1995 | 0 | 20 | 0.0% | 40 | 40 | 100.0% |
| 1996 | 2 | 5 | 40.0% | 110 | 112 | 98.2% |
| 1997 | 0 | 0 | – | 93 | 95 | 97.9% |
| 1998 | 0 | 0 | – | 166 | 171 | 97.1% |
| 1999 | 0 | 1 | 0.0% | 71 | 71 | 100.0% |
| 2000 | 0 | 1 | 0.0% | 104 | 104 | 100.0% |
| 2001 | 0 | 4 | 0.0% | 266 | 277 | 96.0% |
| 2002 | 1 | 7 | 14.3% | 207 | 208 | 99.5% |
| Total | 11 | 91 | 12.1% | 1,125 | 1,146 | 98.2% |

Appendix 2   191

Table A.29.2  Number of successful applications by location for all zones

| Location | Approvals | Total | Success Rates % |
|---|---|---|---|
| Hong Kong | 1,830 | 2,360 | 77.5% |
| Kowloon | 2,090 | 2,732 | 76.5% |
| Development Permission Area | 761 | 1,374 | 55.4% |
| New Towns | 1,835 | 2,285 | 80.3% |
| Rural | 3,061 | 4,412 | 69.4% |
| Total | 9,577 | 13,163 | 72.8% |

Table A.29.3  Number of successful applications by site area for all zones

| Site Area | Approvals | Total | Success Rates % |
|---|---|---|---|
| Smaller than 0.1 ha | 3,739 | 5,095 | 73.4% |
| 0.1 ha to 1 ha | 3,014 | 4,462 | 67.5% |
| Larger than 1 ha | 1,286 | 1,792 | 71.8% |
| N/A | 1,538 | 1,814 | 84.8% |
| Total | 9,577 | 13,163 | 72.8% |

Table A.29.4  Number of successful applications by Gross Floor Area for all zones

| GFA | Approvals | Total | Success Rates % |
|---|---|---|---|
| Smaller than 0.5 ha | 5,313 | 7,067 | 75.2% |
| 0.5 ha to 5 ha | 1,427 | 1,995 | 71.5% |
| Larger than 5 ha | 762 | 959 | 79.5% |
| N/A | 2,075 | 3,142 | 66.0% |
| Total | 9,577 | 13,163 | 72.8% |

# APPENDIX 3
## PROBIT AND LOGIT ESTIMATES OF NON-AGGREGATE STATISTICS REGARDING PLANNING APPLICATIONS

Hypothesis and Results for Tang and Tang (1999).

| Hypotheses Regarding Planning Applications for Uses in R(A) Zones | Test Results | Theoretical/Policy Implications |
|---|---|---|
| (1) Development size is not a major determinant affecting the chance of success in obtaining planning permission in R (A) Zones. | Hypothesis is refuted. | Larger sites lead to a greater chance of success in planning applications. |

Logistic Estimates of the Decision Function: R (A) Zones; Tang and Tang (1999)

| Variable | ß | S.E. | Wald | Df | Significance | R | Exp(B) |
|---|---|---|---|---|---|---|---|
| Area | 0.2677 | 0.0611 | 19.1737 | 1 | 0.0000 | 0.2305 | 1.3069 |
| Constant | -0.6048 | 0.2528 | 5.7237 | 1 | 0.0617 | | |
| Change -2log L | 31.489 | | | 1 | 0.0000 | | |

Notes:
1. N: 242 observations in R(A) Zones of Hong Kong
2. Site area (unit in per 100 sq. m)

## Hypothesis and Results for Tang and Choy (2000)

| Hypotheses Regarding Planning Applications for C/O Use in R(A) Zones | Test Results | Theoretical/Policy Implications |
|---|---|---|
| (1) Additional past application increases the probability of approval. | Hypothesis is not refuted. | Planning applicants have to work out, by trial and error, the acceptable development scheme. |
| (2) Development size is a major determinant affecting the chance of success in obtaining planning permission of C/O use in R (A) Zones. | Hypothesis is not refuted. | Larger sites lead to a greater chance of success in planning applications. |
| (3) It is comparatively more difficult to obtain approval for recent submissions. | Hypothesis is not refuted. | There is a gradual shift towards rejection of the planning applications since the early 1990s due to the government's urban growth restraint policies. |
| (4) Commercial property market is an important decision factor. | Hypothesis is not refuted. | Planning applications are affected by property market conditions. |

## Logistic Estimates of the Decision Function: C/O Use in R (A) Zones; Tang and Choi (2000).

| Variable | β | S.E. | Wald | Df | Significance | R | Exp(B) |
|---|---|---|---|---|---|---|---|
| GFA | 0.188 | 0.067 | 8.007 | 1 | 0.005 | 0.167 | 1.207 |
| RECENCY | -1.540 | 0.352 | 19.181 | 1 | 0.000 | -0.283 | 0.215 |
| PREV | 0.529 | 0.220 | 5.785 | 1 | 0.016 | 0.133 | 1.696 |
| COMM | -0.564 | 0.279 | 4.084 | 1 | 0.043 | -0.099 | 0.569 |
| Constant | 3.145 | 0.687 | 20.963 | 1 | 0.000 | | |
| N | -2log L | | 151.006 | | | | |

Notes:
1. N: 162 observations for C/O use in R(A) Zones in Hong Kong Island and urban Kowloon
2. GFA proposed gloss floor area (in 1,000 sq.m.)
3. RECENCY: How recent the planning application was (denoted by the number of days from 1 January 1986)
4. PREV: the number of previous applications on the same site
5. COMM: completion of new commercial floor space in the past 3 months in Hong Kong (in 100,000 sq.m)
6. Percentage correct Prediction: 77.16%

*Appendix 3* 195

## Hypotheses and Results for Tang, Choy and Wat (2000).

| Hypotheses Regarding Planning Applications for C/O Use in R(A) Zones | Test Results | Theoretical/Policy Implications |
|---|---|---|
| (1) The physical planning criteria stated in the policy guidelines have an influence on the success or failure of the planning applications. | | |
| (a) Site area (expected effect: positive) | Hypothesis is refuted. | Site area has no effect. |
| (b) Site configuration (expected effect: positive) | Hypothesis is refuted. | Site configuration has no effect. |
| (c) Loading facilities (expected effect: positive) | Hypothesis is not refuted. | Providing loading facilities increases the chance of getting approvals. |
| (d) Car park facilities (expected effect: positive) | Hypothesis is refuted. | Providing car park facilities decreases the chance of getting approvals. |
| (e) Frontage (expected effect: positive) | Hypothesis is not refuted. | Frontage has positive effect. |
| (f) Distance to MTR station (expected effect: negative) | Hypothesis is refuted. | Further away from MTR increases the chance of getting approvals. |
| (g) Traffic conditions (expected effect: negative) | Hypothesis is refuted. | Traffic conditions have no effect. |
| (2) The criteria not included in the policy guidelines have no influence on the success or failure of the planning applications. | | |
| (a) Previous applications (expected effect: negative) | Hypothesis is not refuted. | Planning precedent is not a concern. |
| (b) Application year (expected effect: negative) | Hypothesis is not refuted. | Timing has no effect. |
| (c) Intensification (expected effect: negative) | Hypothesis is not refuted. | Intensification has no effect. |
| (d) Development intensity (expected effect: negative) | Hypothesis is refuted at 10% level. | Planning authority has a negative bias against larger office development. |
| (e) Loss of housing space (expected effect: negative) | Hypothesis is not refuted. | The potential loss of housing property has no effect. |
| (f) Decentralisation from CBD (expected effect: negative) | Hypothesis is not refuted. | The distance from CBD has no effect. |
| (g) Positive planning precedent (expected effect: negative) | Hypothesis is not refuted. | No significant advantage in locating close to a successful application site. |
| (h) Negative planning precedent (expected effect: negative) | Hypothesis is refuted. | Shorter distance to the nearest rejected case increases the chance of success. |
| (i) Office market factor (expected effect: negative) | Hypothesis is refuted. | Planning is not autonomous of market. |

**Logistic Estimates of the Decision Function: C/O Use in R (A) Zones; Tang, Choy and Wat (2000)**

| Variable | ß | S.E. | Wald | Df | Significance | R | Exp(B) |
|---|---|---|---|---|---|---|---|
| MTR accessibility | 0.0034 | 0.010 | 10.9532 | 1 | 0.0009 | 0.2492 | 1.0034 |
| Office market factor | -0.0087 | 0.0038 | 5.2180 | 1 | 0.0224 | -0.1494 | 0.9914 |
| Loading facilities | 2.4675 | 0.8677 | 8.0875 | 1 | 0.0045 | 0.2055 | 11.7930 |
| Car park facilities | -2.5624 | 0.9932 | 7.1324 | 1 | 0.0076 | -0.1887 | 0.0705 |
| Frontage | 0.0337 | 0.0129 | 6.8577 | 1 | 0.0088 | 0.1836 | 1.0342 |
| Development intensity | -0.0950 | 0.0571 | 2.7679 | 1 | 0.0962 | -0.0730 | 0.9094 |
| Negative planning precedent | -0.0037 | 0.0013 | 8.2987 | 1 | 0.0040 | -0.2090 | 0.9963 |
| Constant | -0.6218 | 0.5618 | 1.2254 | 1 | 0.2683 | | |

Notes:

1. N: 104 observations for C/O use in R(A) Zones in Hong Kong Island
2. MTR accessibility: distance of the site from the nearest MTR station
3. Office market factor: completion of new commercial floor space in the past 3 months (in 10,000 sq. m)
4. Loading facilities: the availability of such facilities 1, 0 otherwise
5. Car park facilities the availability of such facilities 1, 0 otherwise
6. Frontage: street frontage of the sites (in metres)
7. Development intensity: proposed gross floor area of development (in 10,000 sq. m)
8. Negative planning precedent: distance of the site to the nearest rejected cases (in metres)

## Hypotheses and Results for Lai and Ho (2001a).

| Hypotheses Regarding Planning Applications for Small Houses (Lai and Ho 2001a) | Test Results | Theoretical/Policy Implications |
|---|---|---|
| (1) Planning decisions show no preference for larger development (and arguably developer)? | | A necessary condition for rent-seeking thesis is found absent for this category of applications. |
| (a) Green belt Zones | Hypothesis is not refuted. | Small development has a greater chance of success. |
| (b) Unspecified Use Zones | Hypothesis is not refuted. | Small development has a greater chance of success. |
| (2) Planning decisions insensitive to exogenous housing policies? | | Planning decisions are found insulated from other or wider governmental policies. |
| (a) Green Belt Zones | Hypothesis is not refut. | |
| (b) Unspecified Use Zones | (This is not tested). | |
| (3) Is it not easier to get approvals in Green Belts than in Unspecified Use Zones? | Hypothesis is not refuted. | |
| (4) Is it not more difficult to get approvals in Green Belt Zones in DPA than in Green Belt Zones outside DPA? | Hypothesis is refuted. | DPA is generally more restrictive than Green Belt zoning, though only the latter has an expressed presumption against development. |

## 198 Appendix 3

**Probit Estimates of the Decision Function: GB & U Zones; Lai and Ho (2001a).**

| Model | N | $\beta_0$ | ln(GFA) | POLICY | DPA | Log-Likelihood | Percent Correct Prediction |
|---|---|---|---|---|---|---|---|
| GB | 254 | 1.41860* (3.48714) | −0.13574** (−1.97111) | −0.28018 (−1.53820) | −0.64949* (−2.58413) | −153.413 | 70.0787 |
| U | 572 | 2.91875* (6.88510) | −0.45828* (−5.92026) | | | −345.404 | 69.9301 |

Notes:
Figures in parentheses are *t*-statistics; * indicates significant at 1% confidence level; ** indicates significant at 5% confidence level; GB, Green Belt; U, Unspecified Use Zones.
ln(GFA): natural log of gross floor area.
POLICY: dummy equal to 1 if the application was made during the policy 'to draw up a package of measures to simplify and streamline various government planning, land and building approval process for residential development' was alive, 0 otherwise;
DPA: dummy equal to 1 if application falls in a Development Permission Area Plan, 0 otherwise.

**Probit Estimates of the Decision Function: GB & U Zones; Lai and Ho (2001a)**

| Model | N | $\beta_0$ | ln(GFA) | GB | Log-Likelihood | Percent Correct Prediction |
|---|---|---|---|---|---|---|
| GB and U | 826 | 2.07569* (7.45285) | −0.30433* (−6.05110) | 0.14883 (1.46913) | −505.339 | 70.0969 |

Notes:
Figures in parentheses are *t*-statistics; * indicates significant at 1% confidence level; GB, Green Belt; U, Unspecified Use Zones.
ln (GFA): natural log of gross floor area;
GB: dummy equal to 1 if the site falls in a Green Belt Zone, 0 otherwise.

**Hypotheses and Results for Lai and Ho (2001b)**

| Hypotheses Regarding Planning Applications for Uses in Residential Zones (Lai and Ho 2001b) | Test Results | Theoretical / Policy Implications |
|---|---|---|
| (1) Planning decisions show no preference for larger development (and arguably developer)? | | A necessary condition for rent-seeking thesis is found absent in this category of applications. |
| (a) R(A) Zones | Hypothesis is refuted. | Small development is easier to succeed. |
| (b) R(B) Zones | Hypothesis is not refuted. | Planning applications for uses in larger developments have the same chance of success as those for uses in smaller sites. |
| (c) R(C) Zones | Hypothesis is not refuted. | Planning applications for uses in larger developments have the same chance of success as those for uses in smaller sites. |
| (2) Planning decisions insensitive to exogenous housing policies? Planning application on/after July 1997. | | Planning decisions are found contingent on wider governmental policies, with reference to R (B) and R(C) Zones. |
| (a) R(A) Zones | Hypothesis is not refuted. | Planning decisions are insensitive to exogenous housing policies. |
| (b) R(B) Zones | Hypothesis is refuted. | Planning decisions are sensitive to exogenous housing policies. |
| (c) R(C) Zones | Hypothesis is refuted. | Planning decisions are sensitive to exogenous housing policies. |

## 200  Appendix 3

**Probit Estimates of the Decision Function: R (A), R (B), R(C) Zones; Lai and Ho (2001b)**

| Model | N | $\beta_0$ | RES | ln(GFA) | ln(GSA) | POLICY | HK | KLN | RURAL | DPA | NT | Log-Likelihood | Percent Correct Prediction |
|---|---|---|---|---|---|---|---|---|---|---|---|---|---|
| R(A) | 451 | 2.5647* (6.7998) | | −0.1174* (3.1354) | | 0.3041 (1.2458) | −1.0625* (4.7302) | −0.8536* (2.5823) | | | | −209.787 | 78.7140 |
| R(A) | 597 | −0.0875 (0.2059) | | −0.0320 (0.7790) | 0.2278* (4.6396) | 0.1833 (0.6355) | −1.0102* (3.8910) | −0.9063* (3.4319) | | | | −339.740 | 68.3417 |
| R(B) | 205 | 0.9927* (2.7800) | −0.5119*** (1.6801) | | | 1.5152* (2.7599) | −0.6053* (2.6706) | −0.4328* (1.7091) | | −0.4772 (0.7672) | | −120.249 | 67.8049 |
| R(B) | 147 | 0.2940 (0.5838) | −0.5371*** (1.7145) | | −0.0455 (0.7007) | 1.2167* (2.5267) | | 0.8446** (2.2055) | −0.0340 (0.0393) | 0.0433 (0.0613) | 0.8539* (3.2725) | −82.4133 | 74.1497 |
| R(C) | 229 | −0.6408*** (1.6838) | −0.3110 (1.3207) | 0.0385 (0.6781) | | 0.5256*** (1.7393) | 0.6409* (2.5542) | | 0.4382 (1.2359) | 0.0746 (0.1929) | 0.2211 (0.7295) | −151.708 | 61.1354 |
| R(C) | 209 | −1.1218*** (1.8957) | −0.0546 (0.2553) | | 0.0890 (1.4273) | 0.3616 (1.2872) | 0.4609*** (1.6924) | 0.2114 (0.6145) | 0.0875 (0.2584) | −0.1051 (0.2654) | | −139.915 | 59.8086 |

Notes:
Figures in parentheses are the absolute values of *t*-statistics; *indicates significant at 1 percent level; ** indicates significant at 5 percent level; *** indicates significant at 10 percent level.
RES: dummy equal to 1 if the applied land use is related to residential use;
ln(GFA): natural log of gross floor area;
ln(GSA): natural log of gross site area;
POLICY: dummy equal to 1 if the decision made during the period when the government land use policy 'to draw up a package of measure to simplify and streamline various government planning, land and building approval processes for residential development' was alive, 0 otherwise;
HK, KLN, RURAL, DPA, NT: location dummies equal to 1 if the application site falls in these locations: Hong Kong Island, Kowloon, rural, Development Permission Area or New Towns respectively, 0 otherwise.

## Hypotheses and Results for Lai and Ho (2001c)

| Hypotheses Regarding Planning Applications for Hotel Use | Test Results | Theoretical / Policy Implications |
|---|---|---|
| (1) The chance of success in obtaining planning permission for the use 'school' is the same in both C/R and G/IC Zones. | Hypothesis 1 is not rejected. | A necessary condition for rent-seeking thesis is found absent in this category of applications. |
| (2) The chance of success in obtaining planning permission for the use 'petrol-filling station' is the same in both C/R and G/IC Zones. | Hypothesis 2 is not rejected. | Planning decisions show preference for the hotel use in R(A) Zones. |
| (3) The chance of success in obtaining planning permission for the use 'mass transit railway installation' is the same in both C/R and G/IC Zones. | Hypothesis 3 is left untested due to lack of planning applications. | Nil. |
| (4) The chance of success in obtaining planning permission for all column 2 uses is the same in both C/R and G/IC Zones. | Hypothesis 4 is rejected. | The chance of success in obtaining planning permissions for all or any uses in C/R Zones is found to be relatively higher than that in G/IC Zones. |

## Probit Estimates of the Decision Function: C/R and G/IC Zones; Lai and Ho (2001c)

| Zone | N | $\beta_0$ | SCH | PFS | MTR | Log-likelihood | Percentage correct predictions |
|---|---|---|---|---|---|---|---|
| C/R | 242 | -1.3789* (6.6975) | 0.3722 (1.2632) | -1.4202** (2.1536) | -0.4578 (0.7215) | -47.9831 | 95.0413 |
| G/IC | 551 | 0.5412* (8.2045) | 0.6192* (2.5523) | -0.5410 (0.6088) | nil | -330.832 | 69.5100 |

## Probit Estimates of the Decision Function: C/R and G/IC Zones; Lai and Ho (2001c)

| Zone | N | $\beta_0$ | SCH | PFS | MTR | GFA | C/R | C/R (SCH) | C/R (PFS) | C/R (MTR) | C/R (GFA) | Log-likelihood | Percentage correct predictions |
|---|---|---|---|---|---|---|---|---|---|---|---|---|---|
| C/R & G/C | 793 | 0.5412* (8.2045) | 0.6192* (2.5523) | -0.5410 (0.6088) | nil | 0.000003** (2.2848) | 0.8175* (3.8762) | -0.2130 (0.5649) | -0.8490 (0.7684) | nil | 0.0001 (0.8424) | -379.606 | 77.3041 |

Notes:
Figures in parentheses are the absolute values of $t$-statistics; *indicates significant at 1 percent level; ** indicates significant at 5 percent level.

## Hypotheses and Results for Lai and Ho (2001d)

| Hypotheses Regarding Planning Applications in Green Belt Zones | Test Results | Theoretical / Policy Implications |
|---|---|---|
| (1) The chance of success in obtaining planning permission for 'small houses' and houses are the same in Green Belt Zones. | Hypothesis is refuted. | Planning decisions show preference for the 'small house' use in Green Belt Zones. |
| (2) Planning applications for uses in larger sites do not have a smaller chance of success than those for uses in smaller sites. | Hypothesis is not refuted. | Development size is not considered as a major factor in determining whether an application for small house/house should be approved. |

## Probit Estimates of the Decision Function: Green Belt Zones; Lai and Ho (2001d)

| Zone | N | $\beta_0$ | $ln(GFA)$ | $VTH$ | Log-likelihood | Percentage correct predictions |
|---|---|---|---|---|---|---|
| GB | 379 | −0.03337 (−0.08226) | −0.04906 (−1.05868) | 0.76594* (4.11180) | −239.030 | 67.2823 |

Notes:
Figures in parentheses are $t$-statistics; * indicates statistically significant at 1% confidence level.

## Hypotheses and Results for Yung (2001)

| Hypotheses Regarding Planning Applications for Hotel Use | Test Results | Theoretical / Policy Implications |
|---|---|---|
| (1) Planning decisions show preference for larger development (and arguably developer)? | Hypothesis is not refuted. | A necessary condition for rent-seeking thesis is found present in this category of applications. |
| (2) Planning decisions show preference for R(A) Zones? | Hypothesis is not refuted. | Applications in R(A) Zones will have higher probabilities of getting approvals. |
| (3) Planning decisions show preference for R(B) Zones? | Hypothesis is refuted. | The likelihood of a hotel use approval is independent of R(B) zoing. |
| (4) Planning decisions show preference for CDA Zones? | Hypothesis is not refuted. | Planning decisions show preference for the hotel use in CDA Zones. |
| (5) Planning decisions show preference for OU(CRA) Zones? | Hypothesis is not refuted. | Planning decisions show preference for the hotel use in OU(CRA) Zones. |
| (6) When the demand for hotel rooms is high, the probability of getting planning approval is also high? | Hypothesis is refuted. | |

## Probit Estimates of the Decision Function: Hotel Use (Yung 2001)

| Use | N | Constant | $1/(SA)^2$ | D_CDA | D_RA | D_OU | $ROOM\_3Y^2/(VSTR\_M^*O\ R\ NIGHT\_M^*\_1Y)^2$ | Log-Likelihood |
|---|---|---|---|---|---|---|---|---|
| Hotel | 134 | 0.683043 (1.732851) | −148083* (−2.117455) | 0.997920* (2.431170) | 0.724866* (2.169636) | 1.165094* (2.003412) | −1879.004* (−1.992006) | −65.09514 |

Notes:
Figures in parentheses are *t*-statistics; *indicates statistically significant at 5% confidence level.

## Hypotheses and Results for Lai and Ho (2002a)

| Hypotheses Regarding Planning Applications for Uses in I Zones | Test Results | Theoretical / Policy Implications |
|---|---|---|
| (1) The likelihood of a bank use approval is independent to the rise and fall of the manufacturing sector? | Hypothesis is refuted. | Planning decisions show preference for the use of bank when the manufacturing sector is declining. |
| (2) Planning decisions show no preference for the use of C/O when the manufacturing sector is declining? | Hypothesis is not refuted. | The likelihood of an application for the use of C/O of being approved is independent to the rise and fall of the manufacturing sector. |
| (3) Planning decisions show no preference for the use of I/O when the manufacturing sector is declining? | Hypothesis is refuted. | Planning decisions show preference for the use of I/O when the manufacturing sector is declining. |
| (4) Planning decisions show no preference for the use of office when the manufacturing sector is declining? | Hypothesis is refuted. | Planning decisions show preference for the use of office when the manufacturing sector is declining. |
| (5) Planning decisions show no preference for the use of ancillary office when the manufacturing sector is expanding? | Hypothesis is not refuted. | The likelihood of an application for the use of ancillary office of being approved is independent to the rise and fall of the manufacturing sector. |

## Probit Estimates of the Decision Function: I Zones; Lai and Ho (2002a)

| Zone | N | $\beta_0$ | BANK | C/O | I/O | AOFF | OFF | ln(GFA) | HK | KLN | ln(ECON) | Log-Likelihood | Percent Correct Predictions |
|---|---|---|---|---|---|---|---|---|---|---|---|---|---|
| I | 1552 | 0.76804* (3.98773) | 0.02706 (0.20510) | −0.05576 (−0.36995) | 0.65521* (4.50609) | 0.25553* (1.79546)* | 0.43271* (3.35385) | −0.08161* (−3.94259) | 0.18696 (1.56348) | −0.30697* (−3.35660) | −0.25738* (−3.09449) | −797.175 | 76.9974 |

Notes:
Figures in parentheses are $t$-statistics; * indicates significant at 1% confidence level; ** indicates significant at 5% confidence level.

**Probit Estimates of the Decision Function: I Zones; Lai and Ho (2002a)**

| Use | N | $\beta_0$ | $\ln(GFA)$ | HK | NT | $\ln(ECON)$ | Log-Likelihood | Percent Correct Prediction |
|---|---|---|---|---|---|---|---|---|
| BANK | 131 | −0.36186 (−0.51316) | −0.00019 (−0.00222) | 0.98341** (1.69884) | 0.12184 (0.45229) | −0.54265** (−2.00303) | −77.8965 | 68.7023 |
| C/O | 151 | −0.93729 (−0.92530) | 0.01447 (0.14773) | 1.15048* (4.14420) | 0.93994* (2.82384) | −0.35293 (−1.53115) | −91.5133 | 70.1987 |
| I/O | 298 | −1.36395 (−1.11867) | −0.03172 (−0.30667) | 0.15068 (0.44317) | 0.04888 (0.23721) | −1.35416* (−4.28238) | −130.574 | 81.8792 |
| AOFF | 190 | 1.00282 (1.13615) | −0.20318* (−2.49569) | 0.65719* (2.37560) | | −0.52099 (−1.55544) | −61.5889 | 88.9474 |
| OFF | 203 | −0.58343 (−0.91373) | −0.01944 (−0.23382) | | | −0.94953* (−4.04003) | −85.4437 | 82.2660 |

Notes:
Figures in parentheses are $t$-statistics; * indicates significant at 1% confidence level; ** indicates significant at 5% confidence level.

## Hypotheses and Results for Lai and Ho (2002b)

| Hypotheses Regarding Planning Applications for Uses in OS Zones | Test Results | Theoretical / Policy Implications |
|---|---|---|
| (1) Planning decisions show no preference for the use of open storage of container? | Hypothesis is not refuted. | Planning applications for the use of open storage of container is not especially favoured. |
| (2) Planning decisions show no preference for larger development (and arguably developer)? | Hypothesis is not refuted. | A necessary condition for rent-seeking thesis is found absent for this category of applications. Planning applications for uses in larger developments have the same chance of success as those for uses in smaller sites. |

## Probit Estimates of the Decision Function: OS Zones; Lai and Ho (2002b)

| Zone | $N$ | $\beta_0$ | CTN | NCS | ln(GSA) | Log-Likelihood | Percent Correct Prediction |
|---|---|---|---|---|---|---|---|
| OS | 157 | 1.04477 (1.27256) | 0.29724 (0.65549) | 1.50579* (4.09670) | −0.06874 (−0.59330) | −44.286 | 88.535 |

Notes:
Figures in parentheses are $t$-statistics; * indicates significant at 1% confidence level; ** indicates significant at 5% confidence level.

## Appendix 3  207

### Hypotheses and Results for Lai and Ho (2002c, 2003)

| Hypotheses Regarding Planning Applications for Uses in CDA, G/IC & GB Zones | Test Results | Theoretical / Policy Implications |
|---|---|---|
| (1) Planning decisions show no preference for larger development (and arguably developer)?<br>(a) CDA Zones<br>(b) G/IC Zones<br>(c) GB Zones | Hypothesis is refuted.<br>Hypothesis is not refuted.<br>Hypothesis is not refuted. | A necessary condition for rent-seeking thesis is found present in CDA Zones only.<br>Larger development has a greater chance of success.<br>In fact, small development has a greater chance of success.<br>In fact, small development has a greater chance of success. |
| (2) Planning decisions insensitive to exogenous housing policies?<br>(a) CDA Zones<br>(b) G/IC Zones<br>(c) GB Zones | Hypothesis is not refuted.<br>Hypothesis is not refuted.<br>Hypothesis is not refuted. | Planning decisions are found insulated from other or wider governmental policies. |

### Probit Estimates of the Decision Function: CDA, G/IC & GB Zones; Lai and Ho (2002c, 2003)

| Zones | N | $\beta_0$ | C/R | RES | ln(GFA) | POLICY | HK | KLN | RURAL | NT | Log-Likelihood | Percent Correct Prediction |
|---|---|---|---|---|---|---|---|---|---|---|---|---|
| CDA | 287 | −0.11076<br>(−0.29054) | | −0.29944<br>(−1.60675) | 0.09004**<br>(2.22158) | 0.30161<br>(1.48308) | | | | | −155.767 | 75.6098 |
| G/IC | 551 | 1.25700*<br>(5.37356) | −0.12621<br>(−0.82963) | −0.33021**<br>(−2.36598) | −0.07509*<br>(−2.71392) | 0.15466<br>(0.82354) | | | | | −328.710 | 69.6915 |
| GB | 573 | 0.72450*<br>(2.60865) | 0.62408<br>(1.23656) | −0.78810*<br>(−4.93837) | −0.10182*<br>(−2.96861) | −0.09308<br>(−0.66507) | 0.73493*<br>(3.12969) | 1.15567*<br>(2.91654) | 0.327917<br>(1.46420) | 0.49930*<br>(2.46231) | −335.261 | 71.2042 |

Notes:
Figures in parentheses are the absolute values of *t*-statistics;
* indicates significant at 1% level;
** indicates significant at 5% level.

## Hypotheses and Results for Chiu (2002)

| Hypotheses Regarding Planning Applications for Uses in REC Zones | Test Results | Theoretical / Policy Implications |
|---|---|---|
| (1) Planning decisions show no preference for larger development (and arguably developer). | Hypothesis is not refuted. | A necessary condition for rent-seeking thesis is found absent in this category of applications. |
| (2) Incompatible proposed uses, i.e., open storage uses and container related (port back-up) uses, do not have lower chance of getting approval. | Hypothesis is not refuted. | The current planning system does not necessarily reduce negative externalities (social cost). |
| (3) Planning intention is not significant in affecting the chance of success of the planning application. | Hypothesis is not refuted. | The current planning system does not provide certainty. |

## Probit Estimates of the Decision Function: REC Zones; Chiu (2002)

| Zone | N | $\beta_0$ | Log (GFA/GSA) | C | OS | RES | VTH | Log-Likelihood |
|---|---|---|---|---|---|---|---|---|
| REC | 192 | 0.074773 (0.152621) | 0.039455 (0.620065) | 0.866808* (-2.898105) | -0.299854 (-1.317463) | -1.080138* (-2.939030) | 0.815387** (2.474734) | -114.8134 |

Notes:
Figures in parentheses are *t*-statistics; * indicates statistically significant at 1% confidence level; ** indicates statistically significant at 5% confidence level.

## Probit Estimates of the Decision Function: Small house (VTH) and open storage (OS); Chiu (2002)

| Use | N | $\beta_0$ | Log(GFA) | Log(GSA) | Policy | PR | Size | Log-Likelihood |
|---|---|---|---|---|---|---|---|---|
| VTH | 37 | 4.438348 (2.061767) | -0.619767 (-1.582315) | | 0.082958 (0.151272) | N/A*** (N/A) | | -13.38975 |
| OS | 60 | -0.845511 (-0.849138) | | 0.158356 (1.062596) | | | -0.552322 (-1.138731) | -40.83937 |

Notes:
Figures in parentheses are *t*-statistics; no independent variable here is significant.
*** the variable PR is not incorporated into model 2, as it is found that all observations in the data set have the same value of 1. Obviously, this variable exerts no effect on the chance of success for small house applications.

## Hypotheses and Results for Kwan (2002)

| Hypotheses Regarding Planning Applications for Uses in UNSP and I(D) Zones | Test Results | Theoretical/Policy Implications |
|---|---|---|
| (1) The chance of success in obtaining planning permission for industrial use in I(D) Zones is easier than in UNSP Zones. | Hypothesis is refuted. | In theoretical context, UNSP and I(D) Zones are inseparable with respect to the industrial use. |
| (2) Planning applications for development in I(D) Zones are associated with a higher chance of being approved than those in UNSP Zones. | Hypothesis is not refuted. | There is higher chance of getting planning permission for any development in I(D) Zones than in UNSP Zones. |
| (3) Planning decisions show preference for larger development in UNSP Zones. | Hypothesis is refuted. | Planning applications for uses in larger developments have lower chance of success smaller sites. |

## Probit Estimates of the Decision Function: Unspecified Use and Industrial (Group D) Zones; Kwan (2002)

| Zones | N | $\beta_0$ | IDIND | ID | IND | Ln(GFA) | Log-Likelihood | Percent Correct Predictions |
|---|---|---|---|---|---|---|---|---|
| UNSP & I(D) | 1069 | 1.536966* (10.35796) | 6.454207 (8.53E−06) | 1.651467* (4.780525) | −0.167529* (−0.85696) | −0.221442* (−9.558827) | −648.9839 | 10.4708 |

Note: Figures in parentheses are $t$-statistics.
* indicates significant at 1% level.

## Probit Estimates of the Decision Function: Unspecified Use Zones; Kwan (2002)

| Zones | N | $\beta_0$ | IND | VTH | RES | OS | W | REC | CVP | ln (GFA) | Log-Likelihood | Percent Correct Predictions |
|---|---|---|---|---|---|---|---|---|---|---|---|---|
| UNSP | 1008 | 1.417565* (6.324658) | −0.08989 (−0.422338) | 0.034772 (0.250738) | −0.368658 (−1.865381) | −0.492561* (−2.869245) | −0.282857 (−1.350492) | 0.471017** (2.071309) | −0.494036 (−1.793422) | −0.189148 (−6.191934) | −628.7972 | 8.9417 |

Note: Figures in parentheses are $t$-statistics.
* indicates significant at 1% level;
** indicates significant at 5% level.

## Hypotheses and Results for Ngai (2002)

| Hypotheses Regarding Planning Applications for Uses in REC Zones | Test Results | Theoretical / Policy Implications |
|---|---|---|
| (1) Planning decisions show no preference for larger development (and arguably developer). | Hypothesis is not refuted. | A necessary condition for rent-seeking thesis is found absent in this category of applications. |
| (2) Planning decisions are insensitive to changes in exogenous government land and housing policies towards development. | Hypothesis is not refuted. | Planning decisions are insensitive to changes in exogenous government land and housing policies towards development. |
| (3) Planning applications for the development of VTH use are associated with a greater chance of being approved than other uses. | Hypothesis is not refuted. | Planning decisions show preference to VTH use in AGR Zones. |
| (4) Planning applications for container use are associated with a greater chance of being approved than other uses. | Hypothesis is refuted. | Planning decisions show no preference to container use in AGR Zones. |
| (5) Planning applications for open storage use are associated with a greater chance of being approved than other uses. | Hypothesis is refuted. | Planning decisions show no preference to open storage use in AGR Zones. |

## Probit Estimates of the Decision Function: AGR Zones; Ngai (2002)

| Zone | N | C | Container | OP | VTH | TIME | Log(GFA) | Log-Likelihood |
|---|---|---|---|---|---|---|---|---|
| A | 1392 | −0.061363 (−0.340607) | −0.448806 (−1.656534) | −0.375976** (−2.404341) | 0.424590* (3.061153) | 0.042182 (0.571866) | −8.769662** (−1.981333) | −816.2420 |

Notes:
Figures in parentheses are *t*-statistics; * indicates statistically significant at 1% confidence level; ** indicates statistically significant at 5% confidence level.

## Hypotheses and Results for Chan (2003)

| Hypotheses Regarding Planning Applications for Uses in AGR Zones | Test Results | Theoretical / Policy Implications |
|---|---|---|
| (1) Planning decisions show no preference for VTH use. | Hypothesis is refuted. | TPB treats planning applications for different uses in an asymmetric way that prefers VTH to open storage and car park uses. |
| (2) It is more difficult to get approvals in less accessible sites than in more accessible sites. | Hypothesis is refuted. | Accessibility of the site is one of the decision criteria; more accessible agricultural land tends to be retained. |
| (3) Planning decisions show no preference for larger development. | Hypothesis is refuted. | There is *prima facie* evidence indicating that there are rent-seeking activities within Hong Kong's planning permission system. |
| (4) It is more difficult to get approvals while prime interest rate is lower. | Hypothesis is refuted. | Planning decisions are found sensitive to the overall economic environment in Hong Kong. |

## Probit Estimates of the Decision Function: AGR Zones; Chan (2003)

| Zone | N | C | VTH | OS | CP | GFA | 1/DIST | PIR | Log-Likelihood |
|---|---|---|---|---|---|---|---|---|---|
| AGR | 1226 | 1.141358 (3.668163) | 0.420038** (2.151566) | −0.740369* (−3.743793) | −0.746434** (−2.490644) | 5.02E−05** (2.114360) | −2.473863** (−2.534284) | −0.077321** (−2.488818) | −648.8042 |

Notes:
Figures in parentheses are *t*-statistics; * indicates statistically significant at 1% confidence level; ** indicates statistically significant at 5% confidence level.

## Hypotheses and Results for Liu (2003)

| Hypotheses Regarding Planning Applications for Uses in Undetermined and Open Storage (OS) Zones | Test Results | Theoretical / Policy Implications |
|---|---|---|
| (1) OS and Undetermined Zones for all uses both have the same chance of obtaining planning permission. | Hypothesis 1 is rejected. | Undetermined Zones have greater chance of success than Open Storage Zones. Presumption against development in the zone does not hold. |
| (2) The chance of success in obtaining planning permission for the use of open storage of container related uses is the same in both OS and Undetermined Zones. | Hypothesis 2 is not rejected. | The two dissimilar zones are inseparable with respect to container-related uses. Zone separation does not exist corresponding to such use. |
| (3) The chance of success in obtaining planning permission for the use of open storage of non-container-related uses is the same in both OS and Undetermined Zones. | Hypothesis 3 is rejected. | The two dissimilar zones are separable with respect to non-container related uses. Zone separation exists corresponding to such use. |
| (4) Planning approvals for open storage of container-related uses on or after 11 Oct 2000 (announcement of the Logistics Policy in both OS and Undetermined Zones) are associated with equal or greater likelihood of being approved than those decided before that date. | Hypothesis 4 is rejected. | Internal inconsistency among different planning levels exists. |
| (5) The likelihood of a successful application for a larger site area in both the OS and Undetermined Zones is neither greater nor smaller than that of a smaller site. | Hypothesis 5 is not rejected. | It is contrary to the guidelines stating that larger sites have a favourable factor on approvals. |
| (6) Planning applications for open storage container-related uses enjoy *greater* success when the container trade industry is growing (in terms of the growth of container throughput in previous years) in OS Zones. | Hypothesis 6 is rejected. | Development control decisions are found to be anti-market. |
| (7) Planning applications for open storage container-related uses enjoy *greater* success when the container trade industry is growing (in terms of the growth of container throughput in previous years) in Undetermined Zones. | Hypothesis 7 is rejected. | Development control decisions are found to be anti-market. |

## Probit Estimates of Decision Function: Open Storage and Undetermined Zones; Liu (2003)

| Zone | N | C | CTN | NCS | POLICY | LOG (GFA) | LOG (TEUP) | U | UCTN | UNCS | Log-Likelihood |
|---|---|---|---|---|---|---|---|---|---|---|---|
| OS and Undetermined as a whole | 433 | −6.325405** (−2.184390) | 0.439853 (1.842034) | 0.757466* (3.535954) | 0.631423** (−2.504192) | −0.066601 (−1.576446) | −0.409867** (−2.436091) | 1.44E−06** (2.542050) | 41.10846 (1.062537) | −0.826754* (−4.895970) | −178.2536 |

Notes:
Figures in parentheses are z-statistics; * indicates statistically significant at 1% confidence level; ** indicates statistically significant at 5% confidence level.

## Probit Estimates of the Decision Function: Open Storage Zones; Liu (2003)

| Zone | N | C | CTN | NCS | POLICY | LOG(GFA) | LOG(TEUP) | Log-Likelihood |
|---|---|---|---|---|---|---|---|---|
| OS | 240 | −0.752224 (−0.744170) | 0.364023 (0.867796) | 1.086536* (3.410636) | −0.185982 (−0.586357) | −0.100123 (−1.016122) | −1.002158* (−2.721312) | −68.64746 |

Notes:
Figures in parentheses are z-statistics;
* indicates statistically significant at 1% confidence level;
** indicates statistically significant at 5% confidence level.

## Probit Estimates of the Decision Function: Undetermined Zones; Liu (2003)

| Zone | N | C | CTN | NCS | POLICY | LOG(GFA) | LOG(TEUP) | Log-Likelihood |
|---|---|---|---|---|---|---|---|---|
| Undetermined | 193 | −0.356378 (−0.587627) | 0.591440 (1.930620) | 0.805506* (2.691818) | −0.715305** (−2.444178) | −0.068317 (−1.391621) | −0.469106* (−2.995444) | −109.2359 |

Notes:
Figures in parentheses are z-statistics; * indicates statistically significant at 1% confidence level; ** indicates statistically significant at 5% confidence level.

## Hypotheses and Results for Yu (2003)

| Hypotheses Regarding Planning Applications for Uses in CA, CPA, GB, SSSI, REC and RPA Zones | Test Results | Theoretical/Policy Implications |
|---|---|---|
| (1) Planning applications for development in recreation-related zones (RPA and REC Zones) enjoy greater success in obtaining approval by the Town Planning Board than those in conservation-related zones (GB, CA, SSSI and CPA Zones). | Hypothesis is not refuted. | Recreation-related zones are purposely zoned for low density development, while conservation-related zones are zoned mainly for conservation. |
| (2) The chance of success in obtaining planning permission is higher for applications for change in use in the Northwestern New Territories, Yuen Long, Fanling and Sheung Shui than those in other areas. | Hypothesis is not refuted. | Planning decisions arising from conservation-related and recreation-related zones are found to be sensitive to the degree of urbanization of sites. |
| (3) Planning applications for 'community' uses is likely to be a significant decision criterion for approving planning applications in recreation and conservation related zones. | Hypothesis is not refuted. | Planning decisions arising from conservation-related and recreation-related zones show preference for 'community' uses. |
| (4) Planning applications for 'utility' uses are associated with a greater likelihood of being approved by the Town Planning Board. | Hypothesis is not refuted. | Planning decisions arising from conservation-related and recreation-related zones show preference for 'utility' uses. |

## Hypotheses and Results for Yu (2003) (Cont'd)

| Hypotheses Regarding Planning Applications for Uses in CA, CPA, GB, SSSI, REC and RPA Zones | Test Results | Theoretical/Policy Implications |
|---|---|---|
| (5) The use 'OS' is likely to be a significant decision criterion for disapproval of planning applications. | Hypothesis is not refuted. | In accordance with the statutory planning intentions and administrative guidelines, uses which generate significant adverse environmental impacts are not preferred in conservation-related and recreation-related zones. |
| (6) Planning applications for 'carpark' uses in Recreation Zones are associated with a greater likelihood to be approved than in Conservation Zones. | Hypothesis is refuted. | In accordance with the statutory planning intentions and administrative guidelines, uses which generate significant adverse environmental impacts are not preferred in conservation-related and recreation-related zones. |
| (7) Applications for 'VTH' uses have a greater chance of being approved within recreation- and conservation-related zones than for other uses. | Hypothesis is refuted. | The use 'VTH' has no significant impact on the decisions made by the TPB. |
| (8) Planning applications for 'residential' uses have a lower probability of being approved by the Town Planning Board within recreation and conservation-related zones. | Hypothesis is not refuted. | In accordance with the statutory planning intentions and administrative guidelines, uses which generate significant adverse environmental impacts are not preferred in conservation-related and recreation-related zones. |
| (9) Planning applications for uses on larger sites do not have a smaller chance of success than those on smaller sites. | Hypothesis is not refuted. | |

## Appendix 3

**Probit Estimates of the Decision Function: CA, CPA, GB, SSSI, REC and RPA Zones; Yu (2003)**

| Zones | N | $\beta_0$ | COMMU | CPK | FANLING & SHEUNG SHUI | ISLAND | NORTHERN NT | OS | RES | SA |
|---|---|---|---|---|---|---|---|---|---|---|
| CA, CPA, GB, SSSI, REC & RPA | 1048 | 0.552574* (3.647163) | 0.479370** (2.313696) | −0.413384* (−2.650860) | −0.449643** (−2.092248) | −0.022421 (−0.091318) | −0.905652* (−3.278896) | −0.455998* (−2.853354) | −0.756797* (−5.570537) | 6.07E-07 (1.027404) |

| SAI KUNG | SHA TIN | TUEN MUN | TAI PO | TSUEN WAN & KWAI CHUNG | REC USE | UTILITY | VTH | YUEN LONG | ZRECS | Log-Likelihood |
|---|---|---|---|---|---|---|---|---|---|---|
| −0.336409 (−1.762888) | −0.252359 (−1.074867) | −0.031869 (−0.118585) | 0.030286 (0.159495) | −0.261490 (−1.076642) | 0.140040 (0.790342) | 1.348518* (5.827717) | 0.202489 (1.526857) | −0.464844** (−2.550324) | 0.315586* (2.636048) | −585.7123 |

Notes:
Figures in parentheses are the absolute values of $t$-statistics; * indicates significant at 1% level; ** indicates significant at 5% level.

**Appendix 3** 217

**Probit Estimates of the Decision Function: CA, CPA, GB, REC and RPA Zones; Yu (2003)**

| Zones | N | $\beta_0$ | CPK | COMMU | OS | RES | REC USE | UTILITY | VTH | ZCA | ZGB | ZRECS | Log-Likelihood |
|---|---|---|---|---|---|---|---|---|---|---|---|---|---|
| CA, CPA, GB, REC & RPA | 1042 | 0.219830 (0.972714) | −0.473472* (−3.127038) | 0.556123* (2.634095) | −0.575393* (−3.943556) | −0.711181* (−5.473534) | 0.259975 (1.498587) | 1.495125* (6.577144) | 0.229977** (2.005499) | −0.282159 (−0.928210) | 0.119414 (0.545143) | 0.269660 (1.228311) | −592.8956 |

Notes:
Figures in parentheses are the absolute values of *t*-statistics; * indicates significant at 1% level; ** indicates significant at 5% level.

**Probit Estimates of the Decision Function: Car Park Uses; Yu (2003)**

| Uses | N | $\beta_0$ | SITE AREA | ZRECS | Log-Likelihood |
|---|---|---|---|---|---|
| Car park | 89 | −1.534121 (−6.971516) | −9.122402 (−1.97E−11) | −9.122402 (−1.76E−11) | −18.70333 |

Notes:
Figures in parentheses are the absolute values of *t*-statistics; * indicates significant at 1% level; ** indicates significant at 5% level.

**Probit Estimates of the Decision Function: Car Park Uses; Yu (2003)**

| Uses | N | $\beta_0$ | SITE AREA | ZCA | ZCPA | ZGB | ZSSSI | Log-Likelihood |
|---|---|---|---|---|---|---|---|---|
| Car park | 89 | −1.048308 (−3.189327) | −7.425266 (−1.78E−07) | −6.65E−05 (−1.135648) | −7.453143 (−2.27E−07) | −7.457495 (−2.31E−07) | −7.501452 (−1.78E−07) | −16.11847 |

Notes:
Figures in parentheses are the absolute values of *t*-statistics; * indicates significant at 1% level; ** indicates significant at 5% level.

**Probit Estimates of the Decision Function: VTH Uses; Yu (2003)**

| Uses | N | $\beta_0$ | SITE AREA | ZCA | ZCPA | ZGB | Log-Likelihood |
|---|---|---|---|---|---|---|---|
| VTH | 348 | 1.107781 (4.282431) | −1.46E−05 (−1.904671) | −0.675879 (−0.853418) | −1.093872 (−1.187327) | −0.548462** (−2.032224) | −202.4320 |

Notes:
Figures in parentheses are the absolute values of *t*-statistics; * indicates significant at 1% level; ** indicates significant at 5% level.

## Hypotheses and Results for Yu (2003) (Cont'd)

| Hypotheses Regarding Development Applications for Uses in Country Parks Areas | Test Results | Theoretical / Policy Implications |
|---|---|---|
| (1) The approval of development applications arising from a country park is not associated with any location consideration. | Hypothesis is not refuted. | Development decisions arising from country parks are found to be independent of location consideration. |
| (2) Development applications for overhead line installations are associated with a smaller likelihood to be approved than applications for underground cable laying. | Hypothesis is not refuted. | Development decisions arising from country parks show preference for 'underground cable laying' through other uses. |
| (3) Development applications for 'slope protection' contribute a larger probability to be approved. | Hypothesis is not refuted. | Development decisions arising from parks show preference for 'slope protection'. |
| (4) Development applications for 'emergency telephone-helpline installations' are associated with a greater likelihood to be approved. | Hypothesis is not refuted. | Development decisions arising from country parks show preference for 'emergency telephone-helpline installations'. |
| (5) Development applications for 'drainage system installations' stand higher chances of success. | Hypothesis is refuted. | The Country and Marine Park Authority does not regard this use as a significant criterion when considering applications. |
| (6) Development applications for 'construction of footpaths or trails' are associated with a greater likelihood to be approved. | Hypothesis is refuted. | The Country and Marine Park Authority does not regard this use as a significant criterion when considering applications. |
| (7) Development applications for 'lighting provisions' are associated with a great likelihood to be approved. | Hypothesis is refuted. | The Country and Marine Park Authority does not regard this use as a significant criterion when considering applications. |
| (8) Development applications for 'infrastructure development' are less likely to be approved by the Country and Marine Parks Authority. | Hypothesis is refuted. | The Country and Marine Park Authority does not regard this use as a significant interior when considering applications. |

## Appendix 3

**Probit Estimates of the Decision Function: Agriculture Zones; Chau and Lai (2003)**

| Zones | N | $\beta_0$ | VTH | OS | LGFA | POLICY | SHEUNG SHUI | FANLING | TAIPO | YUEN LONG | Log-Likelihood |
|---|---|---|---|---|---|---|---|---|---|---|---|
| Agriculture | 1371 | −0.631122 (−1.399846) | 0.410713* (2.844353) | −0.423058* (−3.240125) | −0.097449** (−2.111807) | −0.274756* (2.871689) | 1.897947* (5.982363) | 1.439303* (4.801184) | 1.998079* (6.671212) | 1.705292* (5.654277) | −695.3542 |

Notes:
Figures in parentheses are the values of $t$-statistics; * indicates significant at 1% level; ** indicates significant at 5% level.

## Hypotheses and Results for Lai and Ho (2003)

| Hypotheses Regarding Development Applications for Uses in CDA zones | Test Results | Theoretical/Policy Implications |
|---|---|---|
| (1) Planning applications for uses in larger sites (measured in terms of proposed gross floor area [GFA] of the building or use) have no greater chance of success (being approved by the Town Planning Board) than those for uses in smaller sites. | Hypothesis is refuted. | The Town Planning Board discriminates against smaller development (developer). |
| (2) Planning approvals are insensitive to changes in exogenous government policies towards development: a planning application decided on/after 1 July 1997 (on which a major exogenous government policy was announced) is not more likely to be approved by the Town Planning Board than those decided before that date. | Hypothesis is not refuted. | The Town Planning Board is insensitive to exogenous government policies. |
| (3) Planning applications for Residential use (RES) in CDA Zones are not associated with a greater likelihood of being approved by the Town Planning Board than uses permissible for these zones. | Hypothesis is not refuted. | |

## Hypotheses and Results for Lai and Ho (2003)

| Hypotheses Regarding Development Applications for Uses in G/IC zones | Test Results | Theoretical/Policy Implications |
|---|---|---|
| (1) Planning applications for uses in larger sites (measured in terms of proposed gross floor area [GFA] of the building or use) have no greater chance of success (being approved by the Town Planning Board) than those for uses in smaller sites. | Hypothesis is not refuted. | The Town Planning Board discriminates against larger development (developer). |
| (2) Planning approvals are insensitive to changes in exogenous government policies towards development: a planning application decided on/after 1 July 1997 (on which a major exogenous government policy was announced) is not more likely to be approved by the Town Planning Board than those decided before that date. | Hypothesis is not refuted. | The Town Planning Board is insensitive to exogenous government policies. |
| (3) Planning applications for Commercial/Residential use (C/R) or Residential use (RES) in G/IC Zones are not associated with a greater likelihood of being approved by the Town Planning Board than uses permissible for these zones. | Hypothesis is not refuted. | The Town Planning Board discriminates against residential development. |

## Hypotheses and Results for Lai and Ho (2003)

| Hypotheses Regarding Development Applications for Uses in GB zones | Test Results | Theoretical/Policy Implications |
|---|---|---|
| (1) Planning applications for uses in larger sites (measured in terms of proposed gross floor area [GFA] of the building or use) have no greater chance of success (being approved by the Town Planning Board) than those for uses in smaller sites. | Hypothesis is not refuted. | The Town Planning Board discriminates against larger development (developer). |
| (2) Planning approvals are insensitive to changes in exogenous government policies towards development: a planning application decided on/after 1 July 1997 (on which a major exogenous government policy was announced) is not more likely to be approved by the Town Planning Board than decided before that date. | Hypothesis is not refuted. | The Town Planning Board is insensitive to exogenous government policies. |
| (3) Planning applications for Commercial/Residential use against (C/R) or Residential use (RES) in GB Zones are not associated with a greater likelihood of being approved by the Town Planning Board than uses permissible for these zones. | Hypothesis is not refuted. | The Town Planning Board discriminates residential development. |
| (4) Planning permissions in GB Zones are not determined by location factors. | Hypothesis is refuted. | HK, KLN and NT have been found to exert positive influence on the decision making of the Town Planning Board. |

## Probit Estimates of the Decision Function: CDA, G/IC & GB Zones; Lai and Ho (2003)

| Zones | N | $\beta_0$ | C/R | RES | ln(GFA) | POLICY | HK | KLN | RURAL | NT | Log-Likelihood |
|---|---|---|---|---|---|---|---|---|---|---|---|
| CDA | 287 | −0.11076 (−0.29054) | | −0.29944 (−1.60675) | 0.09004** (2.22158) | 0.30161 (1.48308) | | | | | −155.767 |
| G/IC | 551 | 1.25700* (5.37356) | −0.12621 (−0.82963) | −0.33021** (−2.36598) | −0.07509* (−2.71392) | 0.15466 (0.82354) | | | | | −328.710 |
| GB | 573 | 0.72450* (2.60865) | 0.62408 (1.23656) | −0.78810* (−4.93837) | −0.10182* (−2.96861) | −0.09308 (−0.66507) | 0.73493* (3.12969) | 1.15567* (2.91654) | 0.327917 (1.46420) | 0.49930* (2.46231) | −335.261 |

Notes:
Figures in parentheses are the values of $t$-statistics; * indicates significant at 1% level; ** indicates significant at 5% level.

# REFERENCES

## General Readings

### Government Documents

Lands Department, *A Guide to Processing Development Submission*, Hong Kong, Lands Department, unpublished Lands Department handbook, **1998**.

### Published Works

Lai, Lawrence Wai-chung, *Town Planning in Hong Kong: A Review of Planning Appeal Decisions*, Hong Kong, Hong Kong University Press, **1999**, reprinted edition, **2001**.

Lai, Lawrence Wai-chung, *Town Planning in Hong Kong: A Review of Planning Appeal Decisions 1997–2001*, Hong Kong, Hong Kong University Press, **2003**.

Lai, Lawrence Wai-chung and Ho, Daniel Chi-wing, *Planning Buildings in High Density Environment: A Review of Building Appeal Decisions*, Hong Kong, Hong Kong University Press, 2000, reprinted edition, **2002**.

Nissim, Roger, *Land Administration and Practice in Hong Kong*, Hong Kong, Hong Kong University Press, **1998**.

Roberts, P. J., *Valuation of Development Land in Hong Kong*, Hong Kong, Hong Kong University Press, **1975**.

Roberts, P. J. and Siu, J. C. P., *Valuation of Development Land in Hong Kong*, second edition, Hong Kong, Empire Publications International Ltd., **2001**.

Smith, Peter Cookson, 'Town Planning Procedures', in Wong, Wah Sang and Chan, Edwin Hon Wan eds. *Professional Practice for Architects in Hong Kong*, Hong Kong, Pace Publishing Ltd., **1997**, pp. 146–77.

Talbot, Lee M. and Talbot, Martha H., *Conservation of the Hong Kong Countryside: Summary Report and Recommendation by Lee M. Talbot and Martha H. Talbot,* Hong Kong, Government Printer, **1965**.

## Further Readings

### Property Rights and Town Planning

*Published Works*

Cooray, Anton, 'Government as Ground Landlord and Land Use Regulator: The Hong Kong Experience', in Kotaka, Tsugoshi and Callies, David L. eds. *Taking*

*Land: Compulsory Purchase and Regulation in Asia-Pacific Countries*. Hawaii, University of Hawai'i, University of Hawai'i Press, **2002**, pp. 90–143.

Lai, Lawrence Wai-chung, 'The Economics of Land Use Zoning: A Literature Review and Analysis of the Work of Coase', *Town Planning Review*, Vol. 65, No. 1, **1994**, pp. 59–76.

Lai, Lawrence Wai-chung, 'The Leasehold System as a Means of Planning by Contract', *Town Planning Review*, Vol. 69, No. 3, **1998**, pp. 249–76.

Lai, Lawrence Wai-chung, '"Fifty Years No Change?" Land Use Planning and Development in Hong Kong Under Constitutional Capitalism', in Chapter 10, Chan, M. and So, A. eds. *Crisis and Transformation in China's Hong Kong*, Armonk, M. E. Sharpe and Hong Kong, Hong Kong University Press, **2002**, pp. 257–82.

Lai, Lawrence Wai-chung, 'Libertarians on the Road to Town Planning: A Note on the Views of Robert Mundell, Karl Popper, Friedrich Hayek, Robert Nozick, Milton Friedman, and Ronald Coase towards Pollution', *Town Planning Review*, Vol. 73, No. 3, **2002**, pp. 289–310.

Lai, Lawrence Wai-chung, 'Planning and Property Rights in Hong Kong under Constitutional Capitalism', *International Planning Studies*, Vol. 7, No. 3, **2002**, pp. 213–25.

Lai, Lawrence Wai-chung and Yu, Marco Ka-wai, 'The Rise and Fall of Discriminatory Zoning in Hong Kong', *Environment and Planning B: Planning and Design*, Vol. 28, No. 2, **2001**, pp. 295–314.

Webster, Chris J. and Lai, Lawrence Wai-chung, *Property Rights, Planning and Markets: Managing Spontaneous Cities*, Edward Elgar, Cheltenhem, **2003**.

## Land Administration Law

### Published Works

Law, Anthony M. W. 'Judicial Review of Government Leases in the Hong Kong Special Administrative Region', *Hong Kong Law Journal*, Vol. 29, **1999**, pp. 240–66.

## Building Control Law

### Published Works

Glofcheski, R. A. 'Defective Buildings and Defective Law: The Duty of Care in Negligence', *Hong Kong Law Journal*, Vol. 30, Part II, **2000**, pp. 206–22.

## Conveyancing, Land Compensation and Property Management Law

*Published Works*

Cruden, G. N., *Land Compensation and Valuation Law in Hong Kong*, second edition, Hong Kong, Butterworths, **1999**.

Kent, Paul, Merry, Malcolm and Walters, Megan, *Building Management in Hong Kong*. Hong Kong, Butterworths, **2002**.

Lai, Lawrence Wai-chung and Chan, Pearl Yik-long, 'The Formation of Owners' Corporations in Hong Kong's Private Housing Estates: A Probit Evaluation of Mancur Olson's Group Theory', *Property Management*, Vol. 22, No. 1, **2004**, pp. 55–68.

Sihombing, Judith and Wilkinson, Michael, *A Student's Guide to Hong Kong Conveyancing*, 3rd ed., Hong Kong, Butterworths, **1999**.

## Development Control: Statistical Analysis

*Published Works*

Lai, Lawrence Wai-chung and Ho, Winky Kin-on, 'Small Is Beautiful: A Probit Analysis of Planning Applications for Small Houses in Hong Kong', *Environment and Planning B: Planning and Design*, Vol. 28, No. 4, **2001a**, pp. 611–22.

Lai, Lawrence Wai-chung and Ho, Winky Kin-on, 'A Probit Analysis of Development Control: A Hong Kong Case Study on Residential Zones', *Urban Studies*, Vol. 38, No. 13, **2001b**, pp. 2425–37.

Lai, Lawrence Wai-chung and Ho, Winky Kin-on, 'Zone Separation: A Probit Analysis of Hong Kong Planning Application Statistics', *Environment and Planning B: Planning and Design*, Vol. 28 No. 6, **2001c**, pp. 923–32.

Lai, Lawrence Wai-chung and Ho, Winky Kin-on, 'Low-Rise Residential Developments in Green Belts: A Hong Kong Empirical Study of Planning Applications', *Planning Practice and Research*, Vol. 16, No. 3/4, **2001d**, pp. 321–25.

Lai, Lawrence Wai-chung and Ho, Winky Kin-on, 'An Econometric Study of the Decisions of a Town Planning Authority: Complementary & Substitute Uses of Industrial Activities in Hong Kong', *Managerial and Decision Economics*, Vol. 23, No. 3, **2002a**, pp. 121–35.

Lai, Lawrence Wai-chung and Ho, Winky Kin-on, 'Using Probit Models in Planning Theory: An Illustration', *Planning Theory*, Vol. 1, No. 2, **2002b**, pp. 147–63.

Lai, Lawrence Wai-chung and Ho, Winky Kin-on, 'Planning for Open Storage of Containers in a Major International Container Trade Centre: A Quantitative Analysis of Hong Kong Development Control Statistics', *Environment and Planning B: Planning and Design*, Vol. 23, No. 3, **2002c**, pp. 571–87.

Lai, Lawrence Wai-chung and Ho, Winky Kin-on, 'Using Probit Models in Planning Theory: An Illustration', *Planning Theory*, Vol. 1, No. 2, **2002d**, pp. 146–62.

Lai, Lawrence Wai-chung and Ho, Winky Kin-on, 'Modelling Development Control of Residential Development: A Probit Analysis of Rent Seeking and Policy Autonomy in Town Planning in Hong Kong', in Columbus, Frank ed., *Politics and Economics of Asia*, Vol. VII, Nova Science Publishers, **2003**, pp. 155–76.

Tang, B. S. and Choy, L. H. T. 'Modelling Planning Control Decisions: A Logistics Regression Analysis on Office Development Applications in Urban Kowloon, Hong Kong', *Cities*, Vol. 17, No. 3, **2000**, pp. 219–25.

Tang, B. S., Choy, L. H. T. and Wat, J. K. F. 'Certainty and Discretion in Planning Control: A Case Study of Office Development in Hong Kong', *Urban Studies*, Vol. 37, No. 13, **2000**, pp. 2465–83.

Tang, B. S. and Tang, R. M. H. 'Development Control, Planning Incentive and Urban Redevelopment: Evaluation of a Two-tier Plot Ratio System in Hong Kong', *Land Use Policy*, Vol. 16, No. 1, **1999**, pp. 33–43.

*Unpublished Dissertations*

Chan K. W., Development Control in Agriculture Zones: A Probit Analysis of Hong Kong Planning Statistics. Unpublished B.Sc. (Surveying) dissertation, The University of Hong Kong, **2003**.

Chiu S. T. S., An Economic Inquiry on Planning: A Case Study of Recreation Zoning in Hong Kong. Unpublished B.Sc. (Surveying) dissertation, The University of Hong Kong, **2002**.

Kwan K. Y., Modelling Planning Application Statistics in Hong Kong: A Probit Analysis of Zone Separation of Unspecified Use and Industrial (Group D) Zones. Unpublished B.Sc. (Surveying) dissertation, The University of Hong Kong, **2002**.

Liu H. L., Zone Separation: A Probit Analysis of Hong Kong Planning Application Statistics Relating to Open Storage Use. Unpublished B.Sc. (Surveying) dissertation, The University of Hong Kong, **2003**.

Ngai T. H., An Analysis of the Statutory Planning Control Mechanism in Hong Kong: A Probit Study of Agriculture Zones. Unpublished B.Sc. (Surveying) dissertation, The University of Hong Kong, **2002**.

Yu W. C., Modelling Town Planning Statistics for Recreation and Conservation Zones in Hong Kong. Unpublished B.Sc. (Surveying) dissertation, The University of Hong Kong, **2003**.

Yung P., Decisive Criteria in Development Control Decisions: A Probit Inquiry. Unpublished B.Sc. (Surveying) dissertation, The University of Hong Kong, **2001**.

## Lease Enforcement

*Published Works*

Lai, Lawrence Wai-chung, 'Enforcement Against Alleged Breaches of Crown

(Government) Leases in Hong Kong Industrial Premises', *Property Management*, Vol. 18, No. 1, **2000**, pp. 63–73.

## Planning Enforcement

*Government Documents*

Planning Department, *High Court Cases on Enforcement Against Unauthorised Development under the Town Planning Ordinance, Volume One 1991 – March 1995*, unpublished report.

Planning Department, *Planning and Related Cases in Hong Kong, Volume Two May 1995 – July 1996*, unpublished report.

Planning Department, *Town Planning Appeal Cases in Hong Kong 29. 12. 1993 – 31. 7. 2002*, unpublished report.

Town Planning Board, *Guidance Notes: Application for Permission under Section 16 of the Town Planning Ordinance (Cap. 131)*, undated.

Town Planning Board, *Guidance Notes: Application for Permission under Section for Temporary Open Storage and Port Back-Up Uses 16 of the Town Planning Ordinance (Cap. 131)*, undated.

*Published Works*

Lai, Lawrence Wai-chung, 'The Use of Aerial Photographs on Planning Enforcement Against Unauthorised Development', Appendix One in Lai Wai-chung Lawrence, *Zoning and Property Rights: A Hong Kong Case Study*, Hong Kong, Hong Kong University Press, second edition, **1998**.

Lai, Lawrence Wai-chung, *Town Planning in Hong Kong: A Review of Planning Appeal Decisions*, Hong Kong, Hong Kong University Press, **1999**, reprinted edition, **2001**.

Lai, Lawrence Wai-chung, *Town Planning in Hong Kong: A Review of Planning Appeal Decisions 1997–2001*, Hong Kong, Hong Kong University Press, **2003**.

Tang, Bo-sin and Leung, Hing-fung, 'Planning Enforcement in Hong Kong: Implementing New Planning Law Before the Change of Sovereignty', *Town Planning Review*, Vol. 69, No. 2, April **1998**, pp. 153–70.

## Planning Conditions

Lai, Lawrence Wai-chung, Ho, Daniel Chi-wing and Leung, Hing-fung, 'Planning Conditions in Hong Kong: Some Planning, Building, Conveyancing and Property Management Issues', Faculty of Architecture Discussion Paper, The University of Hong Kong, **2004**.

## Building Enforcement

*Published Works*

Lai, Lawrence Wai-chung and Ho, Daniel Chi-wing, *Planning Buildings in High*

*Density Environment: A Review of Building Appeal Decisions*, Hong Kong, Hong Kong University Press, **2000**, reprinted edition, **2002**.

Lai, Lawrence Wai-chung and Ho, Daniel Chi-wing, 'Unauthorised Structures in a High-rise High-density Environment: The Case of Hong Kong', *Property Management*, Vol. 19 No. 2, **2001**, pp. 112–23.

## Aquaculture

### Published Works

Hodgkiss, John and Lai, Lawrence Wai-chung, eds. *Aquaculture Economics and Management*, Vol. 6, Nos. 3 & 4, **2002**.

### Relevant Legislation

*Environmental Impact Assessment Ordinance*, Chapter 499, Laws of Hong Kong
*Country Parks Ordinance*, Chapter 208, Laws of Hong Kong
*Land (Compulsory Sale for Redevelopment) Ordinance*, Ordinance No. 30 of 1998.
*Land Registration Ordinance*, Chapter 128, Laws of Hong Kong.
*Town Planning Ordinance*, Chapter 131, Laws of Hong Kong.

### Relevant Law Cases

*Active Keen Ltd. v Smart Business Ltd.* [1999]
*Attorney General v Firebird Ltd.* [1983] 1 HKC 1, PC
*Attorney General v Melhado Investment Ltd.* [1983] HKLR 327
*Auburntown Ltd. v Town Planning Board* HCMP No. 222 of 1993
*Cavendish Property Development Ltd. v AG and Another* (High Court Miscellaneous Proceedings No. 762 of 1987)
*CC Tse (Estate) Ltd. v AG* HCMP 604/81
*Crozet Ltd. v AG* HCMP 409/73
*Delight World Co. v Town Planning Appeal Board* [1996] MP No. 197 of 1996
*Director of Lands v Yin Shuen Enterprises Limited, Nam Chun Investment Company Limited.* FACV Nos. 2 and 3 of 2002
*Donald Shields (No. 2) v Mary Chan* [1972] HKLR 121
*Head Step Ltd. v Building Authority* [1995] Civil Appeal No. 131 of 1995
*Henderson Real Estate Agency Ltd. v Lo Chai Wan* (for and on behalf of Town Planning Board) [1997] HKLRD 258
*Hinge Well Co. Ltd. v AG* [1998] HKLR 32
*Kwang Kong Co. v Town Planning Board* [1996] 6 HKPLR 237
*Mexx Consolidated (Far East) Ltd. v Attorney General and Another* (High Court Miscellaneous Proceedings No. 2421 of 1986 [1987] HKLR 1210–1220
*Niceboard D Ltd. v China Light and Power Co. Ltd.* [1994] HKDCLR 69, LT
*R. v Town Planning Board ex parte Real Estate Developers' Association of Hong* MP 2457 of 1995

*Raider Ltd. v Secretary for Justice* CACV 115/1999 (judgement on 7 December 1999)
*Singway Co. Ltd. v Attorney General* [1974] HKLR 275.
*Wah Yick Enterprises Co. Ltd. v Building Authority* FACV No. 12 of 1998.
*Wing On Ltd. and Wing On Property and Securities Ltd. v Building Authority* MP 1279 of 1996
*Wotford Construction Co. v Secretary for the New Territories* [1978] HKLR 410, CA

# INDEX

## Law Cases

CC Tze Case, 54
Henderson Case, 65
Melhado Case, 9, 24, 25, 27, 33
Singway Case, 10
Walsh v Longsdale, 68
Yin Shuen Case, 67

## Legislation

Antiquities and Monuments Ordinance, 93
Building (Administration) Regulations, 77, 79
Building (Appeal) Regulations, 81
Building (Construction) Regulations, 77
Building (Demolition Works) Regulations, 77
Building (Energy Efficiency) Regulations, 77
Building (Oil Storage Installations) Regulations, 77
Building (Planning) Regulations, 56, 77, 80, 109
Building (Private Streets and Access Roads) Regulations, 77
Building (Standards of Sanitary Fitments, Plumbing, Drainage Works and Latrines) Regulations, 77
Building (Ventilating Systems) Regulations, 77
Building Regulations, 17
Buildings Ordinance, 3, 4, 5, 6, 15, 17, 19, 24, 25, 26, 27, 29, 33, 43, 52, 54, 55, 56, 57, 58, 63, 70, 75, 76, 77, 78, 79, 80, 81, 82, 83, 85, 91, 92, 99, 100, 105, 108, 109, 110
Buildings Ordinance (Application to the New Territories) Ordinance, 77
Cheung Chau Reservation Ordinance, 15
Conveyancing and Property Ordinance, 7, 8, 56, 68, 70
Country and Marine Parks Ordinance, 20
Country Parks Ordinance, 7, 11, 16, 23, 52, 93, 230
District Court Ordinance, 81
European District Reservation Ordinance, 15
Hill District Reservation Ordinance, 15
Hong Kong Bill of Rights Ordinance (Bill of Rights), 15
Housing Ordinance, 52
Inland Revenue Ordinance, 66
Land (Compulsory Sale for Redevelopment) Ordinance, 43, 230
Landlord and Tenant Ordinance, 100
Lands Resumption Ordinance, 2, 68
New Territories Leases (Extension) Ordinance, 9
Peak District (Residence) Ordinance, 15
Prevention of Bribery Ordinance, 61
Town Planning (Amendment) Bill 2003, 62

234  Index

Town Planning (Amendment)
    Ordinance, 10, 17, 18, 25, 26, 87, 88
Town Planning Bill 1996, 17, 89
Town Planning Bill 2000, 17
Town Planning Ordinance, 2, 3, 4, 7, 10,
    11, 15, 16, 17, 18, 19, 20, 21, 23, 24,
    25, 26, 27, 29, 30, 31, 33, 34, 35, 37,
    38, 39, 51, 52, 54, 56, 57, 58, 61, 63,
    65, 72, 79, 85, 86, 87, 88, 89, 91, 93,
    97, 98, 99, 110, 113, 114, 229, 230

## Terms

Abercrombie Report, 16
access, 15, 53, 56, 57, 59, 77, 78, 79, 83,
    101, 102, 105, 106, 108, 111
    for persons with a disability, 78
administration fee, 67, 68
administrative town plan, 2, 25, 27, 28,
    51, 53, 72
airport height restriction, 78
Appeal Board (under Town Planning
    Ordinance), 4, 10, 11, 18, 46, 51, 65,
    66, 91, 96, 98, 230
approved plan, 21, 55, 79
architect, 4, 42, 103
Architectural Services Department
    (ASD), 43, 44
Authorized Person (AP), 4, 17, 42, 44, 78,
    79, 80, 96, 102

balcony, 107, 108
balcony green feature, 107
barrister, 3, 4, 51
basement, 108
Basic Law, 15, 18
better use, 51
bird net, 104
Block Crown (Government) Lease, 8, 9,
    14, 68, 101
Board of Review (under Inland Revenue
    Ordinance), 66
building, 1, 2, 3, 4, 5, 13, 14, 15, 17, 19,
    20, 20, 21, 24, 25, 26, 27, 29, 30, 31,
    33, 35, 38, 39, 41, 42, 43, 44, 48, 50,
    51, 52, 53, 54, 55, 56, 57, 58, 63, 66,
    67, 68, 69, 71, 72, 75, 76, 77, 78, 79,
    80, 81, 82, 83, 91, 92, 93, 96, 98, 100,
    101, 102, 104, 105, 106, 109, 110, 198,
    200, 221, 222, 223, 225, 226, 227, 230,
    231
Building Appeal Tribunal, 48, 57, 66, 81,
    82, 96
building covenant, 2, 42, 100
building height, 13, 30, 54, 57, 58, 69, 93,
    109
building material, 102
building permission, 41, 54, 55, 71, 79
building plan, 4, 5, 19, 26, 27, 35, 42, 43,
    44, 48, 51, 52, 54, 55, 56, 58, 63, 72,
    75, 77, 78, 79, 80, 92, 96, 100, 102
building restriction, 53, 54
building surveyor, 4, 78
building work, 19, 24, 25, 30, 31, 38, 39,
    76, 77, 78, 79, 80, 91
Buildings Department (BD), 27, 52, 75,
    78, 83, 98

case law, 19
certificate of compliance (CC), 52
change in use, 1, 2, 4, 19, 21, 23, 41, 54,
    71, 72, 100, 101, 107, 214
    of a building, 19
Cheung Chau, 15, 25, 100
Chief Executive (Governor) in Council,
    10, 81
Cho/Tong, 89
Cho/Tong manager, 89
cinema, 100, 106
civil engineer, 41
cladding, 80
cockloft, 108
Column 1, 18, 20, 21, 30, 31, 37, 38, 39,
    88, 104
Column 2, 18, 21, 29, 30, 31, 37, 38, 39,
    61
Committee on Planning and Lands
    (CPLD), 72

## Index

common law, 18, 24, 25, 68
company, 1, 4, 67, 89, 104, 105, 107, 231
compensation, 2, 3, 18, 50, 83, 93, 101, 227
concurrent development permission, 16
condition of renewal, 9, 42
condition of sale, 7, 41, 42, 43, 57, 58
consent to commence work, 79
constitutional capitalism, 226
Consulate General of the United States, 71
consultant study, 41
contractual negotiation, 67
contractual right, 24, 25, 85, 86
conveyancing, 2, 3, 4, 7, 8, 43, 50, 56, 68, 70, 86, 110, 227, 230
conviction, 88, 89
cost, 10, 18, 55, 66, 83, 93, 208
Country and Marine Parks Authority, 11, 16, 28, 218
Country and Marine Parks Board, 11
country park, 7, 11, 16, 17, 23, 27, 51, 52, 93, 218
country park map, 7, 51
Country Parks Authority, 11
Country Parks Board, 11
covered walkway, 76
criminal offence, 89, 91
Crown Lease (see Government Lease) 7, 9, 14, 68, 100, 105, 106, 110

dangerous building, 75, 76
dangerous trade, 80
deed, 3, 7, 8, 42, 56, 68, 63, 70, 71, 104, 105, 106
Deed of Variation, 68, 71, 104
Deed of Mutual Covenant (DMC), 3, 42, 105, 106
deed poll, 70
Deep Bay Buffer Zones, 110
definitions of terms, 15, 17, 38, 39
Demarcation District, 9
Department of Building and Real Estate, 64

depositing matter on land, 20
Deputy Director of Planning, 62
developer, 14, 42, 43, 50, 51, 69, 70, 75, 79, 97, 105, 106, 109, 110, 197, 199, 203, 206, 207, 208, 210, 221, 222, 223
development, 1, 2, 3, 5, 6, 9, 13, 14, 15,16, 18, 20, 23, 24, 25, 26, 27, 28, 29, 33, 34, 35, 38, 39, 41, 42, 43, 44, 45, 46, 47, 48, 49, 50, 51, 52, 53, 54, 55, 56, 57, 58, 59, 61, 62, 63, 68, 69, 70, 71, 72, 75, 76, 77, 78, 85, 86, 88, 89, 91, 93, 102, 104, 108, 109, 110, 111, 113, 114, 116, 118, 119, 120, 123, 127, 129, 133, 136, 139, 142, 144, 147, 149, 151, 155, 157, 160, 163, 166, 168, 170, 172, 175, 177, 180, 183, 185, 188, 191, 193, 194, 195, 196, 197, 198, 199, 200, 202, 203, 206, 207, 208, 209, 210, 211, 212, 214, 218, 220, 221, 222, 223, 225, 226, 227, 228, 229, 230
development blight, 93
development control, 5, 6, 13, 16, 52, 53, 54, 55, 56, 57, 58, 59, 75
development cycle, 41, 44, 45, 46, 47, 48, 49, 50, 75
development drawing, 78
development intensity, 69
Development Permission Area (DPA), 3, 18, 20, 24, 25,, 26, 27, 28, 29, 30, 31, 33, 34, 35, 37, 38, 39, 52, 56, 57, 61, 87, 88, 102, 103, 113, 116, 118, 120, 123, 127, 129, 133, 136, 139, 142, 147, 149, 151, 155, 157, 160, 163, 166, 168, 172, 175, 177, 180, 183, 185, 188, 191, 197, 198, 200
Development Permission Area (DPA) Plan, 20, 26, 27, 28, 29, 30, 31, 33, 34, 35, 37, 38, 39, 52, 88, 102, 103, 113, 198
Direct Access System (DAS), 95
direct professional access, 4
Director of Agriculture, Fisheries and Conservation, 11, 52
Director of Building, 52, 75

## 236  Index

Director of Fire Services, 79
Director of Lands, 7, 52, 67, 231
Director of Planning, 10, 25, 34, 51, 52, 57, 62, 87, 98
Discovery Bay, 24
discretion, 26, 27, 58, 77, 81, 92, 228
discretionary power, 17, 19
Disney World, 24, 41
District Lands Conference, 46, 70, 73
District Lands Office, 67, 68, 70, 73, 87
District Lands Officer (DLO), 73
domestic use, 80
draft DPA plan, 26
draft plan, 10, 20, 21
drainage, 3, 5, 41, 76, 108, 218
dry cultivation, 9, 104
due diligence, 4

economic incentive, 24, 26
economic value, 16
Enforcement Notice (under the Town Planning Ordinance), 2, 3, 31, 38, 87, 88, 90, 91
Engineering Condition, 44
engineering work, 41, 49
environmental impact assessment (EIA), 3
equitable interest, 2
escalators, 105
estate surveyor, 2, 41, 69
  in private practice, 69
European-type house, 14, 53
evidence, 43, 66, 83, 89, 91, 211
excavation, 20, 30, 31, 80
exemption (under the Buildings Ordinance), 80
existing use, 20, 24, 25, 29, 30, 31, 34, 35, 37, 38, 39, 72, 89, 104
external wall, 80, 106, 108

feasibility studies, 42
fines, 2, 89
fine fighting, 78
fire prevention, 57

fire safety, 58, 77, 78
flat, 99, 105, 107, 110
forbearance fee, 58, 86, 87
Form No. PLN-18, 62
forward planning, 5, 6, 52, 53, 54, 57, 58, 59
foundation, 13
free choice, 1
free extension, 42

Gazette, 9, 10, 11, 16, 18, 20, 30, 39, 43, 61, 88, 103
gei wai, 110
general revenue, 83
Geographic Information System (GIS), 95
geotechnical assessment, 78
GN 364 of 1934, 9
GN 365 of 1906, 9
GN 570 of 1924, 9
GN 720 of 1984, 9
good cause, 82
Government Lease (see Crown Lease), vii, 3, 7, 8, 9, 27, 43, 52, 85, 98, 99, 100
grave, 9
green Belt Zone, 18, 113, 197, 198, 201, 202
green field site, 41
Gross Floor Area (GFA), 116, 118, 121, 124, 127, 130, 133, 136, 139, 142, 144, 147, 149, 152, 155, 157, 160, 163, 166, 168, 170, 172, 175, 178, 180, 183, 185, 188, 191
guesthouse, 108
Guidance Notes (see Town Planning Board Guidance Notes), 17, 19, 61, 62, 229

hand-dug caissons, 80
health, 75, 78, 80
highway, 3, 5
hoarding, 76
hobby farmer, 103

home for the elderly, 76
Hong Kong Institute of Engineers (HKIE), 96
Hong Kong Island, 8, 9, 15, 26, 27, 100, 108, 194, 196, 200
Hong Kong Planning Standards and Guidelines (HKPSG), 17, 23, 42, 49, 51
Hong Kong Polytechnic University, 64
Hong Kong Special Administrative Region, 1, 15, 226
house, 9, 14, 15, 18, 24, 105, 106, 116, 121, 169, 172, 176, 183, 185, 186, 188
Housing Department, 43, 45

immediate neighbourhood, 54, 57, 79, 111
indenture, 7
indigenous village, 6, 8, 104
indigenous villager, 6, 8, 104
inquiry hotline, 107
in-situ exchange, 9
inspection, 52, 66, 73, 76, 78, 85, 108
interdepartmental consultation, 70
Interim Development Permission Area (IDPA), 3, 6, 10, 18, 20, 24, 25, 26, 27, 29, 30, 31, 33, 34, 35, 37, 38, 39, 51, 52, 56, 57, 61, 87, 88, 89, 101, 103, 104
Interim Development Permission Area (IDPA) Plan, 6, 20, 24, 25, 26, 29, 30, 31, 33, 35, 37, 38, 39, 52, 57, 87, 88, 101, 103
investor, 1, 5, 6, 71

jogging track, 108
Joint Declaration (Sino-British Agreement), 7, 10
judicial review, 47, 48, 67
June 18th Incident, 93

kindergarten, 114
Kowloon, 8, 9, 10, 26, 27, 114, 116, 118, 120, 123, 127, 129, 133, 136, 139, 142, 144, 147, 149, 151, 155, 157, 160, 163, 166, 168, 170, 172, 175, 177, 180, 183, 185, 188, 191, 200, 228

Lamma, 25, 27
Land Authority, 7, 25, 52, 53, 54, 55, 56, 57, 58
land contract, 2
Land Registry, 63, 68, 69, 95, 96
land sale programme, 42
land surveyor, 41
land use, 6, 7, 9, 13, 14, 15, 18, 19, 21, 24, 25, 27, 29, 41, 43, 51, 53, 56, 57, 95, 200
Lands Department, 10, 14, 24, 41, 42, 44, 46, 52, 55, 67, 68, 69, 72, 73, 85, 86, 87, 95, 101, 109, 225
landslide debris, 80
latent defect, 4
latrine, 9
lawyer, 3, 4
layout plan, 3, 5, 24, 41, 51, 53, 56, 96, 114
lease, 2, 3, 4, 5, 6, 7, 8, 13, 14, 15, 16, 18, 19, 23, 24, 25, 26, 27, 33, 38, 39, 41, 43, 46, 51, 53, 54, 55, 56, 57, 58, 67, 68, 69, 70, 71, 72, 73, 75, 85, 86, 87, 98, 99, 100, 101, 102, 104, 105, 106, 107, 109, 110
lease condition, 3, 5, 7, 13, 14, 16, 24, 25, 27, 55, 58, 71, 72, 85, 86, 99, 100
lease enforcement, 3, 4, 43, 70, 85, 86
lease modification, 2, 24, 25, 26, 27, 41, 46, 51, 54, 55, 56, 67, 68, 69, 70, 71, 72, 73, 75, 86, 105, 106, 109
leasing, 42, 50
legal advice, 87, 91
Legal Advisory and Conveyancing Office (LACO), 73, 87
legal drafter, 18
legal estate, 2
legal practitioner, 65
legal title (of land), 43
Legislative Council, 62

licensing, 76
lighting, 75, 78, 80, 218
list of definitions, 18, 19
litigation, 3, 76, 87
loading requirement, 75
location plan, 68
loss of title, 2
LPG gas, 99

Mai Po Marshes, 104
maintenance of slopes and support, 53
mandatory ceiling, 58
marine lot, 13
master layout (MLP), 3, 5, 24, 53, 56, 96, 114
material change, 16, 20, 30, 31, 34, 35, 39, 88
material change in the use of land or buildings, 16, 20
means of escape (MOE), 15, 57, 76, 78
memorandum of re-entry, 85
mens rea, 89
metal workshop, 105
Metro Planning Committee, 63
Mid-Levels, 93, 108, 110
modification letter, 68, 69
modification premium, 67
motor repair shop, 80
motor vehicle showroom, 100
multiple ownership (of land), 51, 69

natural vegetation, 24
negligent statement, 4
neighbour, 2, 104
new development, 43, 78, 111
new development (under the Country and Marine Parks Ordinance), 11, 16
new grant lot, 9
New Kowloon, 8, 9
New Territories, 2, 3, 6, 8, 9, 10, 17, 23, 24, 25, 77, 87, 97, 99, 100, 101, 102, 106, 133, 214, 220, 231

New Territories Exempted House (NTEH), 24, 25, 77 (*see* small house)
new town development programme, 41
no objection letter, 69
non in-situ exchange, 70
notes (to a statutory town plan), 14, 15, 16, 17, 18, 19, 20, 21, 29, 30, 31, 33, 34, 35, 37, 38, 39, 55, 61, 73, 77, 88, 97, 104, 193, 194, 196, 198, 200, 201, 202, 203, 205, 206, 207, 208, 210, 211, 213, 216, 217, 219, 221, 223
notice of appeal (under the Buildings Ordinance) 81, 82
notice of appeal (under the Town Planning Ordinance) 65

objecting a draft plan, 21
obnoxious trade, 13
occupant (of land or building), 75
occupation permit (OP), 4, 20, 26, 27, 35, 43, 51, 52, 99, 100, 101, 108, 110
offensive trade, 13, 53, 68
offensive trade clause, 13, 68
open kitchen, 107
open storage, 24, 25, 26, 27, 89, 100, 106, 206, 208, 210, 211, 212, 220
open storage of containers, 106
order for demolition, 58, 76, 80, 92, 93
order for repair, 76
Outline Development Plan (ODP), 27, 41, 49, 51, 72, 99, 100, 101
Outline Zoning Plan (OZP), 18, 20, 24, 25, 26, 28, 29, 38, 43, 50, 51, 52, 61, 78, 88, 97, 98, 99, 100, 101, 102, 103, 104, 105, 106, 109, 110

paint shop, 80
parking space, 13, 43, 110
pedestrianization scheme, 110, 111
Peng Chau, 25, 27
Penny's Bay, 24
People's Liberation Army, 76
permit to occupy a new building (see occupation permit), 20

piling work, 80
Ping Chau, Mirs Bay, 24
planning appeal, 2, 4, 17, 47, 51, 65, 82, 91, 96, 97
planning application, 2, 4, 5, 10, 17, 21, 29, 30, 37, 42, 46, 50, 51, 55, 56, 58, 61, 62, 63, 64, 77, 79, 86, 97, 106, 107, 194, 195, 201, 208, 211, 214, 215, 220, 221, 222, 223
planning brief, 52
planning by contract, 56, 99
planning condition, 3, 5, 17, 18, 55, 63, 64, 67, 96, 114, 230
planning consultant, 41, 62, 65
Planning Department, 10, 17, 19, 34, 49, 51, 62, 63, 64, 88, 89, 90, 91, 95, 96, 98, 104, 107, 229
planning intention, 18, 104, 111, 208, 215
planning qualifications, 62
planning review, 2, 46, 62, 64
plea in mitigation, 91
plot ratio, 3, 5, 13, 30, 53, 54, 57, 58, 69, 75, 78, 93, 101, 102, 106, 107, 109
pond filling, 30, 31
positive covenant, 7, 8, 43
potential urban area, 87
practice notes, 14, 17, 77
practice Notes for Authorized Persons (PNAP), 77
precedent, 66, 195, 196
preliminary hearing, 82, 102
premium for BC extension, 42
pre-sale, 42, 50, 99
prescribed fee (for rezoning and planning applications), 62, 79
private agricultural land, 23
private agricultural lot, 8, 24
private building lot, 8
private lane, 57
private property, 1, 18
private property right, 1, 18
private treaty grant, 42
privately owned land, 23
projection, 75

property management, 1, 50
property manager, 2
property owner, 1, 43, 87
prosecution, 76, 88, 91
public body, 61, 65
public officer, 65, 81, 83
Public Works Program, 41, 44

question of law, 82

racial segregation, 15
railway protection, 78
rate and range clause, 99
reasonable steps, 91
reclamation, 3, 5, 41
rectification, 88
re-entry clause, 85
Re-entry Notice, 85
Registered Professional Planner (RPP), 4, 43, 62, 104
Reinstatement Notice, 21, 88, 90
remarks column, 29
restaurant, 99
resumption (of private land), 2, 3, 68, 80, 85, 100, 101
retaining wall, 13, 75
revenue, 93
review (by the secretary), 21
Review of Master Schedule of Notes to Statutory Plans, 15, 19
rezoning, 21, 38, 39, 61, 62
right of way, 2, 53, 57, 105, 106
roots of title, 8
rule in the *Melhado Case*, 24, 25, 27, 33
Rural and New Town Planning Committee (RNTPC), 63
Rural Outline Zoning Plan, 18, 26, 88

s. 16 application (see planning application), 29, 56
safety, 50, 58, 59, 75, 76, 78, 79
Schedule of Notes, 29
Schedule of Uses, 18, 29
security of tenure, 100

## 240 Index

set-back, 13, 53
sewage tunnel work, 80
short-term tenancy (STT), 44
short-term waiver (STW), 2
simple contract, 7, 8, 56
site coverage, 13, 53, 75, 78, 109
Site of Special Scientific Area (SSSI), 93
sky-garden, 109
small house, 6, 24, 25, 77, 104, 202, 208, 220
small house policy, 25, 220
solicitor, 3, 4, 43, 51, 81, 83, 110
Special Area, 93
staircase, 76, 105, 108
statutory body, 18, 56, 61, 65
statutory definitions, 19
statutory town plan, 2, 3, 4, 5, 6, 16, 17, 18, 20, 23, 26, 27, 52, 55, 56, 58, 61, 72
Stop Notice, 88, 90
storage of dangerous good, 80
street work, 79
strict liability, 89
structural engineer, 4, 78
structural stability, 76, 80
subdivision, 54, 69
Sub-Regional Development Strategy, 49
Survey and Mapping Office (SMO), 10
survey map, 9

Tai Tam Country Park, 28
Talbots Report, 16
temporary use, 27, 29, 30, 31, 33, 34, 38, 39, 42, 61, 100, 102
tender, 42, 44, 56
Territorial Development Strategy (Review) (TDS [TDSR]), 23, 51
title defeasibility of, 3
title defect, 2
title document, 8, 68, 69, 95
title requisition, 4
toilet, 80
town planner, 18, 43, 50, 51, 53
    in private practice, 43, 51

Town Planning Board, 10, 11, 15, 16, 17, 18, 19, 21, 29, 34, 38, 43, 46, 50, 51, 52, 53, 54, 55, 56, 57, 58, 61, 62, 63, 64, 65, 79, 81, 86, 88, 91, 95, 96, 98, 111, 113, 114, 214, 215, 220, 221, 222, 223, 229, 230, 231
Town Planning Board Guidance Notes, 17
Town Planning Board Guidelines, 17, 19, 34, 62, 113, 114
Town Planning Board Paper, 63, 64

unauthorized building work, 6, 76, 104
unauthorized development, 10, 20, 88, 91, 103, 104
University of Hong Kong, The 64, 228, 230
unrestricted lease (999-year lease), 13, 99
urban environment, 16
urban fringe, 16
Urban Renewal Agency, 93
urbanization, 16, 214
use, 1, 2, 3, 4, 5, 6, 7, 13, 14, 15, 16, 18, 19, 20, 21, 24, 25, 29, 30, 31, 33, 34, 35, 37, 38, 39, 41, 42, 43, 63, 67, 68, 69, 70, 71, 72, 75, 76, 79, 80, 85, 86, 87,, 88, 89, 91, 93, 95, 97, 98, 99, 100, 101, 103, 104, 105, 107, 108, 109, 110, 113, 114, 116, 118, 121, 124, 127, 130, 133, 136, 139, 142, 144, 147, 149, 150, 152, 155, 157, 160, 163, 166, 169, 170, 172, 176, 178, 183, 184, 185, 188, 194, 195, 196, 197, 198, 200, 201, 202, 203, 204, 205, 206, 208, 209, 210, 211, 212, 215, 218, 220, 221, 222, 223, 225, 226, 228, 229
use of a building, 19, 20, 35
use of land, 1, 13, 35, 88
user, 1, 2, 3, 5, 13, 14, 27, 53, 54, 71, 85, 86, 87, 89, 99, 100, 101, 106, 107
user clause, 13, 14, 99
user restriction, 27, 53, 85, 99

valuation, 1, 2, 3, 42, 44, 46, 68, 69
value appraisal, 1
vending machine, 107
ventilation, 75, 78, 80
Vesting Notice, 85
visual impact, 58

waiver, 56, 67, 68, 69, 70, 86
waiver letter, 69
Western District, 108
wet cultivation, 9
witness, 81, 83

zone, 15, 18, 19, 29, 37, 38, 39, 64, 102, 105, 106, 111, 212
Zone (under Town Planning Ordinance), 18, 20, 103, 104, 113, 114, 133, 198, 201, 202, 206, 208, 210, 211, 212, 213, 227, 228
zoning, 2, 4, 15, 18, 25, 34, 38, 39, 41, 61, 79, 89, 93, 98, 100, 102, 104, 107, 139, 152, 197, 226, 228, 229